BROWN
FOR THE COUNT

BROWN FOR THE COUNT

A COMPENDIUM OF CLEVELAND BROWNS LISTS

DAVE ALGASE

© 2015 by David M. Algase

All rights reserved. No part of this publication may be reproduced, distributed, or transmitted in any form or by any means without the prior written permission of the publisher, except in the case of brief quotations embodied in critical reviews and certain other noncommercial uses permitted by copyright law.

For permission requests or ordering information, including quantity discounts, contact the publisher shown below.

Library of Congress Control Number: 2015909652

ISBN 978-0-9961248-0-5

A publication of
Interspiral Press
Saline, MI 48176
www.interspiralpress.com

First edition.

First printing, 2015.

Printed in the United States of America.

For all the men who lost
more than just games
being Cleveland Browns.

TABLE OF CONTENTS

PREFACE xii
CHAPTER 1: BROWNS BIOGRAPHICAL FACTS 1
    47 Birthdays Shared by Several Browns.................................. 1
    8 Holidays and their Browns Birthdays 4
    15 Foreign-Born Browns... 4
    23 Sets of Browns from the Same High School 6
    Browns Who Were Also College Teammates 8
    14 Browns Notable for Playing Other Sports....................... 17
    The 8 Tallest Browns.. 19
    The 15 Heaviest Browns 20
    4 Browns with Physical Anomalies 21
    11 Sets of Relatives Affiliated with the Browns 22
    9 Browns Accomplished in Other Fields............................. 24
    18 Browns Players Who Became
        Head Coaches or Team Executives................................ 25
    30 Browns Who Died Young 30
CHAPTER 2: COMINGS AND GOINGS 35
    20 Outstanding Draft Value Picks 35
    25 Career-Long Browns 36
    12 Great Browns Who Played Only For Other Teams........ 37
    16 "Sandwich" Browns... 39
    3 Original Browns Who Returned in 1999.......................... 43
    13 Tail-Enders.. 44
    The 7 Browncos 47
    10 Best Trades of the Paul Brown Era 48
    8 Worst Trades of the Paul Brown Era 50
    10 Best Trades of the Modell Era 52
    14 Worst Trades of the Modell Era 54
    8 Best Trades of the New Browns Era................................. 57

 7 Worst Trades of the New Browns Era 59

CHAPTER 3: MOMENTS AND MEMORIES 63
 12 Superb Goal-Line Stands 63
 15 Non-Quarterbacks Who Threw for Touchdowns 67
 8 Most Noteworthy Hits By and Upon Browns 69
 13 Once-in-a-Career Touchdowns 71
 6 Significant Two-Point Conversions 73
 12 Browns Who Scored Touchdowns on Offense and Defense 74
 21 Browns Safeties 75
 9 Notable Browns-Related Pro Bowl Moments 78

CHAPTER 4: FRANCHISE FACETS AND FEATURES 81
 17 Browns Who Made the Pro Bowl At Least Half the Time 81
 14 Seasons, 14 Browns Players of the Year 82
 8 Heisman Trophy Winners Who Became Browns 83
 11 Best Rookie Seasons 85
 17 Ways the Browns' Record Book Would Improve
   by Including the AAFC Years 88
 39 Starting Guards Since 1999 90
 9 NFL Rule Changes Inspired by Browns 91
 6 Browns Coaching Careers Hurt by Losing to Cincinnati 93
 7 Uniform and Equipment Oddities 95
 10 Ownership Changes in Browns History 96
 The 21 Best Brief Browns Careers 98
 Browns Who Wore Each Jersey Number the Most 100

CHAPTER 5: THE BEST OF THE BROWNS 103
 8 Best Quarterbacks in Browns History 103
 17 Best Running Backs in Browns History 105
 7 Best Tight Ends in Browns History 111
 15 Best Wide Receivers in Browns History 112
 11 Best Offensive Tackles in Browns History 116
 8 Best Offensive Guards in Browns History 119
 8 Best Centers in Browns History 121

    9 Best Defensive Tackles in Browns History................................123
    11 Best Defensive Ends in Browns History....................................126
    13 Best Linebackers in Browns History...128
    14 Best Cornerbacks in Browns History..132
    14 Best Safeties in Browns History..136
    9 Best Kickers and Punters in Browns History............................138
    10 Best Kick and Punt Returners in Browns History....................141

CHAPTER 6: FANDOM AND FRIVOLITY..145
    10 Somewhat Apt Anagrams...145
    19 Browns Players with Interesting Names...................................145
    8 Name-Related Browns Coincidences..147
    23 *Sports Illustrated* Covers Depicting Browns..............................148
    The 10 Best Cleveland Browns Books...151
    11 Other Brown and Orange Teams...154
    SEMBB's Top 10 Reasons I'm a Browns Fan................................155
    19 Freaky Browns Coincidences..156

PREFACE

Browns fandom is far from a Cleveland-only phenomenon. With the number of Browns Backers Worldwide fan clubs approaching 400 in over a dozen countries, the team's supporters have truly fanned out. This book is both for and from this diaspora.

I first took notice of the Browns at age ten, growing up near Toledo. It was 1978. The backfield featured two Pruitts and a gutsy gunslinger named Brian Sipe. Newcomers included head coach Sam Rutigliano and rookies Clay Matthews and Ozzie Newsome, who would often run an end-around or two from his tight end position. It was the first season of 16 games, and while three of them went into overtime, legendary sportswriter Hal Lebovitz wouldn't bestow the nickname of the Kardiac Kids on these Browns until the next season.

As I would write much later in the first blog post of the first Browns blog, my dad was a little dynamo, always on the go with work, side gigs and projects around the house. Even his recreation choices were energetic. But on fall Sunday afternoons, he settled in to watch those brown and orange hulks from his hometown. He didn't exactly settle down though. Nothing else on TV drew more animated reactions than the Browns' various feats and defeats. "HIT HIM!" he would yell at the defense as opponents advanced the ball, which they did quite often in those days. I soon learned that the Browns, like my dad's emotions, were something I could neither predict nor control, but together we could try to understand them and hope for the best.

So my passion for the Browns — a test of loyalty and perseverance that eventually fueled the creation of this book — is rooted is my love for my father. I'm sure that's true of many, probably most, Browns fans. While my own fandom has taken on a life of its own, I honor the many memories of watching and attending games with dad. I also appreciate my mom's forbearance during those formative football Sundays and all the bowls of chili mac and pans of brownies that sustained us. For their backing on so many levels, my deep gratitude goes to Drew and Donna.

This book would not exist without the steadfast encouragement, support, love, patience and devoted friendship of my wife, Terrie, whose assistance with the manuscript I also appreciate. She's also responsible for the existence of our wonderful son Elliot, 11 already, who inspires me to do and be my best. One of my main intentions with this project has been to write the Browns book I would have wanted to read at his age. I hope he finds it a fraction as interesting as he is to me.

Back in 2002, during the Browns' only playoff season of the new era, I followed a friend's advice to focus my blogging on a particular topic. The choice was obvious, especially since I found no other blogs devoted to the Browns at the time. Validation soon came from the extraordinary Browns fan Barry McBride, who invited me to write for his influential website, now known as The Orange & Brown Report — browns.scout.com — and its (dearly departed) magazine. A shout-out goes to Barry and the community of Browns fans he's hosted since the dark days surrounding The Move.

I also want to acknowledge this project's early supporters, including such dear friends as Heidi Rotheim and Jane Wu. For their artistic talents and efforts, I thank graphic designer Cullen Whitmore and photographer Karen Hockley. And among all the others who have provided technical, legal and promotional advice and assistance, I want to single out my home club, the vibrant Southeast Michigan Browns Backers, for helping in a variety of ways, including granting permission to use one of their lists in this book.

My aim herein is not to provide a comprehensive account of every aspect of the Cleveland Browns, nor an overview of the team's essential history. There are other fine sources for such big-picture perspectives. *Brown for the Count* is an eclectic reference book with a viewpoint. For the most part, the lists here synthesize a great deal of research in original ways. They cover the Browns from their origins in 1946 through the 2014 season. The asterisk (*) is used throughout to identify Browns playing careers which remain active as of June 2015.

I hope you find that the format makes for a digestible read that is easy to pick up again and again, regardless of age, prior knowledge or attention span. However, a few lists are intended more for pure reference than straightforward readability, as they present information never before assembled as such.

Sources consist of a wide variety of print and online materials. Several of the books included in the list that begins on page 151 were particularly useful. Many valuable facts were also gleaned from the following:

- *Day By Day in Cleveland Browns History* by Morris Eckhouse, Leisure Press, 1984, especially for details of Browns trades
- The Cleveland Browns' official media guides, especially for team records
- pro-football-reference.com, for statistical data
- *Cleveland Plain Dealer* content and cleveland.com, especially the history database of stories from nearly every Browns game
- *Browns News/Illustrated*, a now-defunct official team serial publication that began in 1981
- fanbase.com and lostletterman.com, for college information.

PREFACE

While indebted to all the reporters, writers and content creators who helped inform this work, I take responsibility for all opinions and any factual errors herein. Feel free to send me any corrections, feedback, questions or other comments at acedavis@gmail.com or through the contact methods on my blog at clevelandbrowns.blogspot.com.

Thank you for sharing in this appreciation of the Browns' fascinatingly rich and complex history.

CHAPTER 1
BROWNS BIOGRAPHICAL FACTS

47 Birthdays Shared by Several Browns

Birthdays, to twist a familiar saying, are like opinions: everyone's got one. So it's no great surprise that many Cleveland Browns over the ages were born on the same date. To present a small slice of these calendar coincidences:

January 2 — Calvin Hill, Raymond Clayborn and Madre Hill.

January 10 — Jake Delhomme, Clarence Weathers, Dwight Walker, Leon Clarke and Yamon Figurs.

January 20 — Milt Plum, Darnell Dinkins, Michael Myers and Terry Kirby.

January 23 — A trio of special teams standouts were born on this date: K Phil Dawson, KR/PR/RB Eric Metcalf and C/LS Frank Winters.

February 6 — Three alliterative names and an assonant one share this birthday: Tom Tupa, Houston Hoover, James Jones and Don Cockroft.

February 15 — Gene Hickerson, Brian Brennan, Walter "The Flea" Roberts, Paul Kruger and Bob Whitlow.

March 16 — Veteran CB Tramon Williams, a 2015 free agent signee, joins some good company, as Browns alumni born on this date include Hall of Famers Ozzie Newsome and Joe DeLamielleure, as well as Darnell Sanders.

March 22 — Cody Risien, Cliff Lewis, John Rienstra, Kaluka Maiava, Rahim Abdullah and Ben Hawkins.

April 3 — Mike Pruitt, Lyle Alzado and Cleveland Crosby.

April 14 — Joe Haden, Herschel Forester, and — both in 1984 — Blake Costanzo and Tyler Thigpen.

April 27 — John Hughes, John Morrow, Ray Ellis and Allen Aldridge.

April 28 — Scott Fujita, Earl Holmes, Mark Bavaro, Tony Peters, Bob Briggs and Dick Deschaine.

May 8 — Bill Cowher, Doug Atkins, Lawrence Vickers and Usama Young.

May 20 — Leroy Kelly, Chris Ogbonnaya, Lawyer Tillman, Brad Smelley and D.D. Hoggard.

May 29 — Three defensive linemen share this spring birthday: Ebenezer Ekuban, Nick Eason and Sam Clancy.

June 9 — Josh Cribbs, John Brown, Alvin McKinley, Hugh McKinnis and Ken Rose.

June 12 — Receiver teammates Frisman Jackson and Andre' Davis were both born on this date in 1979, as was OL Seth McKinney. Longtime tackle Ryan Tucker, who split the duties at right guard with McKinney in 2007, also shares this birthday, along with two drafted receivers who didn't pan out: Paul Hubbard and Eugene Rowell.

June 20 — Len Dawson, Dave Mays, Gerald Dixon, Najee Mustafaa, Rocky Belk, Vernon Joines and Therrian Fontenot.

June 21 — Mike McCormack, Bob Gain, Ernie Blandin, Don Goode and Dale Walters.

July 12 — Frank Ryan, Carl Barisich, Jason Wright, K'Waun Williams, Paul Zukauskas, Bobby Jones, Darius Eubanks and Luke McCown.

July 15 — Kevin Johnson, John St. Clair, Ricky Dudley, Dave Jacobs, Al Jenkins and Scott Young.

July 21 — Kellen Winslow II, Barry Redden, Mike Sellers, Kendrick Mosley and Clifton Smith.

July 31 — Tim Couch, Antonio Langham, Larry Poole and Nick Sorensen.

August 6 — Brian Kinchen, Seneca Wallace, C.J. Mosley and Mike Frederick.

August 7 — Tashaun Gipson, Jordan Cameron, Scott Nicholas and Clarence Williams.

August 16 — Bill Glass, Mack Mitchell, Bobby Garrett and Stacey Hairston.

August 19 — Randy Baldwin, David Patten, Mike Robinson and Shaun Smith.

August 20 — Gary Collins, Brian Schaefering, James-Michael Johnson and Hamza Abdullah.

August 27 — Three of the better defensive lineman in Browns history share this birthday: Michael Dean Perry, Rob Burnett and Derrell Palmer.

August 29 — Jamal Lewis, Carl Banks, Oliver Davis, Stephen Braggs and Steve Nave.

BROWNS BIOGRAPHICAL FACTS

August 31 — It was a good day for linebackers, as Chris Kirksey, Matt Stewart, Ben Taylor, Mike Caldwell, Gene Fekete and Allen Bradford (2014 practice squad) all share this birthday.

September 5 — Jason Pinkston and Colt McCoy were born on the same day in 1987. Warren Lahr, Cleo Miller and Duane Putnam preceded them.

September 20 — Eric Turner and David McMillan were born exactly 13 years apart. Sadly, they each passed away at the young age of 31.

September 21 — Charlie Harraway (1944), Reggie Rucker (1947), Richard Brown (1965), Steve Heiden (1976), Hank Fraley (1977) and Tim Carter (1979).

October 4 — The Browns tenures of Owen Marecic (1988) and Barkevious Mingo (1990) overlapped during the 2013 training camp.

October 13 — Brad Goebel, Amon Gordon, Brian Hoyer, Lou Saban, Irv Smith and Kamerion Wimbley.

October 26 — Bob Golic, Ross Fichtner, Shawn Lauvao, Dave Zastudil, Leon McFadden, Brian Hansen and Nick Miller.

October 27 — Brady Quinn, Jim Leonhard and Cosey Coleman.

November 3 — Karlos Dansby, Anthony Henry, Jim Houston and Leslie Shepherd.

November 13 — Walter Johnson, Vinny Testaverde, Charley Ferguson, Derrick Alexander (the DE, not the WR), Chad Beasley and Chris Kelley.

November 19 — Mike Phipps, Jamir Miller and Alex Mack, all former first-round draft picks.

November 22 — Brian Hartline, Marvin Upshaw, Mel Long, Keith Adams and Warrick Holdman.

November 25 — Bernie Kosar, Michael Lehan, Bob Matheson and Kendall Ogle.

November 27 — Don Strock, Curtis Dickey, Ron Green, Lee Johnson and Duriel Harris.

December 6 — Otto Graham, Johnny Manziel, Mike Baab, Dino Hall, Mark Campbell and Marshall Harris.

December 15 — Carl Hairston, Jerry Ball, Desmond Bryant and Frank Hartley.

December 29 — Dub Jones, Travis Benjamin, Mike Lucci, Kevin Bentley and Mike Teifke.

8 Holidays and their Browns Birthdays

1. Frank Minnifield, the All-Pro cornerback, was born on New Year's Day, 1960.

2. His equally excellent counterpart, Hanford Dixon, was born on Christmas Day in 1958.

3. Courtney Brown's birthday is made for courting. He was born February 14, 1978. The Browns loved him enough to draft him first overall in 2000, but an injury-shortened career left fans brokenhearted. (Born exactly 15 years later was the Texans' Jadeveon Clowney, who like Brown is a top draft pick, a defensive lineman, a South Carolina native, and a microfracture surgery patient.)

4. It's no joke that Robert E. Jackson, the longtime offensive lineman, was born on April 1, 1953.

5. July 4 is America's birthday, but also a German's. Jammi German, a backup receiver in 2001, arrived in Fort Myers, Florida, on Independence Day, 1974. Also born on this date were fellow Browns alumni Erich Barnes and Clifton Smith as well as quarterback Josh McCown.

6. For the mothers of Pete Brewster (born September 1, 1930) and Cleo Miller (September 5, 1952), Labor Day became a double entendre.

7. The Browns got both a trick and a treat with offensive lineman Ross Verba, born October 31, 1973.

8. Tax breaks arrived just in time for the families of New Year's Eve babies Jim Dray, Jason Campbell, Joe Righetti, Ollie Cline and Commodore Perry Kemp.

15 Foreign-Born Browns

1. Tim Manoa (1987-89) — The fullback, a third-round pick out of Penn State, was born in Tonga, a Polynesian monarchy in the south Pacific. His family relocated to Hawaii in 1974, and he moved to the Pittsburgh area for high school. He scored a career-high two touchdowns in the 51-0 win over the Steelers in 1989.

2. Roman Oben (2000-01) — The Browns' starting left tackle in the middle of his 12-year career, Oben hails from Cameroon in west Africa. At age five, he came to the Washington D.C. area with his mother, who

worked for her home nation's embassy. He earned a master's degree while with the Browns. Benched by Butch Davis, he signed with Tampa Bay and started for their Super Bowl championship team.

3. **Pierre Desir (2014*)** — The cornerback drafted in the fourth-round out of tiny Lindenwood was born in Haiti and grew up playing soccer. His family emigrated from the politically turbulent nation when he was four and settled in the St. Louis area.

4. **Karim Barton (2014*)** — The offensive lineman who spent his first year on the Browns' practice squad was actually born in Brooklyn but grew up in Kingston, Jamaica. At age 13, he lost his mother to a blood clot that would be treated routinely in any first-world country. He moved in with an older brother in a rough area of Los Angeles and began playing football as a high school junior.

5. **Ebenezer Ekuban (2004)** — The pass rushing defensive end was born in the west African nation of Ghana. His father, Ebenezer Sr., left the family in 1981 but brought seven-year-old Ebenezer and his three sisters to the Washington D.C. area two years later.

6. **Mark Rypien (1994)** — Born in Calgary, Alberta, and raised in Spokane, Washington, he's the only Canadian-born quarterback to become a full-time NFL starter. The MVP of Super Bowl XXVI began the journeyman phase of his career in Cleveland, where he won two of three unspectacular starts in relief of the injured Vinny Testaverde.

7. **Otis James "O.J." Santiago (2001)** — The 6'7", 265-pound tight end had a six-year NFL career. Born in Whitby, Ontario, and raised there in the Toronto area, he attended Kent State and was a third-round draft choice of the Atlanta Falcons, where he became known for originating the "Dirty Bird" touchdown dance.

8. **John Jurkovic (1999)** — The defensive tackle's nine-year NFL journey ended on Cleveland's expansion roster. His official first name is Ivan, and while ethnically Croatian, he was born in Friedrichshafen, near the Swiss and Austrian borders of what was then West Germany. He grew up near Chicago and in recent years has co-hosted a radio sports talk show there.

9. **Adimchinobe Echemandu (2004)** — Born in Lagos, Nigeria, the running back grew up in California and went by the name Joe Echema for a time. The cousin of standout cornerback Nnamdi Asomugha bounced around the league for four years but never started or scored.

10. **Israel Idonije (2003)** — Born in Lagos, Nigeria and raised in Manitoba from age four, he joined the Browns as an undrafted free agent and made the practice squad as a defensive lineman. Waived midseason, he went on to enjoy ten more years in the NFL, mostly with Chicago.

11. **Jerry Kauric (1990)** — He succeeded Matt Bahr as the Browns' kicker and scored 66 points in his sole NFL season. Born in Windsor, Ontario, Kauric had more success in the Canadian Football League, where he kicked a game-winning field goal to give Edmonton the Grey Cup in 1987.

12. **Goran Lingmerth (1987)** — A kicker who holds the NCAA single-game record with eight field goals, he appeared in just one NFL game and never attempted a placekick. He was born in Nassjo, Sweden.

13, 14 & 15. **Gerald McNeil (1986-89)**, **Ray Mickens (2005)** and **Mike Sellers (2001)** were all born in Frankfurt, where the U.S. had a major military presence in the pre-reunification West Germany.

23 Sets of Browns from the Same High School

The United States has over 37,000 high schools, public and private. Only a select few are privileged to count among their alumni multiple Cleveland Browns. Even fewer of them are featured here.

1. The high school most associated with the Browns is, of course, **Massillon Washington**, where Paul Brown graduated in 1925 and coached from 1932-40, winning six state titles. His early Browns teams included three fine players he coached at Massillon: Tommy James, Horace Gillom and Lin Houston. Linebackers Jim Houston and Chris Spielman are other Tiger alums who succeeded in the NFL.

2. **Bishop Amat High School** in La Puente, California, once featured Brian Russell at quarterback and Daylon McCutcheon at running back. McCutcheon scored 33 touchdowns (his jersey number) as a senior in 1994. Ralph Brown took over as the primary tailback the next year, when they won the state title. All three would later play in the Browns' defensive backfield, as Brown was signed in 2006 to fill in for the injured McCutcheon at cornerback, while Russell started at safety. QB Paul McDonald also attended the school in the 1970s.

3. The Browns' two regular kickers between 1991 and 2012, Matt Stover and Phil Dawson, both attended **Lake Highlands High School** in Dallas.

4. Center Jeff Faine and linebacker D'Qwell Jackson both attended **Seminole High School** in Sanford, Florida. The Browns traded Faine to New Orleans to move up in the second round of the 2006 draft and select Jackson.

5. Cleveland's **Benedictine High School** is the alma mater of former Browns Chuck Noll (1953-59), Stan Sczurek (1963-65), Pat Moriaty (1979) and David Marshall (1984). Longtime northeast Ohio sportswriter Terry Pluto, whose long list of books includes four Browns-related titles, is a Benedictine alum, class of 1973.

6. Two Browns quarterbacks attended **Alliance High School**, located between Canton and Youngstown. John Borton was Cleveland's third-stringer in 1957, and Len Dawson joined the team in 1960. He too was a backup, until moving to the AFL two years later and building Hall of Fame credentials.

7. Massillon's big football rival, **Canton McKinley**, is the alma mater of former Browns Marion Motley, Nick Roman and Ray Ellis.

8. Hall of Famer Bill Willis (1946-53) and iron man Jim Marshall, a Brown in 1960, both attended **Columbus East High School**.

9. Cleveland St. Joseph's Tom Schoen played four games for the 1970 Browns two years after being drafted out of Notre Dame. NT Bob Golic (1982-88) followed the same high school and college path. Schoen later returned to his alma mater as head coach and athletic director.

10. Pro Bowl S Thom Darden (1972-81) and Ed Bettridge, a member of the 1964 championship team, are both graduates of **Sandusky High School**.

11. Three former teammates at **Toledo St. John's Jesuit** — Mark Krerowicz, Mike Teifke and Dave Butler — briefly reunited as Browns strike replacement players in 1987. Krerowicz and Teifke were part of a makeshift offensive line that helped Larry Mason rush for 133 yards in a victory at New England that proved to be important in the standings, as the Browns won the division by one game. Former head coach Rob Chudzinski is also a St. John's alum, as is this book's author.

12. **Glades Central** in Belle Glade, Florida, is the alma mater of the Browns' 2001 third-round pick James Jackson, 2012 fourth-rounder Travis Benjamin and undrafted DL Santonio Thomas (2008). All three attended the University of Miami.

13. **Cincinnati Princeton** produced S Harlon Barnett (1990-92) and DT Jesse Turnbow (1978).

14. Los Angeles' **Susan Miller Dorsey High School** has produced dozens of NFL players over the years, including WR Dennis Northcutt (2000-06), RB Karim Abdul-Jabbar (1999) and CB Chris Owens (2013)

15. Former Browns DE Frostee Rucker (2012) and LB Beau Bell (2008) are both products of **Tustin High School** in southern California.

16. Long Beach (Cal.) Polytechnic: LB Willie McGinest (2006-08), Marquez Pope (1999) and Kirk Jones (1987).

17. Roy Barker and Marlon Forbes, teammates on the expansion Browns' 1999 defense, both hail from **Central Islip High School** on Long Island.

18. QB Mike Tomczak (1992) and DT John Jurkovic (1999) both attended **Thornton Fractional North** in Calumet City, Illinois.

19. New Jersey's **Bergen Catholic** helped develop DT Carl Barisich (1973-75) and TE Jim Dray (2014*).

20. **DeMatha High School** in Maryland: LB Mike Johnson (1986-93) and T Mike Graybill (1989).

21. **Bryan (Texas) High School**'s NFL alumni include RB Curtis Dickey (1985-86), DB Odie Harris (1991-92) and WR Syndric Steptoe (2008).

22. **South Oak Cliff** in Dallas, Texas: TE Oscar Roan (1975-78) and Joe King (1991).

23. **Longview** (Texas): DT Forrest "Chubby" Grigg (1948-51) and RB Earnest Hunter (1995).

Browns Who Were Also College Teammates

This is the most complete listing known of players who were teammates both in college and with the Browns.

Browns years are based on appearing in a regular season game, except as noted. Strike replacement players from 1987 are excluded.

College years are generally based on letters earned or other evidence of varsity participation. (Several early Browns — including Lou Groza, Horace Gillom, Bob Gaudio and Spiro Dellerba — played together on Ohio State freshman teams of 1941 and 1942 but left for academic or military service reasons.)

The list is ordered chronologically by the players' first year as Browns teammates, then alphabetically by college. Some especially noteworthy sets of teammates are indicated in boldface.

John Harrington & Mel Maceau — Marquette 1941-42, Browns 1946
Frank Gatski & Ed Ulinski — Marshall 1941, Browns 1946-49
Don Greenwood & Bob Steuber — Missouri 1940-2, Browns 1946
Otto Graham & Alex Kapter — Northwestern 1941-43, Browns 1946

BROWNS BIOGRAPHICAL FACTS

Fred "Dippy" Evans & Lou Rymkus — Notre Dame 1940-42, Browns 1946
Evans, Rymkus & John Yonakor — Notre Dame 1942, Browns 1946
Rymkus & Yonakor — Notre Dame 1942, Browns 1946-49
George Cheroke, Jim Daniell & Lin Houston — Ohio State 1941, Browns 1946
Gene Fekete, Houston, Dante Lavelli & Bill Willis — Ohio State 1942, Browns 1946
Houston, Lavelli & Willis — Ohio State 1942, Browns 1946-53

Bob Cowan, Jim Dewar & Lou Saban — Indiana 1942, Browns 1947
Cowan & Saban — Indiana 1942, Browns 1947-48
Greenwood & Marshall Shurnas — Missouri 1941-42, Browns 1947

George Terlep & Yonakor — Notre Dame 1943, Browns 1948
Houston, Tommy James, Lavelli & Willis — Ohio State 1942, Browns 1948-53
James & Lavelli — Ohio State 1942, Browns 1948-55
Tony Adamle & James — Ohio State 1946, Browns 1948-51, 1954
Ollie Cline & Willis — Ohio State 1944, Browns 1948

Les Horvath, Houston, James, Lavelli & Willis — Ohio State 1942, Browns 1949
Horvath & Willis — Ohio State 1942, 1944, Browns 1949

Abe Gibron & Ken Gorgal — Purdue 1947-48, Browns 1950, 1953-54

Don Shula & Carl Taseff — John Carroll 1948-50, Browns 1951

Bob Gain & Don "Dopey" Phelps — Kentucky 1947, 1949, Browns 1952
Darrel "Pete" Brewster & Joe Skibinski — Purdue 1949-51, Browns 1952

Brewster & Gorgal — Purdue 1949, Browns 1953-54

Quincy Armstrong & Ray Renfro — North Texas 1949-50, Browns 1954
Adamle, James & Fred "Curly" Morrison — Ohio State 1946, Browns 1954
James & Morrison — Ohio State 1946, Browns 1954-55

Sam Palumbo & Johnny Petitbon — Notre Dame 1951, Browns 1955-56
James, Morrison & Pete Perini — Ohio State 1946, Browns 1955
Morrison & Perini — Ohio State 1946-49, Browns 1955

Galen Fiss & Mike McCormack — Kansas 1950, Browns 1956-62

Gain & Vito "Babe" Parilli — Kentucky 1949-50, Browns 1956
Art Hunter, Palumbo & Petitbon — Notre Dame 1951, Browns 1956
Hunter & Palumbo — Notre Dame 1951-53, Browns 1956
Herschel Forester & Donald "Tiny" Goss — SMU 1951, Browns 1956

Joe Amstutz & Milt Campbell — Indiana 1954-55, Browns 1957
Chet "The Jet" Hanulak & Ed Modzewlewski — Maryland 1951, Browns 1957

Leroy Bolden & Fred Quinlan — Michigan State 1952-53, Browns 1958

Frank Clarke & John Wooten — Colorado 1956, Browns 1959
Rich Kreitling & Bobby Mitchell — Illinois 1957, Browns 1959-61
Jim Ninowski & Fran O'Brien — Michigan State 1956-57, Browns 1959

Don Fleming & Bernie Parrish — Florida 1956-57, Browns 1960-62
Bobby Franklin & Gene Hickerson — Mississippi 1957, Browns 1960, 1962-66
Jim Houston, Jim Marshall & Dick Schafrath — Ohio State 1957-58, Browns 1960
Houston & Schafrath — Ohio State 1957-58, Browns 1960-71
Ross Fichtner & Gene Selawski — Purdue 1957-58, Browns 1960

Johnny Brewer & Franklin — Mississippi 1957, 1959, Browns 1961-66
Bobby Crespino & Franklin — Mississippi 1958-59, Browns 1961-63
Brewer & Crespino — Mississippi 1959-60, Browns 1961-63
Brewer, Crespino & Franklin — Mississippi 1959, Browns 1961-63

Bill Glass & Jim Ray Smith — Baylor 1954, Browns 1962
Brewer, Franklin & Hickerson — Mississippi 1957, Browns 1962-1966
Brewer & Hickerson — Mississippi 1957, Browns 1962-67
John Brown & Ernie Davis — Syracuse 1959-61, Browns 1962 (Davis inactive)

Gary Collins & Roger Shoals — Maryland 1960-61, Browns 1963-64
Fichtner & Stan Sczurek — Purdue 1959, Browns 1963-65

Mike Howell & Clifton "Sticks" McNeil — Grambling 1961, Browns 1965-67
Tom Hutchinson & Dale Lindsey — Kentucky 1962 (Lindsey quit this infamous "Thin Thirty" team in the spring), Browns 1965
Brewer, Franklin & Ralph "Catfish" Smith — Mississippi 1959, Browns 1965-66
Brewer & Smith — Mississippi 1959-60, Browns 1965-67
Erich Barnes and Fichtner — Purdue 1957, Browns 1965-67

BROWNS BIOGRAPHICAL FACTS

Charlie Harraway & Walter "The Flea" Roberts — San Jose State 1963, Browns 1966

Jim Battle & Sid Williams — Southern 1962-63, Browns 1966

Collins & Dick Shiner — Maryland 1961, Browns 1967

Walter Johnson & George Youngblood — Los Angeles State 1964, Browns 1967

John Demarie & John Garlington — LSU 1965-66, Browns 1968-75

Chip Glass & Walt Sumner — Florida State 1966-68, Browns 1969-73
Paul Warfield & Bo Scott — Ohio State 1962, Browns 1969
Al Jenkins & Chuck Reynolds — Tulsa 1967-68, Browns 1969-70

Mike Phipps & William Yanchar — Purdue 1967-69, Browns 1970

Dave Jones & Clarence Scott — Kansas State 1968, Browns 1971
Stan Brown & Phipps — Purdue 1968-69, Browns 1971

Thom Darden & Paul Staroba — Michigan 1969-70, Browns 1972
Rich Jackson & Frank Pitts — Southern 1962-63, Browns 1972

Fair Hooker & Hugh McKinnis — Arizona State 1968, Browns 1973-75
Chuck Hutchison & Nick Roman — Ohio State 1967, 1969, Browns 1973-74
Cliff Brooks & "Turkey" Joe Jones — Tennessee State 1968-69, Browns 1973

Tom DeLeone, Hutchison & Roman — Ohio State 1969, Browns 1974
DeLeone & Hutchison — Ohio State 1969, Browns 1974-75

Terry Brown & Jerry Sherk — Oklahoma State 1968-69, Browns 1976
Brian Duncan & Oscar Roan — SMU 1972-74, Browns 1976-77
Duncan, Roan & Henry Sheppard — SMU 1973-74, Browns 1976-77
Roan & Sheppard — SMU 1973-74, Browns 1976-78

Bob Lingenfelter & Terry Luck — Nebraska 1974-75, Browns 1977

Johnny Evans & Tom London — North Carolina State 1974-77, Browns 1978

Oliver Davis & John Smith — Tennessee State 1976, Browns 1979
Robert L. Jackson & Cody Risien — Texas A&M 1976, Browns 1979-81
Rich Dimler & Clay Matthews — USC 1975-77, Browns 1979

Judson Flint & Keith Wright — Memphis 1977, Browns 1980

Bill Cowher & Evans — North Carolina State 1975-77, Browns 1980
Davis & McDonald Oden — Tennessee State 1976, Browns 1980
Matthews, Paul McDonald & Charles White — USC 1976-77, Browns 1980-84
Matthews & McDonald — USC 1976-77, Browns 1980-85
McDonald & White — USC 1976-79, Browns 1980-84

Johnny Davis & Ozzie Newsome — Alabama 1975-77, Browns 1982-87
Keith Baldwin, Risien & Mike Whitwell — Texas A&M 1978, Browns 1982-83
Baldwin & Risien — Texas A&M 1978, Browns 1982-83, 1985
Baldwin & Whitwell — Texas A&M 1978-81, Browns 1982-83
Larry Braziel, Matthews & McDonald — USC 1977, Browns 1982-85
Larry Braziel, Matthews, McDonald & White — USC 1977, Browns 1982-84
Chip Banks, Braziel & McDonald — USC 1978, Browns 1982-85
Banks, Braziel, McDonald & White — USC 1978, Browns 1982-84
Banks & McDonald — USC 1978-79, Browns 1982-85
Banks, McDonald & White — USC 1978-79, Browns 1982-84

Dave Logan & Rod Perry — Colorado 1973-74, Browns 1983
Rocky Belk & Scott Nicolas — Miami 1980-81, Browns 1983
Vagas Ferguson & Bob Golic — Notre Dame 1976-78, Browns 1983
Lawrence Johnson & Tim Stracka — Wisconsin 1978, Browns 1983-84

Eddie Johnson & Frank Minnifield — Louisville 1979-80, Browns 1984-90

Curtis Dickey & Risien — Texas A&M 1976-78, Browns 1985-86
Baldwin & Dickey — Texas A&M 1978-79, Browns 1985
Baldwin, Dickey & Risien — Texas A&M 1978, Browns 1985

Tony Baker & Earnest Byner — East Carolina 1982-83, Browns 1986, 88

Bernie Kosar & Gregg Rakoczy — Miami 1983-84, Browns 1987-90
Darryl Sims & George Winslow — Wisconsin 1982, Browns 1987

Ron Middleton & Lawyer Tillman — Auburn 1985, Browns 1989
Kevin Simons & Daryle Smith — Tennessee 1985-86, Browns 1989
Stephen Braggs & Eric Metcalf — Texas 1985-86, Browns 1989-91

Ben Jefferson & Vernon Joines — Maryland 1985, 87-88, Browns 1990
Harlon Barnett & Kevin Robbins — Michigan State 1987-88, Browns 1990
Marcus Cotton & Scott Galbraith — USC 1986-87, Browns 1990

BROWNS BIOGRAPHICAL FACTS 13

Derrick Douglas & Matt Stover — Louisiana Tech 1986-89, Browns 1991
Richard Brown & Webster Slaughter — San Diego State 1984-85, Browns 1991
Brown, Randy Kirk, Alfred Jackson & Slaughter — San Diego State 1985, Browns 1991
Brown, Kirk & Jackson — San Diego State 1985-86, Browns 1991
Jackson & Pio Sagapolutele — San Diego State 1988, Browns 1991-92
Brown & Jackson — San Diego State 1985-86, Browns 1991-92
Rob Burnett, Frank Conover & Todd Philcox — Syracuse 1988, Browns 1991
Burnett & Conover — Syracuse 1988-89, Browns 1991
Burnett & Philcox — Syracuse 1987-88, Browns 1991-93

Ed King & Tillman — Auburn 1988, Browns 1992-93
Bobby Abrams & Leroy Hoard — Michigan 1987-89, Browns 1992
Barnett, Alan Haller & Bill Johnson — Michigan State 1988-89, Browns 1992
Haller & Johnson — Michigan State 1988-91, Browns 1992
Fred Foggie & Chris Thome — Minnesota 1988-90, Browns 1992
Cedric Figaro & Frank Stams — Notre Dame 1984-87, Browns 1992
Mark Bavaro, Figaro & Stams — Notre Dame 1984, Browns 1992
Bob Dahl & Stams — Notre Dame 1988, Browns 1992-95
Eric Turner & Lance Zeno — UCLA 1987-90, Browns 1992-93

Kosar & Vinny Testaverde — Miami 1984, Browns 1993
Steve Everitt & Hoard — Michigan 1989, Browns 1993-95
Patrick Rowe & Sagapolutele — San Diego State 1990, Browns 1993

Derrick Alexander (WR), Everitt & Hoard — Michigan 1989, Browns 1994-95
Pepper Johnson & Tom Tupa — Ohio State 1984-85, Browns 1994-95

Andre Rison & Lorenzo White — Michigan State 1985-87, Browns 1995

Rahim Abdullah & Jim Bundren — Clemson 1996-97, Browns 1999-2000
Darius Holland & Rashaan Salaam — Colorado 1993-94, Browns 1999
Derrick Alexander (DE) & Corey Fuller — Florida State 1992, 1994, Browns 1999
Damon Gibson & Sedrick Shaw — Iowa 1995-96, Browns 1999
Karim Abdul-Jabbar & Jamir Miller — UCLA 1992, Browns 1999
Terry Kirby & Ryan Kuehl — Virginia 1991-92, Browns 1999
Tarek Saleh & Mike Thompson — Wisconsin 1993-94, Browns 1999-2000

Chester Burnett & Dennis Northcutt — Arizona 1996-97, Browns 2000
Rashidi Barnes, Brad Bedell & Darrin Chiaverini — Colorado 1998, Browns 2000
Barnes & Bedell — Colorado 1998-89, Browns 2000
Barnes & Chiaverini — Colorado 1996-98, Browns 2000
Fuller & Orpheus Roye — Florida State 1994, Browns 2000-02
Mark Campbell, Chris Floyd & Aaron Shea — Michigan 1996-97, Browns 2000
Campbell & Floyd — Michigan 1995-97, Browns 2000
Campbell & Shea — Michigan 1996-98, Browns 2000, 2002
Bobby Brown & Marc Edwards — Notre Dame 1996, Browns 2000
Courtney Brown & Kevin Thompson — Penn State 1996-99, Browns 2000
Percy Ellsworth & Kuehl — Virginia 1994, Browns 2000-01
Noel LaMontagne & Wali Rainer — Virginia 1997-98, Browns 2000

Devin Bush & Fuller — Florida State 1992, Browns 2001-02
Fuller, Roye & Greg Spires — Florida State 1994, Browns 2001
Roye & Spires — Florida State 1994-95, Browns 2001
Jeremy McKinney & Ross Verba — Iowa 1994-96, Browns 2001
Dyshod Carter, Lamar Chapman & Quincy Morgan — Kansas State 1999, Browns 2001
Carter & Chapman — Kansas State 1997-99, Browns 2001
Carter & Morgan — Kansas State 1999-2000, Browns 2001, 2004
Jammi German & Derrick Ham — Miami 1995, Browns 2001
German & Earl Little — Miami 1993-95, Browns 2001
Ham & Little — Miami 1995-96, Browns 2001
Andre King & James Jackson — Miami 1997-2000, Browns 2001-04
Ham, King & Jackson — Miami 1997-98, Browns 2001
Saleh & Tony Simmons — Wisconsin 1994-96, Browns 2001

William Green & Paul Zukauskas — Boston College 1999, Browns 2002-04
Andra Davis & Gerard Warren — Florida 1998-2000, Browns 2002-04
Melvin Fowler & Lewis Sanders — Maryland 1999, Browns 2002-04
Kenard Lang & Little — Miami 1994-06, Browns 2002-04
Joaquin Gonzalez, King & Jackson — Miami 1998-2000, Browns 2002-04
Cedric Scott & Raymond Walls — Southern Miss 1997-2000, Browns 2002
Lenoy Jones & Ryan Tucker — TCU 1993-05, Browns 2002
Andre' Davis & Ben Taylor — Virginia Tech 1998-2001, Browns 2002-04

Antonio Garay, Green & Zukauskas — Boston College 1999, Browns 2003
Garay & Green — Boston College 1999-01, Browns 2003
Enoch Demar & Craig Osika — Indiana 1999-2001, Browns 2003
Kevin Bentley & Barry Gardner — Northwestern 1998, Browns 2003-04
Courtney Brown & Brett Conway — Penn State 1996, Browns 2003
Chad Beasley, Davis, Lee Suggs & Taylor — Virginia Tech 1999-2000, Browns 2003
Beasley, Davis & Taylor — Virginia Tech 1998-2001, Browns 2003
Davis, Suggs & Taylor — Virginia Tech 1999-2000, Browns 2003-04
Suggs & Taylor — Virginia Tech 1999-2000, Browns 2003-5

Terrelle Smith & Mason Unck — Arizona State 1999, Browns 2004-06
Gonzalez & Kellen Winslow — Miami 2001, Browns 2004
Kirk Chambers & Amon Gordon — Stanford 2001-03, Browns 2004
Warrick Holdman & Michael Jameson — Texas A&M 1997-98, Browns 2004

Gary Baxter & Jody Littleton — Baylor 1997, Browns 2005
Baxter & Ethan Kelley — Baylor 1999-2000, Browns 2005-06
Antonio Perkins & Brodney Pool — Oklahoma 2002-04, Browns 2005-06
Daylon McCutcheon & Billy Miller — USC 1995-98, Browns 2005

Ken Dorsey, Orien Harris, Leon Williams & Winslow — Miami 2002, Browns 2006
Dorsey, Williams & Winslow — Miami 2002, Browns 2006-08
Dorsey & Winslow — Miami 2001-02, Browns 2006-08
Williams & Winslow — Miami 2001-03, Browns 2006-08
Harris, Williams & Winslow — Miami 2002-03, Browns 2006
Harris & Williams — Miami 2002-05, Browns 2006
Michael Hawkins, Perkins, Pool & Travis Wilson — Oklahoma 2002, Browns 2006
Perkins, Pool & Wilson — Oklahoma 2002-04, Browns 2006

Daven Holly & Antwan Peek — Cincinnati 2001-02, Browns 2007

Dorsey, Winslow & Santonio Thomas — Miami 2001, Browns 2008
Dorsey & Thomas — Miami 2000-01, Browns 2008
Thomas, Williams & Winslow — Miami 2003, Browns 2008
Thomas & Williams — Miami 2003-04, Browns 2008
Thomas & Winslow — Miami 2001, 2003, Browns 2008
Braylon Edwards & Shantee Orr — Michigan 2002, Browns 2008
Derek Anderson & Gerard Lawson — Oregon State 2004, Browns 2008-09

Jamal Lewis & Donte' Stallworth — Tennessee 1999, Browns 2008
Phil Dawson & Shaun Rogers — Texas 1997, Browns 2008-10
Beau Bell & Eric Wright — UNLV 2006, Browns 2008
Hamza Abdullah & Jerome Harrison — Washington State 2004, Browns 2008

Anthony Madison & Ramzee Robinson — Alabama 2003-05, Browns 2009
Eric Steinbach & Matt Roth — Iowa 2001-02, Browns 2009-10
Steinbach & Derreck Robinson — Iowa 2002, Browns 2009-10
Roth & Robinson — Iowa 2002-04, Browns 2009-10
Joshua Cribbs & Abram Elam — Kent State 2004, Browns 2009-10

James Davis & Chansi Stuckey — Clemson 2005-06, Browns 2010
Eric Alexander & Robert Royal — LSU 2001, Browns 2010
Evan Moore & Alex Smith — Stanford 2003-04, Browns 2010-11
Eric King & Steve Vallos — Wake Forest 2003-04, Browns 2010

Mohammed Massaquoi & Kiante Tripp — Georgia 2008, Browns 2011
Cribbs & Usama Young — Kent State 2003-04. Browns 2011-12
Jordan Norwood & Scott Paxson — Penn State 2005, Browns 2011
Jason Pinkston & Jabaal Sheard — Pittsburgh 2007-10, Browns 2011-13
Owen Marecic & Moore — Stanford 2007, Browns 2011
Colt McCoy & Chris Ogbonnaya — Texas 2006-08, Browns 2011-12
Jordan Cameron & Kaluka Maiava — USC 2008, Browns 2011-12

Trent Richardson & Brad Smelley — Alabama 2009-11, Browns 2012
Josh Gordon & Phil Taylor — Baylor 2009-10, Browns 2012-2014*
Alex Mack & Mitchell Schwartz — California 2008, Browns 2012-2014*
Massaquoi & Prince Miller — Georgia 2006-08, Browns 2012
Brandon Weeden & Josh Cooper — Oklahoma State 2008-11, Browns 2012-13
Johnson Bademosi & Marecic — Stanford 2008-10, Browns 2012
Maiava & Frostee Rucker — USC 2005, Browns 2012

Rashad Butler & Willis McGahee — Miami 2002, Browns 2013
Tori Gurley & Spencer Lanning — South Carolina 2009-10, Browns 2013
Brian Sanford & Martin Wallace — Temple 2010, Browns 2013
Ogbonnaya & Fozzy Whittaker — Texas 2008, Browns 2013

Robert Nelson & Gerell Robinson — Arizona State 2011, Browns 2014
Jaccobi McDaniel & Rodney Smith — Florida State 2009-11, Browns 2014*
Travis Benjamin & LaRon Byrd — Miami 2008-11, Browns 2014

BROWNS BIOGRAPHICAL FACTS   17

Shaun Draughn & Ryan Taylor — North Carolina 2007-08, Browns 2014
Lanning & Connor Shaw — South Carolina 2010, Browns 2014
Bademosi, Jim Dray & Sione Fua — Stanford 2008-09, Browns 2014
Bademosi & Dray — Stanford 2008-09, Browns 2014*
Dray & Fua — Stanford 2006, 2008, Browns 2014
Bademosi & Fua — Stanford 2008-10, Browns 2014
John Greco & Andrew Hawkins — Toledo 2005-07, Browns 2014*
Jim Leonhard & Joe Thomas — Wisconsin 2003-04, Browns 2014

Cameron Erving & Kevin Haplea — Florida State 2012-14, Browns 2015* (draftee/UDFA)
Hayes Pullard & Randall Telfer — USC 2011-14, Browns 2015* (draftees)
Xavier Cooper & Vince Mayle — Washington State 2013-14, Browns 2015* (draftees)

14 Browns Notable for Playing Other Sports

1. **John Havlicek** — The Hall of Fame guard for Boston Celtics, who won eight NBA titles in his 16 years with the team, was a seventh-round Browns draft pick in 1962. He competed as a receiver in training camp until the final cutdown. An all-state quarterback at Bridgeport High School in eastern Ohio, Havlicek focused on basketball at Ohio State, where his teammates included Jerry Lucas and Bobby Knight.

2. **Dave Logan** — The rangy receiver was the Browns' third-round pick in 1976, and he eventually thrived in the pass-happy Sam Rutigliano offense. Coming out of high school, the pitcher/infielder was a 19th-round pick of the Cincinnati Reds but never signed. He lettered in both football and basketball at Colorado, where he averaged 14.1 points in 58 collegiate games. Also a ninth-round pick of the NBA's Kansas City Kings, Logan is among a very select group of athletes to be drafted in all three major sports.

3. **Milt Campbell** — One of the greatest — and most overlooked — American athletes ever, Campbell won the gold medal in decathlon at the 1956 Olympic Games in Melbourne, besting Rafer Johnson, the 1960 champion, with a record point total in the ten-event competition. He was also the silver medalist in 1952 while still in high school, and he set world records in the 60- and 120-yard high hurdles in 1957. That fall Campbell broke into the NFL as the Browns' kick returner and backup to

fellow rookie Jim Brown. An African American from New Jersey who served in the Navy and attended Indiana University, he later claimed Paul Brown cut him in 1958 after confronting him for marrying a white woman. He then played several seasons in Canada.

4. **Jim Brown** — It's well-known how dominant he was as a running back, but he earned 13 varsity letters in high school and ten more at Syracuse in four different sports: football, basketball, track and lacrosse. In the latter, he was a first-team All-American, capping his career by scoring five goals in a single half of an all-star game. In addition to his enshrinement in Canton, he's a member of the National Lacrosse Hall of Fame in Baltimore.

5. **Otto Graham** — It's not uncommon for gridiron stars to have diverse athletic backgrounds, but only a scarce few have won championships in another major pro sports league. That's what the legendary quarterback did between his Navy discharge and the first Browns training camp in 1946. Graham went to Northwestern as a music major on a basketball scholarship, becoming a first-team All-American in two sports in the same year. He joined the Rochester Royals of the National Basketball League, a precursor to the NBA. In their inaugural season, they beat Fort Wayne and Sheboygan in the playoffs to claim the league title. Averaging 5.2 points per game as a guard/forward, "Automatic Otto" was a 64% free-throw shooter.

6. **Ron Brown** — Cleveland drafted this Los Angeles native in the second round of 1983 to bolster their weakening wide receiver corps. He pursued Olympic glory instead, winning a gold medal as part of the 4 x 100 relay team at the L.A. games in 1984. The Browns traded his rights to the L.A. Rams, where he played eight seasons and made the 1985 Pro Bowl as a kick returner.

7. **Brandon Weeden** — This Oklahoman's strong right arm led to a two-sport career, beginning as a pitcher the New York Yankees drafted in the second round in 2002. In five minor-league seasons with three organizations, Weeden rose no higher than A ball, finishing 19-26 with a 5.02 ERA. So he enrolled at Oklahoma State and eventually broke many of the school's passing records in quarterbacking the team to 12-1 record, including a BCS bowl win, in 2012. Cleveland made him the oldest first-round pick in NFL history at age 28, but he failed to find consistency as a starter and was released after two seasons.

8. **Eric Metcalf** — The shifty speedster was every bit as good in track as he was in football. He was a four-time track All-American at Texas and twice won the NCAA title in long jump, with a career mark of 27' 8.25".

9. **Bobby Mitchell** — Unlike Ron Brown, this college track star signed with the Browns rather than chasing Olympic dreams. He ran the 70-

yard low hurdles in 7.7 seconds in 1958, setting an indoor world record, though it lasted just six days. His bust in Canton endures far longer.

10. Sam Clancy — He never played college football, but the 6'7" Pittsburgh native was worth an 11th-round flyer by the Seahawks in 1982 based on his basketball résumé. The first Pitt player to top 1,000 points and rebounds, he remains their all-time rebound leader. He racked up 14 of his 30 career sacks during his four-year stint as a Brown.

11. Galen Fiss — A roommate of legendary basketball coach Dean Smith on the Kansas Jayhawk baseball team, Fiss signed with the Cleveland Indians in 1953 after the Browns didn't offer him a contract despite drafting him in the 13th round. The catcher/outfielder hit .275 for the Indians' farm team in Fargo/Moorhead, where his teammates included a young Roger Maris. After two years in the Air Force, Lieutenant Fiss joined the Browns for an 11-year career as a dependably durable linebacker who became team captain and a two-time Pro Bowler.

12. Bernie Parrish — The two-sport star from Florida took a $90,000 bonus to sign with the Cincinnati Reds. The outfielder hit .219 for Albuquerque and Topeka in two minor-league seasons before writing to Paul Brown of his intention to focus on football. He quickly became a solid starting cornerback.

13. Mike Baab — The fine center who served two tours of duty as a Brown later won a Masters World Championship and set several world records in his age class in the Scottish Highland Games.

14. Andre King — Eight years before Butch Davis drafted his former Miami receiver in the seventh round of 2001, King was a second-round pick of the Atlanta Braves. The outfielder played five years in the low minors, hitting just .237.

The 8 Tallest Browns

These Browns players' heights were each listed at six feet, eight inches or greater.

1. Ben Jefferson (OG, 1990) — 6'9", 330 pounds.
The undrafted Maryland lineman claimed he'd been that height since ninth grade. A nickname of "Big Ben" seems obvious, but Jefferson proposed that he be called "The House." Like his NFL career, it never quite got established.

2. Jerry Wilkinson (DE, 1980) — 6'9", 265.

He appeared in Super Bowl XIV for the Rams as a rookie but was cut the next summer. Signed to replace rookie second-round bust Cleveland Crosby, he was flagged for offsides three times in seven games before being released midseason.

3. Scott Rehberg (OL, 1999) — 6'8", 325.

The Browns' third pick in the expansion draft, he started a career-high 13 games at guard and tackle but was criticized by team veterans after sitting a game out with the flu. Cleveland didn't offer him a contract for 2000, so he signed with Cincinnati and spent four seasons there.

4. Reid Fragel (OT, 2013) — 6'8", 308.

The former Buckeye was on the Browns' active roster but has yet to appear in an NFL game.

5. Chris Pike (DT, 1989-90) — 6'8", 280.

A one-time recruit of Dean Smith for North Carolina basketball, Pike started 11 games as a Brown after arriving via trade with Philadelphia.

6. Greg Estandia (TE, 2009) — 6'8", 265.

The tallest man to catch a pass for the Browns, he had four receptions in four games here before injuries caught up with him.

7. Doug Atkins (DE, 1953-54) — 6'8", 257.

Browns assistant Weeb Ewbank recommended him to Paul Brown as the finest physical specimen he'd ever seen. The rowdy pass rusher was a first-round pick and, two years later, one of three future Hall of Fame defenders that Brown traded away.

8. Mack Mitchell (DE, 1975-78) — 6'8", 246.

The fifth-overall pick in the 1975 draft out of Houston, Mitchell was perhaps just shy of 6'8", not including his Afro. His pass rushing speed flashed at times, as he twice racked up four-sack games. But he was inconsistent over his four seasons here and was cut in 1979. His NFL career ended a year later in Cincinnati with the arrival of his former Browns coach, Forrest Gregg, whose disciplinarian ways Mitchell did not recall fondly.

The 15 Heaviest Browns

The listed weights of NFL players are notoriously inaccurate, as body mass measurement is prone to fluctuate and often a touchy topic anyway.

The list below illustrates the increasing bulk of athletes in recent years. The exception that proves the rule is the early Brown Forrest Grigg (1948-51), listed at 6'2" and 294 pounds. Widely known as "Chubby," he eventually dieted down to 275 after being benched for ballooning as high as 330, which wouldn't even make this list's top ten.

The Browns' top draft pick in 2015, Danny Shelton (also 6'2"), tipped the scales at the scouting combine at 339 pounds.

1. DT Ted Washington (2006-07) — 365 pounds
2. OT Orlando "Zeus" Brown (1994-95, 1999) — 360
3. G Kelvin Garmon (2004) — 350
4. DT Shaun Rogers (2008-10) — 340
5. (tie) OT Tony Pashos (2010-11) — 337
    DT Phil Taylor (2011-2014*) — 337
7. (tie) G Damion Cook (2004) — 335
    OT L.J. Shelton (2005) — 335
9. DT Ishmaa'ily Kitchen (2012-2014*) — 334
10. G Floyd "Pork Chop" Womack (2009-10) — 333
11. OL Freddie Childress (1992) — 331
12. (tie) DT Jerry Ball (1993, 1999) — 330
    OT James Brown (2000) — 330
    DT Darius Holland (1999-2000) — 330
    G Ben Jefferson (1990) — 330

4 Browns with Physical Anomalies

1. Mac Speedie (WR, 1946-52) — A childhood condition called Perthes Disease affecting blood supply to the femoral head required him to wear a brace for four years. Speedie's legs ended up different lengths, but his athletic determination, once freed from the brace, proved boundless. With an odd gait that proved deceptively fast, he led the AAFC in receptions for three straight years, among his many remarkable but underrated professional accomplishments.

2. Paul Kruger (LB, 2013-14*) — A car accident at age 13 cost him a kidney and his spleen. A Jeep driven by his uncle overturned and rolled onto his stomach, which put him on life support for two days and in critical condition for five. In college, he was stabbed twice by gang members, suffering a nicked artery and collapsed lung and leaving him with two long scars.

3. George Young (DE, 1946-53) — Doctors found a large calcium growth on his right thigh bone in 1945 and wanted to operate. He declined out of fear of the surgery causing functional impairment. The deposit was over nine inches before it stopped growing, but it didn't turn out to be a career impediment.

4. Jason Pinkston (G, 2011-13) — A fifth-round draft pick who became an instant starter, Pinkston was sidelined midway through his second year with what turned out to be a life-threatening blood clot in a lung. Despite needing blood thinners and months of diet and exercise restrictions, he was cleared to return for the 2013 season. However, a preseason ankle sprain limited him to three games. Unfortunately blood clots returned in the summer of 2014, leading the Browns to release him with an injury settlement.

11 Sets of Relatives Affiliated with the Browns

These family members who played and/or coached with the Browns are listed alphabetically.

1. Ball/Malbrough — Massive defensive tackle Jerry Ball, who played for the Browns in 1993 and again briefly in 1999, is the half-brother of Anthony Malbrough, a sixth-round pick of the Browns who played here in 2000. The defensive back later played several seasons in Canada.

2. Hilgenberg — Center Jay joined the Browns for the 1992 season following a trade with Chicago, where he was coming off seven straight Pro Bowl years. His father Jerry, also a center, was a Browns fourth-round draft choice in 1954 but never appeared in a pro game. Each had a younger brother who also played in the NFL. All four were University of Iowa standouts.

3. Houston — Brothers Lin and Jim were nearly 17 years apart and represented the family on the Browns roster for 21 of the franchise's first 27 years. Lin played for Paul Brown in high school at Massillon, on a national championship team with Ohio State, and for the first eight

seasons of the Cleveland Browns, one of the original messenger guards. Jim eventually outgrew him, becoming a first-round draft pick and earning Pro Bowl honors at linebacker four times in 13 pro seasons, all with the Browns.

4. Jones — Wide receiver Homer finished his career in Cleveland in 1970, the year they drafted his cousin, "Turkey" Joe, a Browns defensive end for two stints totalling six-and-a-half years. Hall of Fame receiver Charley Taylor is Homer's cousin and Joe's half-brother.

5. Kruger — Linebacker Paul signed a hefty free agent deal with the Browns in 2013. His brother David joined him two months later as an undrafted rookie free agent, but the defensive end was waived late in training camp.

6. McCown — Quarterback Luke, a fourth-round draft pick in 2004 pressed into service late in his rookie year, was traded to Tampa Bay the next April. A decade later, the Buccaneers released his older brother, Josh, and the 35-year-old free agent QB signed with the Browns, his ninth NFL team, on February 27, 2015.

7. Modzelewski — Two sons of a Polish-born coal miner each became world champs during different eras of Browns football. Fullback Ed, or "Big Mo," was the team's second-leading rusher in 1955 and 1956, then backed up Jim Brown for three seasons. His younger brother Dick, or "Little Mo," was actually larger by some 33 pounds. The defensive tackle was a key veteran pickup in 1964. He played three years in Cleveland and stayed with the organization through 1977. A third brother, Gene, was drafted by both the Browns and the U.S. Army in 1966. He served in Vietnam and never appeared in an NFL game.

8. Montgomery — Cleotha filled in for the injured Dino Hall as a return specialist early in 1981, the year his older brother, Wilbert, enjoyed his third 1,000-yard rushing season for the Eagles. Wilbert was hired as the Browns' running backs coach in 2014.

9. Richardson — Gloster, a wide receiver, caught 22 passes for 448 yards in three seasons as a Brown. Three of his brothers also played pro football, including Ernie, a tight end who played two games for Cleveland in 1974. They are the only set of brothers to take the field for the Browns in the same regular season.

10. Robiskie — NFL veteran Terry spent six seasons with the Browns, as offensive coordinator and interim head coach in 2004, and coaching wide receivers both before and after. Meanwhile, his son, Brian, served as a training camp ball boy, starred at Chagrin Falls High School and moved on to Ohio State. The receiver was the Browns' second-round choice in 2009 (drafted by another former Browns ball boy, Eric Mangini) but was released midway through his third season.

11. Saban — It's believed that two longtime coaches with Browns connections were distant cousins, though their paths didn't cross until both were engaged in their professions. The late Lou Saban was an early Browns captain and standout linebacker for their first four seasons before embarking on a well-traveled coaching career. Nick Saban, born in 1951, was given Lou as a middle name. The Kent State product was Bill Belichick's defensive coordinator for the 1991-94 Browns.

9 Browns Accomplished in Other Fields

Football is a young man's game, so it behooves players to use their college scholarships and high playing-days incomes to prepare for life's next chapters. Here's a sampling of the many Browns who succeeded in fields other than sports.

1. **Frank Ryan** (QB, 1962-68) — Well-known for earning his Ph.D. in mathematics during his playing career, he enjoyed a successful post-football profession life in academia and business. He is credited with helping establish the first electronic voting system for the U.S. House of Representatives.

2. **Ernie Green** (HB, 1962-68) — The blocker for feature backs Jim Brown and Leroy Kelly became a headliner beyond football, co-founding and running Ernie Green Industries, Inc., an Ohio-based auto parts maker and supplier with several plants throughout the state and beyond. In recent years it's been diversifying into other markets with plastics contract manufacturing.

3. **Dick Ambrose** (MLB, 1975-83) — The impact "Bam Bam" has these days is with a gavel. Since 2004, he's served as a judge of the Cuyahoga County Court of Common Pleas.

4. **Tony Adamle** (LB/FB, 1947-51, 1954) — The former Browns captain earned two degrees while an active player, retiring in 1951 to attend medical school. He returned to fill a gap at linebacker for the 1954 championship team, then earned his medical degree from Western Reserve University in 1956. He practiced in Kent for most of the rest of the century, specializing in knee and neck injuries.

5. **Bill Glass** (DE, 1962-68) — He spent off-seasons in seminary studies, then after retirement founded a still-active prison ministry now known as Bill Glass Champions for Life.

6. Mike Lucci (LB, 1962-64) — The backup linebacker on the Browns' last title team became a Pro Bowler in Detroit following the three-team trade that brought DB Erich Barnes to the Browns. Lucci's post-football titles included president of the industry-leading Bally division that owned and operated several hundred fitness centers under various names.

7. Dick Schafrath (OT, 1959-71) — The durable left tackle won election to the Ohio State Senate in 1986 with the help of former college coach Woody Hayes. The Republican retired in 2003. He then completed his bachelor's degree at OSU and wrote his autobiography, *Heart of a Mule*.

8. Matt Miller (T, 1979-82) — A fourth-round draft pick and reserve offensive lineman during the Sam Rutigliano era, Miller returned to school after knee problems shortened his playing career. He's currently a full professor at Cornell University's Sibley School of Mechanical and Aerospace Engineering.

9. Les Horvath (HB, 1949) — The 1944 Heisman Trophy winner used his Ohio State education to become a dentist and was practicing as such in the off-season while a Los Angeles Ram in 1947 and 1948. Upon his release, he signed with the Browns and played the 1949 season on offense, defense and special teams. He retired to resume his dentistry career in the L.A. area.

18 Browns Players Who Became Head Coaches or Team Executives

1. Don Shula — The Lake County native played defensive back for the Browns for two seasons, intercepting four passes as a rookie in 1951, before Paul Brown included him in a 15-player swap with the Baltimore Colts. Four days after his 33rd birthday, he succeeded the fired Weeb Ewbank, his former coach, to become, at the time, the youngest head coach in the league's modern history. He went 71-24-4 in seven years at Baltimore but was upset in his two biggest games, the 1964 NFL championship in Cleveland and Super Bowl III to Ewbank's New York Jets. He moved to Miami and became a fixture there over the next 26 years, which included two Super Bowl titles and a perfect 17-0 season. A preeminent name in the history of the sport, Shula earned numerous honors and records, including most career wins as a head coach (347).

2. Chuck Noll — The whip-smart Clevelander served as one of Paul Brown's messenger guards and linebackers but retired at age 27 to

pursue coaching. After nine years as a defensive assistant under the Chargers' Sid Gillman and Shula in Baltimore, he was hired in 1969 to turn around the perennial sad-sack Steelers as their head coach. The low-key Noll masterminded Pittsburgh's dominant Steel Curtain, won four Super Bowls, and earned Hall of Fame induction in 1993.

3. **Ara Parseghian** — The Akron back's playing career was cut short by a hip injured early in 1949, his second season with the Browns. Woody Hayes, his college coach at Miami of Ohio, brought him in to coach their freshman team, and he soon took over the varsity when Hayes left for Ohio State. Winning there led him to Northwestern, where he succeeded former teammate Lou Saban and over eight seasons turned an 0-8-1 team into a Big Ten force. The Wildcats were the top-ranked team for a while in 1962 after beating Ohio State and Notre Dame back to back. The Fighting Irish had been in football famine when Parseghian arrived in 1964. He promptly restored the program's lost luster and won two national championships in 11 successful seasons. He resigned at age 51 with a 170-58-6 coaching record. He then became a TV color commentator, served on Miami's Board of Trustees, and worked on behalf of medical causes close to his heart. As of June 2015, Parseghian, born May 21, 1923, is the oldest living former Browns player.

4. **Ozzie Newsome** — Many Browns fans have mixed feelings about the team's all-time leader in receptions and receiving yards. After all, while Art Modell abandoned Cleveland and its fans in 1995, he stayed loyal to Newsome, and Newsome returned the favor. After 13 seasons as the Browns' game-changing tight end, he rose through the front office ranks in Cleveland and then with the Baltimore Ravens. There he became the league's first African American general manager. His acumen, leadership and disciplined approach have made him one of football's most successful and respected executives. Their track record of drafting Pro Bowlers — nearly one a year on average — has proven an extension of Newsome's wizardry, much as it pains Browns fans to see his work benefit a rival that rose from the heartbreak of the original Browns' devoted fans.

5. **Bill Cowher** — Browns defensive coordinator Marty Schottenheimer must have seen something of himself in Cowher. Both were 6'3", 225-pound linebackers from the Pittsburgh area. Cowher's playing career was injury-shortened and not especially noteworthy, except that his two Browns seasons, 1980 and 1982, featured their only playoff appearances in a 12-year span. Traded to the Eagles for a ninth-round pick, he returned in 1985 as special teams coach for Schottenheimer, who had risen to head coach, and followed him to Kansas City as defensive coordinator. Modell interviewed him for the Browns' head coaching vacancy in 1991 but chose Bill Belichick instead. A year later, the Steelers hired him at age 34 to succeed the retiring Noll. After just one wildcard bid in seven

years, the Steelers under Cowher reached the playoffs six straight times on the strength of their aggressive defense and strong running game. They got their long-awaited "one for the thumb" by winning Super Bowl XL in his 14th season. Since resigning after the 2006 season at age 49, the man known for his gung-ho motivational style and jutting chin has resisted all offers — including at least one from the Browns — to return to the sidelines.

6. Lou Saban — The World War II veteran was team captain as a rookie on the inaugural Browns squad. He played mostly linebacker for the four years Cleveland dominated the All-America Football Conference. (The stat sheets also show a smattering of pass and rush attempts, one 45-yard reception, and 21 extra points as a fill-in for another fellow named Lou.) He retired to become head coach at Cleveland's Case Tech in 1950, launching a colorful and extremely well-traveled career of five decades at virtually every level of the sport. He served two stints as head coach of the Buffalo Bills, twice winning the AFL title. His rosters there included Schottenheimer, O.J. Simpson, Jack Kemp, and Cookie Gilchrist.

7. Mike McCormack — One of Paul Brown's favorites, he combined toughness and technique during his outstanding career, mostly at right tackle. As a coach, he assisted with the College All-Star Game and for the likes of Otto Graham, Vince Lombardi and George Allen in Washington and Brown in Cincinnati. His own head coaching stints in Philadelphia and Baltimore failed to yield a winning record, but he succeeded splendidly in front office roles with Seattle and Carolina. After filling in for fired head coach Jack Patera in 1982, McCormack was named team president/general manager, and the Seahawks immediately made their first playoff appearance, followed by his Hall of Fame induction and three more playoff seasons over the next six years. He then played a key role in starting the expansion Panthers, who went 12-4 in their second season, after which he retired as president/GM.

8. Walt Michaels — Born Wladek Majka to Polish immigrants, he rose from Pennsylvania coal country to the peak of pro football as both player and coach. The linebacker called signals for NFL's stingiest scoring defense, winning two titles and earning Pro Bowl honors five straight years in the 1950s. He later joined former Browns assistant Weeb Ewbank as the Jets' defensive coordinator. His unit held the Raiders — the AFL's leading offense — to 50 rushing yards for the 1968 league championship and then forced five Colt turnovers in the legendary upset of Super Bowl III. When Ewbank hand-picked his son-in-law to succeed him, Michaels spent three years under former Browns teammate McCormack in Philadelphia. He got the long-awaited Jets top job when Lou Holtz crashed and burned after less than a year. His up-and-down six-year tenure included AFC Coach of the Year honors in 1978 and an AFC title game appearance in 1982. Donald Trump hired him to coach

the USFL's New Jersey Generals — including Brian Sipe, Doug Flutie and Herschel Walker — for two winning seasons.

9. **Paul Wiggin** — After 11 years as a fixture at defensive end, this cerebral Stanford grad turned to coaching, starting as an assistant to Dick Nolan with the 49ers. His first head-coaching gig was to follow Hank Stram in Kansas City. He brought in former Browns teammate Vince Costello as defensive coordinator but couldn't restore the Chiefs' winning ways. He was fired midway into 1977 after a 44-7 loss to the Browns, whom they had beaten 39-14 the year before. After two more years with Nolan, this time in New Orleans, Wiggin took the helm at his alma mater, where he coached John Elway and suffered the surreal spectacle of "The Play," a series of last-ditch laterals that gave archrival Cal a most unlikely win. The famous play damaged Stanford's football program, and athletic director Andy Geiger (later with Ohio State) fired Wiggin less than a year later. Wiggin then settled into a long tenure with the Vikings, where his roles included Director of Player Personnel.

10. **Monte Clark** — The steady right tackle of the 1960s Browns later helped coach the Miami Dolphins' great rushing offenses of the early '70s. He was the runner-up for the Browns' head coaching job in 1975, but Modell chose Forrest Gregg instead. Clark instead got chances with the 49ers (the team that originally drafted him) and the Lions. In seven years with Detroit, coaching future Browns Al "Bubba" Baker and Gary Danielson, Clark led his team to the playoffs twice but was fired after a 1984 tailspin that included a career-ending injury to star RB Billy Sims.

11. **Otto Graham** — The greatest of all Browns quarterbacks spent much of his post-playing career with the Coast Guard Academy as their football coach and athletic director (though Modell briefly considered him before hiring Blanton Collier to replace Paul Brown). The Division III program improved under Graham, earning a Tangerine Bowl berth in 1963. His service at the Coast Guard flanked a three-year hitch as an NFL head coach in Washington, where his teams went 17-22-3 before Vince Lombardi replaced him. Graham also coached College All-Star teams ten times in pre-season exhibition games against the defending NFL champs, an annual tradition that ended in 1976. The last victory for collegians came under Graham's leadership in a 1963 upset of Lombardi's Packers.

12. **John Wooten** — This fine Browns guard of the 1960s has remained engaged with pro football throughout his adult life. He's been an agent, a scout, a league executive focused on player programs and chair of the Fritz Pollard Alliance, which has helped spur the NFL to make strides in minority hiring. His front office duties have included high-ranking personnel roles with the Cowboys, Eagles and Ravens.

13. **Lou Rymkus** — The great lineman for the earliest Browns teams spent most of two decades coaching in several leagues. He helped develop Forrest Gregg and Jim Ringo as line coach for the Packers. He assisted Sid Gillman with the Rams, but when his former coach at Notre Dame, Frank Leahy, chose Gillman rather than Rymkus to head the new AFL Los Angeles Chargers, Rymkus took the top job in Houston. The Oilers beat the Chargers to win the first AFL championship, and Rymkus was the league's Coach of the Year. But he soon butted heads with owner Bud Adams and was fired five games into the next season. He then bounced around as an assistant in the AFL and NFL and as head coach of a high school team and two others in the Continental Football League, including the financially failing Akron Vulcans.

14. **Abe Gibron** — The great guard of the Browns' early '50s dynasty spent 41 straight years affiliated with various pro football teams. He had lengthy stints coaching linemen on both offense and defense. His term as head coach of the Chicago Bears from 1972-74 was ill-fated, as Gale Sayers and Dick Butkus were injured, and Walter Payton was drafted the year after he was fired with a record of 11-30-1.

15. **John Sandusky** — The Browns' second selection in their first NFL draft played 70 games as a lineman on both offense and defense before embarking on his long coaching career, much of it as an assistant to former teammate Shula. His 14-year run with the Colts ended after 1972, when he replaced the fired Don McCafferty as head coach midseason, benched the aging Johnny Unitas, and won four of nine games before being fired. He then went to Philadelphia to assist McCormack, who had succeeded him years earlier as the Browns' right tackle, before rejoining Shula in Miami, where he followed Clark as the offensive line coach and remained 19 years.

16. **Jim Shofner** — The Browns' first-round pick in 1958, he played cornerback for six years, retiring just before the 1964 championship season. His long coaching career included two stints with the Browns. He was Brian Sipe's quarterback coach from 1978-1980 and as such was a key contributor to the frequent last-minute heroics of the Kardiac Kids. He returned in 1990 as offensive coordinator and served as interim head coach upon Bud Carson's dismissal, winning just one of seven games in the worst Browns season to that point. Ten years prior to Sipe's 1980 MVP award, Shofner coached 49ers' QB John Brodie to the same career pinnacle. His other coaching stops included the Cowboys, Oilers, Cardinals and Bills, along with his alma mater, Texas Christian, where he endured a 20-game losing streak as head coach in the 1970s.

17. **Mac Speedie** — The AAFC's overall receiving leader also earned Pro Bowl honors in two of his three NFL seasons. But he left for Canada to double his salary and escape Paul Brown, whose lifelong grudge probably kept Speedie out of the Hall of Fame. Former teammate Rymkus

brought him into coaching as an assistant with the first Houston Oilers squad in 1960. He resigned after Rymkus' midseason firing in 1961. Speedie then caught on with Denver and rose to head coach, compiling a 6-19-1 record. He remained a Broncos scout through 1982.

18. Dick Modzelewski — The longtime Giants defensive tackle ended his playing career with three seasons as a Brown, then stayed in Cleveland for another 11 years, most of them as defensive line coach under three different head men. In 1977, he became the first former Browns player to serve as their head coach. Forrest Gregg was fired before the last game, and Modzelewski led the team on an interim basis to a 20-19 loss to the Seattle Seahawks. He later rejoined Gregg's staff in Cincinnati and Green Bay.

30 Browns Who Died Young

This list, arranged alphabetically, pays respects to those Browns struck down too soon. Though the causes varied, it's always a sad irony when an athlete celebrated for physical vitality succumbs at an early age. Yet, as expressed in A.E. Housman's poem, "To an Athlete Dying Young," this irony can itself be a blessing for the "Smart lad, to slip betimes away/ From fields where glory does not stay[.]" Alas, this consoling sentiment applied to all too few of these departed young men.

1. Harry Agganis (April 20, 1929 - June 27, 1955, age 26) was drafted to succeed Otto Graham, but he instead chose a baseball career in his native state. The 12th overall pick in 1952, "The Golden Greek" never signed with the Browns, opting to finish at Boston University and join the Red Sox organization. During his second season in the majors, he was stricken with pneumonia and later died of a pulmonary embolism.

2. Lyle Alzado (April 3, 1949 - May 14, 1992, age 43), the All-Pro defensive end for the Kardiac Kids, lost his battle with brain cancer. With a personality larger than life, Alzado was both fierce and friendly, reviled and rewarded, during his 14-year career that began in Denver and ended with the Raiders. After his diagnosis, he admitted to decades of steroid use, though this was not definitively linked with his ultimately fatal lymphoma, a rare type of tumor associated with suppressed immunity.

3. Anthony Lovett "Rocky" Belk (June 20, 1960 - July 15, 2010, age 50) played just ten games in the NFL, scoring two touchdowns among five receptions for the 1983 Browns. The leading receiver for the 1982 Miami Hurricanes was Cleveland's seventh-round draft pick. He left a bigger

mark as a longtime educator and coach in his native Virginia. He died after an illness of several months.

4. **Ernie Blandin** (June 21, 1919 - Sept. 16, 1968, age 49) was one of the original Cleveland Browns, a part-time starter at left tackle for the championship 1946 and 1947 teams. The Tulane All-American and Navy veteran then went to the Colts as part of the AAFC's parity effort. He lived in the Baltimore area at the time of his death.

5. **Tom Bloom** (July 19, 1941 - Jan. 18, 1963, age 21) never had the chance to suit up for the Browns, as the sixth-round draft pick was killed in a one-car accident on I-70 near Vandalia, Ohio. The highway patrol blamed excessive speed. Bloom and two Purdue teammates were headed home during a school break when his vehicle rammed into a concrete bridge abutment.

6. **Orlando Bobo** (Feb. 9, 1974 - May 14, 2007, age 33) passed away from complications during surgery to remove his spleen. After two seasons in Minnesota, he joined the Browns in 1999 as their 27th expansion draft pick. He played nine games at right guard, starting one, before being released after the season. He then joined the Baltimore Ravens in time for their first Super Bowl championship.

7. **Orlando Brown** (Nov. 12, 1970 - Sept. 23, 2011, age 40), who played offensive right tackle for both the original and reborn Browns, died of diabetic ketoacidosis. An undrafted free agent whose massive presence prompted the nickname "Zeus," Brown became a quality starter, mostly for the benefit of the Ravens. The Washington D.C. native twice left the Browns involuntarily, once due to "The Move" and once after a referee's penalty flag injured his eye in 1999, costing him three full seasons.

8. **Damion Cook** (April 16, 1979 - June 26, 2015, age 36) died of a heart attack at his home in Maryland, where he was the head football coach for Atholton High School. The 6'5", 335-pound offensive lineman started six games at guard for the 2004 Browns, one of several teams he played for in the NFL and other pro leagues.

9. **Ernie Davis** (Dec. 14, 1939 - May 18, 1963, age 23) was to have partnered with his Syracuse predecessor, Jim Brown, to form the most formidable backfield in football. The first black Heisman Trophy winner was the top pick of the 1962 draft, and Paul Brown obtained him in exchange for the Browns' first-rounder plus star halfback Bobby Mitchell. As portrayed in the 2008 film *The Express*, Davis' story turned tragic, as leukemia prevented him from ever playing a down for the Browns. If he was destined not to play in it, then no Brown thereafter would ever wear his jersey number 45.

10. **Spiro Dellerba** (Jan. 25, 1923 - Aug. 19, 1968, age 45) was an Ashtabula native and a linebacker/fullback for the 1947 Browns. He was a resident of nearby Lake County at the time of his death.

11. **Rich Dimler** (July 18, 1956 - Sept. 30, 2000, age 44), a defensive tackle for the Browns in 1979, died of pancreatitis. The fifth-round pick was co-captain of Southern Cal's national championship team in 1978, a team that included future Browns Chip Banks, Paul McDonald and Charles White and future Hall of Famers Ronnie Lott and Marcus Allen.

12. **Don Fleming** (June 11, 1937 - June 4, 1963, age 25) was a three-year starter and emerging star safety when he and another worker were electrocuted at an off-season construction job in Winter Park, Florida. He was close friends with Bernie Parrish, a teammate at the University of Florida and in the Browns' secondary. His was the third off-season death of a Browns player in 1963, and the jersey number 46 is retired in his honor. His wife and a son survived him.

13. **Len Ford** (Feb. 18, 1926 - March 13, 1972, age 46) passed away from heart failure after a month's hospitalization. He worked for Detroit's city recreation department after a stellar football career. The greatest defensive end in Browns history, Ford spearheaded a ferocious defense that allowed the fewest or second fewest points in the league each of his eight years here. Sadly, though a finalist in 1971, Ford was not inducted into the Hall of Fame until four years after his death.

14. **Harry "Chick" Jagade** (Dec. 9, 1926 - Nov. 24, 1968, age 41) suffered a fatal heart attack while hauling a deer he had felled hunting. A fullback whose reckless style and exuberance impressed Paul Brown, he averaged five yards a carry in three seasons as a Brown and rushed for over 100 yards in both the 1952 and 1953 NFL title games.

15. **Eddie Johnson** (Feb. 3, 1959 - Jan. 21, 2003, age 43), the undersized linebacker who beat out future All-Pro Sam Mills as a rookie and stuck around for a decade of hard tackling and inspirational leadership, died of colon cancer. His dedication and community-mindedness survive through the volunteer work of the Eddie Johnson Memorial Foundation.

16. **Kirk Jones** (January 5, 1965 - June 9, 2001, age 36), a strike replacement player who appeared in just one 1987 game and registered no statistics, died of a heart attack at his California home. He was a star running back at UNLV, where his teammates included Randall Cunningham and Ickey Woods.

17. **Tom Jones** (June 22, 1931 - Aug. 30, 1978, age 47) was a Cincinnati native who appeared in two games with the 1955 Browns, having been their ninth-round pick a year earlier. He played several seasons in Canada, mostly for Ottawa. Known as "The Emperor," he was one of the

BROWNS BIOGRAPHICAL FACTS

largest linemen in the CFL. He died of a heart attack at his central Ontario cottage.

18. Henry Jordan (Jan. 26, 1935 - Feb. 21, 1977, age 42) played two seasons as a Brown before Paul Brown traded him to Green Bay in 1959. The defensive tackle became a key cog in the Packers' 1960s dynasty, along with linemate Willie Davis, who arrived from Cleveland a year later. The former roommate of QB Bart Starr was inducted into the Hall of Fame in 1995, 18 years after passing away from a heart attack he sustained while jogging.

19. Warren Lahr (Sept. 5, 1923 - Jan. 19, 1969, age 45), one of the finest cornerbacks (then called defensive halfbacks) in team history, left behind a wife and five daughters after a fatal heart attack. Three days prior, his doctor had given him a clean bill of health. A sales rep at the time, he earlier did color commentary for Browns telecasts from 1963-67.

20. Errol Linden (Oct. 21, 1937 - March 10, 1983, age 45) was a reserve tackle for the Browns in 1961, the first of his ten NFL seasons, before being packaged in a trade with Minnesota. He died of cancer in New Orleans, where he had finished his playing career.

21. Bob Matheson (Nov. 25, 1944 - Sept. 5, 1994, age 49) was Cleveland's first-round choice in 1967 out of Duke. A converted running back, he was an All-American at linebacker and the team's placekicker. He played four seasons for the Browns before a trade sent him to Miami, where he became a key cog in the Dolphins' No Name defense. The 13-year veteran died of complications from Hodgkin's disease 12 years after his first diagnosis.

22. David McMillan (Sept. 20, 1981 - May 18, 2013, age 31) was shot and killed not far from his home in DeKalb County, Georgia, in an apparent robbery attempt. The reserve linebacker played in 28 games for Romeo Crennel's 3-4 defense from 2005-07 after being drafted in the fifth round out of Kansas.

23. Wayne Mehlan (March 2, 1946 - June 26, 1987, age 41), a Nebraska All-American, played for the Browns as a linebacker on the playoff teams of 1968 and 1969. The fourth-round pick later started an industrial cleaning company and flew WWII fighter planes as a hobby. The Michigan native died when his P-51 Mustang crashed in Ludington.

24. Nick Pietrosante (Sept. 10, 1937 - Feb. 6, 1988, age 50) died of prostate cancer near Detroit, where he spent the bulk of his outstanding NFL career. The 1959 Rookie of the Year was featured on the cover of *Sports Illustrated* in 1962 as "The Complete Fullback." He became a Brown in 1966 via waivers and backed up Ernie Green for two seasons.

25. Don Rogers (Sept. 17, 1962 - June 27, 1986, age 23) was to be married on a Saturday. He died on a Friday of a cocaine-induced heart attack. His death was beyond shocking, and its impact transcended football, as chronicled in the 2007 book *One Moment Changes Everything: The All-America Tragedy of Don Rogers*. The former UCLA star was the 18th overall pick in 1984 and had already helped the Browns into the playoffs by his second season. Big things were expected from him, and many feel "The Drive" would not have happened the next season had Rogers been patrolling the secondary.

26. **Pio Sagapolutele** (Nov. 28, 1969 - June 9, 2009, age 39) died two days after suffering a brain aneurysm, leaving behind a wife and four children. The American Samoa native grew up in Hawaii and played 63 games as a Brown, starting 34 of them. The defensive lineman was Bill Belichick's fourth-round draft pick in 1991.

27. **Don Steinbrunner** (April 5, 1932 - July 20, 1967, age 35) was a tackle drafted in the sixth round in 1953 who appeared in eight games that year. After a knee injury ended his football career, he joined the Air Force as a navigator. His plane was shot down during a mission to defoliate a Vietnamese jungle, killing him and four crewmates.

28. **Ed Sustersic** (Jan. 7, 1922 - Jan. 18, 1967, age 45) was a Cleveland native who played a backup role as a fullback and linebacker on the 1949 Browns team. The University of Findlay graduate pursued a coaching career, becoming the athletic director of Brecksville-Broadview Heights High School. He suffered a fatal heart attack while running in the gym during school, leaving behind a wife and four sons.

29. **Eric Turner** (Sept. 21, 1968 - May 28, 2000, age 31) lost his life to intestinal cancer while still a member of the Oakland Raiders. The first draft pick of the Belichick era in Cleveland (second overall in 1991), Turner was first-team All-Pro in 1994, the most recent season that the Browns have won a playoff game. He became the second UCLA safety drafted by the Browns in the first round to die in California during his playing career.

30. **George Young** (May 10, 1924 - Sept. 21, 1969, age 45) tried out for the inaugural Browns team in 1946 and became the second-youngest player to make the squad. The defensive end stuck around for eight great seasons. He later officiated ten years in the American Football League and was the umpire in Super Bowl I. He died of a brain tumor.

CHAPTER 2
COMINGS AND GOINGS

20 Outstanding Draft Value Picks

This list focuses on those players the Browns drafted who provided the team with the most value relative to their draft position. Contributions while playing for other teams are not considered. We'll also overlook the fact that many other Browns greats weren't drafted at all. See Chapter 5, The Best of the Browns, for descriptions of these players' careers.

1. RB Leroy Kelly, drafted in 1964 in Round 8 (110th overall), out of Morgan State.
2. G Gene Hickerson, 1957 7(78), Mississippi
3. QB Brian Sipe, 1972 13(330), San Diego State
4. LB Galen Fiss, 1953 13(155), Kansas
5. RB Earnest Byner, 1984 10(280), East Carolina
6. LB Dick Ambrose, 1975 12(290), Virginia
7. LB Walt Michaels, 1951 7(86), Washington & Lee
8. OL Cody Risien, 1979 7(183), Texas A&M
9. WR Reggie Langhorne, 1985 7(175), Elizabeth City State
10. LB Billy Andrews, 1967 13(333), SE Louisiana
11. T Doug Dieken, 1971 6(142), Illinois
12. DE Jack Gregory, 1966 9(139), Delta State
13. OL Paul Farren, 1983 12(316), Boston University
14. DB Ben Davis, 1967 17(439), Defiance
15. LB Eddie Johnson, 1981 7(187), Louisville
16. CB Bernie Parrish, 1958 9(108), Florida
17. LB Dale Lindsey, 1965 7(97), Western Kentucky
18. DT Ahtyba Rubin, 2008 6(190), Iowa State
19. DB Mike Howell, 1965 8(111), Grambling
20. DE Rob Burnett, 1990 5(129), Syracuse

25 Career-Long Browns

These are the Browns who played in the most regular-season AAFC or NFL games for Cleveland while never appearing for another professional team in a regular-season or playoff game:

1. Lou Groza (K/LT, 1946-59, 1961-67)	268 games
2. Doug Dieken (LT, 1971-84)	203
3. Gene Hickerson (OG, 1958-60, 1962-73)	202
4. Ozzie Newsome (TE, 1978-90)	198
5. Don Cockroft (K/P, 1968-80)	188
6. Clarence Scott (CB/S, 1971-83)	186
7. Jim Houston (LB/DE, 1960-72)	177
8. Dick Schafrath (LT, 1959-71)	176
9. Robert E. Jackson (OG, 1975-85)	160
10. Eddie Johnson (LB, 1981-90)	148
11. Jerry Sherk (DT, 1970-81)	147
12. (tie) Charlie Hall (LB, 1971-80)	146
Cody Risien (RT/LG, 1979-83, 1985-89)	146
Paul Wiggin (DE, 1957-67)	146
15. Ray Renfro (FL/HB, 1952-63)	142
16. Galen Fiss (LB, 1956-66)	139
17. Ryan Pontbriand (LS, 2003-11)	134
18. Paul Farren (LT/G, 1983-91)	132
19. Hanford Dixon (CB, 1981-89)	131
20. Milt Morin (TE, 1966-75)	129
21. (tie) Joe Thomas (T, 2007-2014)	128*
Thom Darden (S, 1972-74, 1976-81)	128
John Garlington (LB, 1968-77)	128
24. Otto Graham (QB/DB, 1946-55)	126
25. Warren Lahr (DB, 1949-59)	125

12 Great Browns Who Played Only For Other Teams

The following standout players were all with the Browns at one time or another but never appeared in a single regular-season game for them.

1. Art Donovan — The jocular, crew-cutted defensive tackle was chosen in three different NFL drafts: by the Giants in 1947 (he stayed at Boston College); by the original Baltimore Colts in 1950 (they went defunct after the season); and by the Browns in the fourth round of 1951. Hurt in a scrimmage, he was soon traded to the New York Yanks, who became the Dallas Texans, who folded after one year but were then included in a new version of the Colts. In 1968, the nimble 300-pounder was the first pure defensive lineman to be inducted into the Hall of Fame.

2. Y.A. Tittle — Paul Brown (perhaps keen to a kinship of hairlines) induced the star LSU quarterback to sign a $12,000 contract in late 1947. He became a Browns asset despite the NFL's Detroit Lions drafting him sixth overall. But Cleveland already dominated the All-America Football Conference with Otto Graham starring at QB, so before training camp, commissioner Jonas Ingram assigned Tittle to Baltimore as part of a parity program. There he began his 17-year Hall of Fame career, in which he made seven Pro Bowls as a 49er and Giant. In Brown's memoir he called it "the most critical loss in Browns history."

3. Dick LeBeau — The Ohio State defensive back was the Browns' fifth-round choice in 1959, but he didn't make the opening day roster. He soon latched on in Detroit, where he spent the entire 14-year career that would much later get him enshrined in Canton. His 62 career interceptions are 37% more than Thom Darden's Browns career record. LeBeau, later the Steelers' longtime defensive coordinator, was one of several great Paul Brown castoffs, including Jim Marshall, Bobby Mitchell, Len Dawson, Doug Atkins, Willie Davis and Henry Jordan.

4. Sam Mills — The 5'9" linebacker was an undrafted free agent from Montclair State in 1981, back when former linebacker Marty Schottenheimer ran the Browns defense. Mills just missed the cut; the Browns kept another undersized rookie, Eddie Johnson, instead. Samuel Davis Mills Jr. went on to enjoy a long career in the USFL and with the Saints and Panthers, earning Pro Bowl honors five times. Sadly, both he and Johnson became victims of colon cancer in their mid-40s.

5. **Carlton Chester "Cookie" Gilchrist** — Conflicting accounts exist about how this talented Pennsylvania high school fullback ended up taking part in — and taking off from — the Browns' 1954 training camp, before he was eligible to join the league. Paul Brown implied in his autobiography that Gilchrist was never signed. Other sources say he was, but that the deal was invalidated. The colorful iconoclast furthered his legend with a tremendous career in Canada and with the Buffalo Bills, making ten straight All-Star teams in the CFL and AFL.

6. **Chris Spielman** — The former Ohio State star made four Pro Bowls as a Lions linebacker. Following neck fusion surgery, he tried to resurrect his career just as the Browns returned from their three-year hiatus. Along with top draftee Tim Couch, Spielman was marketed as the face of the new franchise. But a blindside block by the Bears' Casey Wiegmann in an exhibition game left him momentarily paralyzed, and his playing career ended then and there.

7. **Fred Cox** — In 1961 Brown spent an eighth-round pick on this Pitt pre-med major who played offense, defense and special teams. Brown convinced him to focus on kicking after a rookie camp back injury took him out of the offensive backfield. Veteran Lou Groza mentored him before he was traded to Minnesota, where he played 15 seasons, appearing in four Super Bowls and two Pro Bowls. The Vikings' all-time leading scorer's biggest professional success, though, may have been inventing the Nerf football.

8. **David Lee** — This lanky Louisianan signed his Browns contract at Dub Jones' home in 1965 and spent the season on the taxi squad. But Cleveland's punting duties were ably handled by flanker Gary Collins, who had the league's highest average that season, so they traded Lee to Baltimore. Lee succeeded Collins as the league's punting leader in 1966, made All-Pro in 1969, and didn't miss a game for the Colts over his 13-year career. With the Colts' fifth-round pick in 1968, the Browns drafted Clemson RB Jackie Jackson, who never made it as a pro.

9. **Lance Moore** — The Westerville, Ohio, native was signed by rookie GM Phil Savage as a undrafted free agent in 2005. He would have been the first Toledo Rocket to play for the Browns since Mel Long in 1974. But the 5'9" receiver was cut in late August, as Cleveland kept five wideouts: top draftee Braylon Edwards; veteran starters Antonio Bryant and Dennis Northcutt; perennial project Frisman Jackson; and another UDFA from a MAC school, converted Kent State quarterback Joshua Cribbs. Moore developed into a popular, productive option for Drew Brees in New Orleans, catching 346 passes and scoring 39 touchdowns over eight seasons. No Browns WR has as many receptions since they joined the NFL in 1950.

10. Jim McMahon — The brash, oft-injured quarterback was on the verge of his 36th birthday, nearly a decade removed from his Super Bowl championship year, when he signed with his sixth team, the Browns, in 1995. He reportedly turned down more money from Green Bay so that he could compete for a starting job with Vinny Testaverde. But he was waived mid-season after falling behind even rookie Eric Zeier on the depth chart, so he joined the Packers and ended his career with another Super Bowl ring as Brett Favre's backup the next season.

11. LeCharles Bentley — The former Cleveland St. Ignatius and Ohio State offensive lineman made the Pro Bowl twice in four seasons with the New Orleans Saints. As the top-ranked free agent in 2006, he was eager to come home, and the Browns were pleased to have him. He famously sported a Browns "00" jersey upon signing a six-year, $36-million deal with $12.5 million guaranteed, the centerpiece of GM Phil Savage's off-season haul that included Willie McGinest, Kevin Shaffer, Joe Jurevicius, Dave Zastudil, and Ted Washington. But on the first full-contact play of training camp, he ruptured his patellar tendon. A subsequent staph infection greatly complicated his recovery and even threatened his life. Bentley retired in 2008 and settled a lawsuit against the Browns in 2010. He now runs a well-regarded training center focused on developing offensive linemen.

12. Bob Mischak — Vince Lombardi had recruited this lineman to Army, and the Browns made him a 23rd-round pick in 1954 despite his upcoming service commitment. At training camp in 1957, he was a contender to succeed aging star Len Ford at defensive end, but he withdrew from the team. Cleveland recouped a sixth-round pick from the Giants (where Lombardi was now offensive coordinator) for his rights. Mischak became the first captain of the AFL's New York Jets, then known as the Titans. He played guard for three teams in seven seasons and was twice a first-team All-AFL honoree.

16 "Sandwich" Browns

Several notable Browns have found their way back to Cleveland after stints with other teams. These cases are listed in order of increasing significance. The stories of several "sandwich" Browns carry bittersweet aftertastes, as Cleveland fans missed out on many great years from players of known excellence.

16. **Brian Sanford**, an undrafted defensive lineman out of Temple, shuttled between the Browns' practice squad and active roster, playing in six games in 2011-12. He made his only start in 2013 for the Oakland Raiders but was later waived and picked up by the Browns, for whom he played one last game that year.

15. **Thaddeus Lewis**, former Duke quarterback, was the emergency starter in the 2012 season finale, playing reasonably well in a loss to Pittsburgh. A new Browns regime waived him the next May. He had some moments as a Bill in 2013, but he bounced to Houston in 2014 and back into the mix with the Browns in March 2015.

14. **Jamie Caleb** was the backup fullback to Jim Brown in 1960, scoring his only career touchdown late in a rout of the expansion Dallas Cowboys. The next year, he was traded to another expansion team, the Minnesota Vikings. From there he went south to Canada, playing two seasons for Hamilton in the CFL. After a year teaching in his native Louisiana, he returned to appear in five games for Blanton Collier's Browns in 1965 but never touched the ball. He and Brown were both done at age 29.

13. Kicker **Billy Cundiff** filled in for the injured Phil Dawson for five games in 2009. He then made first-team All-Pro as a Raven in 2010, but a crucial 32-yard miss in the playoffs at New England ended their 2011 season. After Dawson left via free agency, the Browns had two kickers in camp for 2013, Shayne Graham and Brandon Bogotay. They cut both and instead re-signed Cundiff, who rebounded with a fine year but was replaced by Garrett Hartley during the 2014 season.

12. **Jeff Gossett** joined the Browns in 1983 to take over as punter from big-legged Steve Cox, who stayed as a kickoff specialist. Gossett left for the USFL, playing for the Chicago Blitz in 1984 and the Portland Breakers in 1985. Cox resumed punting duties in '84. His average improved, but his low, long motion remained a problem: he had five punts blocked in three Browns seasons. Gossett, with more efficient footwork, returned in '85 and kept the job until midway through the 1987 season, when rookie George Winslow beat him out. Winslow lasted all of five games with the Browns, while Gossett stayed in the league another nine years.

11. **Chet "The Jet" Hanulak** played just two NFL seasons: 1954 and 1957. In between, he served in the U.S. Air Force, playing on its first football team. A star halfback on a national champion University of Maryland squad, the swift rookie scored four touchdowns and averaged five yards per carry for the league champs. As a returning veteran, he shared the backfield with Jim Brown, scoring three more TDs and passing for one as well, a 32-yarder to Ray Renfro to break the ice in a victory at Pittsburgh. But a knee injury from his service days lingered, and he left

football for a more conventional career selling tires, easily topping his $10,000 Browns salary.

10. Jim Ninowski, a fourth-round pick from Michigan State, couldn't beat out quarterback Milt Plum in 1958 or 1959. Paul Brown traded him to Detroit, where he battled Earl Morrall for the top job, tossing nine touchdowns and 36 interceptions in two seasons. Meanwhile Plum made two Pro Bowls and kept future Hall of Famer Len Dawson on the bench. Then Brown reacquired Ninowski in an important six-player deal that included the disgruntled Plum. Ninowski began 1962 as the starting quarterback but broke his collarbone midseason, opening the way for Frank Ryan's emergence. He remained with the Browns through '66 and in the NFL through '69 as a backup.

9. Al "Bubba" Baker hit quarterbacks early and often, earning Pro Bowl honors his first three seasons as a Detroit Lion defensive end. His stints with the Browns came at the back end of his 13-year career. He arrived in 1987 from the Cardinals for a fifth-round pick, though the 6'6", 265-pound sack specialist didn't quite fit the 3-4 defensive scheme. He started just one game and was among the final cuts in 1988. The Vikings picked him up, but the Browns lured him back a year later in free agency. He started all 25 games of Bud Carson's reign, racking up 10.5 sacks until Carson was fired and Baker gave way to rookie Rob Burnett.

8. Gern Nagler was the Browns' 14th-round draft pick in 1953, but two months later he was included in a massive 15-player swap with the Baltimore Colts. The offensive end didn't play there either. He was a Chicago Cardinal most of his career, including his Pro Bowl 1958 season. His '59 year in Pittsburgh featured a last-minute touchdown catch to beat Cleveland. The Browns soon traded with the Steelers to acquire Nagler and quarterback Len Dawson. Both spent two years in brown and orange, Nagler's being more successful than the future Hall of Famer's, as he led the 1960 squad in receiving yards.

7. John Kissell (1950-52, 1954-56) was a physical defensive tackle who impressed Paul Brown as an AAFC foe in Buffalo and became a solid starter for Cleveland's stellar unit. The Canadian Football League began competing hard for many NFL players. In 1953, Kissel signed with the Ottawa Rough Riders for $9,500 plus bonuses, a raise of over 25%. But unlike star end Mac Speedie's defection, Kissell's move left fewer lingering hard feelings with Paul Brown, who dropped a lawsuit and welcomed him back a year later. The Browns won the next two NFL championships.

6. "Turkey" Joe Jones, part of a very good Browns defensive line in the early 1970s, was traded just before the 1974 season for Eagles WR Ben Hawkins. Hawkins was clearly past his prime and was jettisoned a month later, ending his career after just two games and no catches as a Brown. Jones, meanwhile, managed seven sacks that season as an edge

rusher. When he was waived midway through the '75 season, the Browns claimed him. He followed up with two solid seasons before fading and getting traded again. Along with Kissell, Jones is among the most balanced of the "sandwich" Browns, as his two stints with the team were roughly equal in duration and quality.

5. **Jack Gregory** outperformed his ninth-round draft status by plenty, racking up 103 career sacks (unofficially) over 13 seasons. After five fine years in Cleveland, including one Pro Bowl selection and another season with 14 sacks, a contract dispute with Art Modell prompted a 1972 trade to the Giants, where his sturdy combination of size and speed paid dividends for seven more seasons. The draft pick used for Greg Pruitt was part of the deal, so it wasn't a total loss for the Browns. Gregory returned for his final season, 1979, in exchange for a seventh-rounder.

4. **Walt Michaels** was Cleveland's seventh-round draft pick in 1951 out of Washington and Lee. Paul Brown traded the linebacker to Green Bay in August of his rookie year for Dan Orlich, who was traded back to the Packers a month later. Brown, realizing his mistake, managed to re-acquire Michaels the next April in exchange for three players. He played ten years for the Browns, missing only two games, and earned selection to the Pro Bowl five straight seasons.

3. **Mike Baab**, a fine center on those ascendant mid-'80 Browns offenses, was popular with teammates and fans alike. Star of the campy "Masters of the Gridiron" video, the "Baabarian" was shipped to New England right before the 1988 season for a mere fifth-round pick. The 24-year-old sidearm slinger he had helped to the Pro Bowl was not pleased, and Bernie Kosar would suffer a career-changing injury on a failed blitz pickup in his first game without Baab calling out line assignments. Successor Gregg Rakoczy never quite filled Baab's shoes, and Baab returned as a free agent in 1990 to start two more seasons. After Bill Belichick's tough choice to cut him, Baab got one last chance in the league from the Chiefs' Marty Schottenheimer, the Browns' coach when Cleveland traded him.

2. **Earnest Byner**, whose professional story is among the most compelling and dramatic in Browns history, was shipped off to Washington in a straight-up swap for another running back, Mike Oliphant, on draft day in 1989. It didn't seem fair at the time, and it proved to be one of Cleveland's worst trades ever. Oliphant may have been faster, but he was never in Byner's class as a football player, even before injury shortened his career. After several outstanding seasons in Washington — two Pro Bowls and a Super Bowl championship among them — Byner returned to Browns Town in 1994 as a backup. In the last

game at Cleveland Municipal Stadium, Byner mustered 147 yards in the saddest victory ever.

1. **Paul Warfield**, the graceful receiver from Warren, Ohio, should've been a lifelong Brown. Instead, he was sacrificed for a prospect who played the game's most important position. Fresh off two straight Pro Bowl seasons, he was still only 27 when the infamous trade to Miami brought the Browns the third overall pick of 1970, QB Mike Phipps. Warfield made the Pro Bowl the next five seasons with the Dolphins and won two Super Bowls. With Dolphin teammates Larry Csonka and Jim Kiick, Warfield defected to Memphis of the ill-fated World Football League in 1975. He rejoined the Browns for his final two seasons, just in time to catch his sole touchdown from Phipps in his first game back in brown and orange.

3 Original Browns Who Returned in 1999

The trio below constitutes a unique variety of "Sandwich" Browns. They are the only players to suit up for both the original franchise and the new version that began play in 1999.

3. The aptly-named **Jerry Ball** had his best years with the team that drafted him, the Detroit Lions. The 6'1", 330-pound nose tackle earned Pro Bowl honors three times in six years there. Traded to Cleveland for a third-round pick, Ball had a trying year in 1993 under coach Bill Belichick. Whether his fluctuating weight or contract issues were to blame, he started just seven of 16 games, registering three sacks and two forced fumbles. He signed with the Raiders as a free agent after the season. The new Browns signed him in 1999, the third defender (after Corey Fuller and Derrick Alexander) the Carmen Policy/Dwight Clark braintrust brought in from a Vikings team coming off a 15-1 year. Just three games into the season, they traded him back to Minnesota for a younger defensive lineman, Stalin Colinet, who was eventually also traded back to the Vikings in 2001.

2. Alabama All-American **Antonio Langham** was Cleveland's top draftee in 1994, the ninth overall pick. Winner of the Jim Thorpe Award as the nation's top collegiate defensive back, he nonetheless caused the Crimson Tide to forfeit most of its 1993 season for having earlier signed with an agent and applied for the NFL draft, making him ineligible. Following a frustrating negotiation process on his original contract, he started every game for two years with Belichick's Browns. He earned

some rookie honors, but Langham never developed into an elite pro. After two years in Baltimore, he signed for five years and $17 million with San Francisco in 1998, a deal the 49ers soon regretted. He was repeatedly beaten deep by receivers and racked up seven penalties before being benched. Former 49ers exec Carmen Policy bailed out San Francisco by selecting Langham in the last round of the Browns' expansion draft, taking on his $3 million salary cap charge. He started just two of 13 games for the 1999 Browns before being released. Belichick then brought him to New England, where he played his final season at age 28.

1. **Orlando "Zeus" Brown** built himself from an undrafted project out of South Carolina State into one of the game's most imposing offensive linemen. He joined the original Browns in 1993 just a year after switching over from defense. Mentored by left tackle Tony Jones, the raw rookie from D.C.'s mean streets didn't see the field until the following year, when he worked his way into the starting lineup at right tackle. Listed at 6'7" and 360 pounds, his size and physical style of play made him a mighty tough matchup. He moved with the team to Baltimore and three years later returned to Cleveland with a six-year, $27 million free agent contract. The reborn team's best lineman started every game in 1999 into Week 15, when Jeff Triplette's errant, BB-weighted penalty flag struck Brown's right eye. Zeus' last image as a Brown was him shoving the referee to the ground. Brown, temporarily blinded, was hospitalized for six days and couldn't play again until 2003, when he returned for three more seasons with the Ravens.

13 Tail-Enders

This list recognizes players who had long and successful careers mostly for other teams, and who finished their playing days with at most two years as members of the Browns. They're ranked by overall accomplishment rather than their contributions in Cleveland, which range from notable to negligible.

1. **Tommy McDonald** — This crafty little playmaker, the last non-kicker to play without a facemask, ended his Hall of Fame career with seven catches in nine games for the 1968 Browns.

2. **Ted Washington** — He made four Pro Bowls as a stout run-stuffer for seven teams in 17 years, concluding rather ineffectively as the Browns' nose tackle in 2006-07. He remains the oldest non-kicker (39) and the heaviest player in Browns history.

COMINGS AND GOINGS 45

3. Everson Walls — A Pro Bowl cornerback four of his first five seasons, this longtime Cowboy and Giant was a midseason pickup by the 1992 Browns. He started the first seven games of 1993 before Bill Belichick released him during the bye week.

4. Raymond Clayborn — The great Patriots corner was 35 when the Browns signed him to a two-year, $1.9 million free agency deal to replace Hanford Dixon. He started all 16 games for the woeful 1990 squad but hurt his ankle in the 1991 season opener and never returned.

5. Brad Van Pelt — The best player on some poor Giants teams, the rangy linebacker made every Pro Bowl from 1976 to 1980. Browns coach Marty Schottenheimer, his position coach and defensive coordinator in New York, brought him to Cleveland in 1986 and gave him number 50 soon after waiving Tom Cousineau. His last game became known for "The Drive," but an earlier Denver touchdown came on fourth-and-goal at the one, with Van Pelt on the sideline and the Browns one man short.

6. Carl Banks — Another great former Michigan State and New York Giant outside linebacker brought to Cleveland by his former coordinator, in this case Belichick, Banks remained a full-time starter for the Browns during his final two NFL seasons, 1994-95, alongside fellow ex-Giant Pepper Johnson.

7. Homer Jones — A terrific track star and deep threat with the 1960s Giants, this cousin of "Turkey" Joe Jones is credited with inventing the spike as a touchdown celebration. He remains the NFL career leader in yards per reception with 22.3. The Browns traded promising young runner Ron Johnson and others for Jones in 1970 to help replace the great Paul Warfield. But aside from scoring on a kickoff return in the debut of Monday Night Football, Jones didn't do much in what turned out to be his final season at age 29.

8. John Jefferson — "J.J." was a fantastic receiver on some great offenses: Air Coryell in San Diego and later with the Packers' Lynn Dickey and James Lofton. With the 1985 Browns, not so much. Acquired by trade after holding out in Green Bay, Jefferson started two of seven games and caught just three passes before being waived in November.

9. Willis McGahee — One of only two players to post 1,000-yard rushing seasons with three different teams (Ricky Watters is the other), he arrived in Cleveland during the 2013 season to provide veteran stability in the wake of the Trent Richardson trade. Coming off a torn MCL and compression fracture in his right knee, McGahee was largely ineffective, gaining a career-worst 2.7 yards per carry. He led the Browns with 377 rushing yards, their lowest team-leading total in 61 years.

10. Mark Moseley — The 38-year old placekicker — the last of the straight-on variety — had been released by his longtime team, Washing-

ton, midway through the 1986 season. The former league MVP answered Cleveland's call when Matt Bahr suffered a season-ending knee injury tackling a Steeler returner. His Browns tenure is best known for his role in the epic playoff game against the Jets, in which he missed three field goals but redeemed himself by making three others, including the game-winner in the second overtime period. It was the Browns' first playoff victory since Moseley was in college.

11. Rich Jackson — During the 1972 season, the Browns traded for this three-time All-Pro defensive end from Denver, where his ferocity inspired a young Lyle Alzado. Cleveland had lost starter "Turkey" Joe Jones, second-round rookie Lester Sims and veteran Ron Snidow to serious injuries. Though never fully recovered from his own knee problem, "Tombstone" Jackson toughed it out in his final year to help the Browns recover and make the playoffs.

12. Joe Morris — The diminutive tailback was the Giants' all-time leading rusher but missed 1989 with a foot injury and 1990 when no club would sign him after his release. Belichick brought him onto his first Browns squad, and the former Syracuse star shared snaps with Kevin Mack, Leroy Hoard and Eric Metcalf in a lackluster comeback season, his last.

13. Rod Perry — The two-time Pro Bowl cornerback for the Rams started four of 24 games as a Brown on the wrong side of age 30. He had one interception each in 1983 and 1984, the last of his 30 career picks. He was later the position coach at Oregon State for Jordan Poyer, who joined the Browns in 2013.

Other notable tail-enders:

- G George Buehler (1978-79)
- LB Eric Barton (2009-10)
- DL Bobby Hamilton (2007)
- WR Ben Hawkins (1974)
- LB Lucius Sanford (1987)
- G Joe Andruzzi (2005-06)
- RB Lorenzo White (1995)
- LB Johnie Cooks (1991)
- FB Nick Pietrosante (1966-67)
- WR/TE Gern Nagler (1960-61)
- RB Curtis Dickey (1985-86)
- T James Brown (2000)
- S Vince Newsome (1991-92)
- LB Don Goode (1980-81)
- S Keith Bostic (1990)
- DT John Jurkovic (1999)
- WR Joe Jurevicius (2006-07)

- OL Eric Moore (1995)
- S Ray Ellis (1986-87)
- G Cosey Coleman (2005-06)
- DE/LB David Bowens (2009-10)
- P Brad Maynard (2011)
- QB Don Strock (1988)
- G Doug Dawson (1994)
- P Scott Player (2007)
- T John St. Clair (2009-10)
- RB Errict Rhett (2000)
- WR/S Mike Furrey (2009)
- S Terry Brown (1976)

The 7 Browncos

It's almost beyond belief that one team could so thoroughly absorb a unit of players from another team, but that's what Denver did to the Cleveland defensive line a decade ago. As the Browns switched from the Butch Davis regime to the Phil Savage/Romeo Crennel collaboration, no fewer than seven defensive tackles and ends made their way to the Mile High city, transferees who became known as the "Browncos."

Although the 2004 Browns allowed more rushing yards than anyone, their departed D-line coach, Andre Patterson, earned the ear of his new boss, Denver's Mike Shanahan, and these acquisitions ensued.

1. Ebenezer Ekuban — The former Cowboy first-rounder led the 2004 Browns with eight sacks, but he didn't fit the incoming 3-4 scheme and was part of the trade that yielded RB Reuben Droughns. He racked up 16 more sacks in three seasons in Denver.

2. Michael Myers — Another former Cowboy, he was included in the Ekuban/Droughns deal and started at defensive tackle for two seasons for the Broncos.

3. Gerard Warren — The self-styled "Big Money" ultimately failed to vindicate his lofty draft position. The new regime dumped him for Denver's fourth-round pick, used to acquire QB Trent Dilfer via trade. Though the talented tackle played 11 years, he never improved on his rookie stats.

4. Courtney Brown — The Browns released the top pick of the 2000 draft after five injury-ravaged seasons. Denver picked him up, but the

once-promising pass rusher played only 14 games before his body gave out for good.

5. Amon Gordon — A Broncos waiver pickup in March 2006, Gordon was one of four Browns draftees in 2004 whose careers were slowed at the outset by injury. He played 33 NFL games for eight teams.

6. Kenard Lang — A solid starter as a 4-3 defensive end, Lang was miscast as a linebacker in Crennel's 3-4 scheme and released early in 2006. He recorded six of his 50 career sacks for the Broncos that year, his last in the league.

7. Alvin McKinley — A backup DT under Butch Davis, he started for two season as a 3-4 end under Crennel. Denver signed him for four years and $8 million in 2007, but he lasted just one more season.

10 Best Trades of the Paul Brown Era

1. 1951: DT Bob Gain from Green Bay for DE Dan Orlich, FB Bill Schroll, DB/HB Ace Loomis, and HB Dom Moselle.

Green Bay failed to offer enough money to their first-round pick, so he went to Canada for a year before Paul Brown acquired his rights. The Packers' loss was the Browns' Gain. He became a mainstay at defensive tackle, making five Pro Bowl appearances during his decade of service. Aside from Loomis' 12 career interceptions, the four players sent packing were largely irrelevant.

2. 1948: HB Dub Jones from Brooklyn Dodgers for draft rights to TB Bob Chappuis.

Jones emerged as an offensive weapon with the Browns, scoring 40 times (including six in one game) over eight years. Chappuis, a Toledoan and top runner-up in the 1947 Heisman Trophy voting, played just two pro seasons.

3. 1952: LB Walt Michaels from Green Bay for DT Forrest "Chubby" Grigg, T Dick Logan and T Elmer Costa.

Paul Brown had traded Michaels away the previous year but made up for the lapse in judgment. Grigg and Costa didn't survive that season's cutdown with the Packers, and Logan played just two years. Michaels became one the best linebackers in Browns history over the next decade.

4. 1962: HB Ernie Green from Green Bay for a seventh-round draft pick. Pick used on Wisconsin DB/K Gary Kroner.

Green was an ideal backfield partner for stars Jim Brown and Leroy Kelly, amassing 5,240 yards from scrimmage in seven years at 4.8 yards per rush and 10.4 per reception. Kroner played three years for Denver of the AFL.

5. 1952: WR Darrel "Pete" Brewster from the Chicago Cardinals for LB Burl Toler.

For some reason, the Cardinals decided to ship off their rookie second-round pick from Purdue for the Browns' ninth-rounder from the year before. Toler had injured his knee in a college all-star game and never played a pro game. The University of San Francisco star became the NFL's first black official in 1965. Brewster made two Pro Bowls and led the Browns in receiving three straight years.

6. 1962: QB Frank Ryan and HB Tommy Wilson from the L.A. Rams for DL Larry Stephens and third- and six-round draft picks.

Ryan had completed less than half his passes with more interceptions than touchdowns in four years of part-time duty. An injury to recently reacquired Jim Ninowski opened the door for him in Cleveland. He's the last quarterback to earn multiple (three) Pro Bowl honors as a Brown and, more importantly, to win a championship. Wilson was a productive backup on the downside of his career. Stephens, a former second-round pick, played six more seasons, mostly with Dallas. Neither of the two draft picks helped the Rams at all.

7. 1947: G Weldon Humble from Baltimore for G George Cheroke, OL Al Klug, QB/K Steve Nemeth and T Hal Mullins.

Humble, an All-American at Rice and a Marine veteran, was a former sprinter whose character impressed Paul Brown from the beginning. Thoroughly Texan in style, he struck up a strong friendship with teammate Bill Willis, the great lineman who was among the first African Americans to reintegrate pro football. The trade was classic quality for quantity, as Humble helped establish the Browns' offense dominance and played in the first Pro Bowl.

8. 1955: C Art Hunter from Green Bay for G Joe Skibinski and DT Bill Lucky.

Hunter was an Akron native one season removed from being drafted third overall. While Skibinski and Lucky lasted just three more seasons between them, Hunter played nine. The 1959 Pro Bowler was traded for Rams C John Morrow, who manned the pivot capably for seven seasons.

9. 1959: Fourth-round pick from Green Bay for DB Bobby Freeman. Pick used on Johnny Brewer.

Freeman had emerged as a starting cornerback, but Bernie Parrish's arrival led to this July deal. Brewer would start four seasons as a tight end and two more at linebacker for the Browns. Freeman spent one year as a Packer and played for two other teams over the next three years.

10. 1948: G/LB Alex Agase and DT Forrest "Chubby" Grigg from the Chicago Rockets for HB Bill Lund and G Joe Signaigo.

Both incoming players spent four successful seasons with the Browns, while Lund never appeared in another game. Signaigo was a quality lineman but played only three years.

8 Worst Trades of the Paul Brown Era

1. 1960: DE Willie Davis to Green Bay for WR A.D. Williams.

Davis was an incredible find as a 15th-rounder out of Grambling. The pass rushing phenom was thought to have too many holes in his game for full-time duty under Paul Brown. But Vince Lombardi knew how to maximize his talents. Davis played every game of the 1960s for Green Bay, winning five titles. Though sack statistics were unofficial, he easily averaged double digits during that dynastic decade. He became, quite simply, one of the very greatest defensive ends of all time. As for Williams, he had 15 career receptions, just one for Cleveland.

2. 1962: HB Bobby Mitchell and the rights to RB Leroy Jackson to Washington for the rights to RB Ernie Davis.

Paul Brown infuriated young owner Art Modell by not consulting him on this blockbuster trade. The fleet Mitchell, after four fine years paired with Jim Brown, enjoyed a string of stellar seasons at receiver, cementing his Hall of Fame credentials. Jackson, drafted at Washington's behest with the Browns' 11th overall pick, played just 15 NFL games. But that was 15 more than Davis did. "The Elmira Express" was the first African American to win the Heisman Trophy. Jim Brown's successor at Syracuse was drafted first overall, but died of leukemia without ever taking the field for the Browns. There are indications that Paul Brown considered the possibility of trading Jim Brown, and it might have happened had Davis not taken ill.

3. 1955: DE Doug Atkins and S Ken Gorgal to Chicago for third- and sixth-round draft choices in 1956.

The 6'8" Atkins was the Browns' first-rounder in 1953 and showed promise as a disruptive pass rusher. But Brown's concern about disruptions to the organization's disciplined culture led to this trade with George Halas. Gorgal, one of Atkins' best friends on the team, was included in the deal. Atkins became an embodiment of the "Monsters of the Midway," wreaking havoc for a dozen years there, followed by three more with New Orleans, which retired his number 81. The eight-time Pro Bowler was a 1982 Hall of Fame inductee. Gorgal had been a solid starter with the Browns for three seasons. As a Bear, he tied a career high with six interceptions in 1955. With the modest draft capital received, the Browns selected E Larry Ross, who never made it, and T Sherman Plunkett. He was soon drafted into the Army and, after the Browns released him, played ten years for other teams.

4. 1959: DT Henry Jordan to Green Bay for a fifth-round draft choice. Pick used on Purdue FB Bob Jarus.

After two seasons as a reserve, Jordan became one of several gifts from Brown to his friend Lombardi, the Packers' rookie head coach. Though listed at just 248 pounds, the former wrestling star was a formidable foe at defensive tackle. First-team All-Pro for five seasons running, Jordan played 11 seasons spanning the Packers' great dynasty and was inducted into the Hall of Fame posthumously. Jarus, a Parma, Ohio, product, was soon traded to Packers for a lower pick, but his only pro experience would come in Canada.

5. 1961: DE Jim Marshall, T Paul Dickson, DT Jim Prestel, FB Jamie Caleb, LB Dick Grecni and DB Billy Gault to Minnesota for 1962 second- and 11th-round picks. Cleveland selected DT Charles Hinton and E Ronnie Myers.

Hinton had an eight-year NFL career, mostly for the Steelers, but neither draftee played a game for the Browns. Meanwhile, Marshall became a legendary iron man as a founding member of the Purple People Eaters, never missing a game in 19 seasons. Dickson and Prestel were the Vikings' defensive tackles for ten and five years, respectively. The Vikings' 1961 expansion roster included eight players originally drafted by the Browns.

6. 1951: LB Walt Michaels to Green Bay for DE Dan Orlich.

This trade would rank higher had Brown not reacquired the great linebacker eight months later. Michaels played his rookie year for the Packers, joined by the man he was traded for, as Orlich returned to Green Bay just a month later as part of the Bob Gain deal.

7. 1957: QB Vito "Babe" Parilli, DB John Pettibon, DB Billy Kinard, OL John Macerelli and LB Sam Palumbo to Green Bay for QB Bobby Garrett and LB Roger Zatkoff.

The quarterbacks are the most significant pieces in this deal. Garrett was the Browns' first-overall draft choice in 1954. It's widely believed that his stuttering problem made him a pro washout, but the truth is more complicated. Brown didn't realize that Garrett had a two-year military commitment to serve until after he had drafted him and paid a $5,000 signing bonus. Before Garrett ever reported to Cleveland, he was traded to Green Bay in a deal involving Parilli. After Garrett completed his Air Force obligation, Brown reacquired him in this deal. But the coach's sharp tongue exacerbated Garrett's previously manageable speech impediment, and the Stanford star suddenly quit the sport at age 25 for a more conventional life in his native Golden State. Parilli proved to be a late bloomer who emerged as a three-time Pro Bowler with the Boston Patriots. One of the most prolific passers in AFL history, he earned a Super Bowl ring as Joe Namath's 38-year-old backup.

8. 1962: K Fred Cox, OL Errol Linden, DB Tom Franckhauser and WR Charley Ferguson to Minnesota for a sixth-round draft pick. Pick used on Pitt T Ernie Borghetti.

Another Paul Brown gesture that helped the Vikings establish themselves amid the expanding pro football landscape, this trade did nothing for the Browns. Borghetti was a Youngstown native but signed with the AFL's Chiefs and never played due to injury. The four departing players subsequently appeared in a combined 414 games.

10 Best Trades of the Modell Era

For these purposes, the Art Modell era dates from January 1963, when he fired Paul Brown, through the end of the original Browns' run in 1995.

1. 1977: First-round pick in 1978 and fourth-rounder in 1977 from Chicago for QB Mike Phipps.

This proved significant salvage for a failed franchise quarterback. Cleveland used the Bears' first-rounder to trade down with the Rams and select TE Ozzie Newsome, the Browns' all-time leading receiver. The lower pick was used on DT Mickey Sims, who started 23 games in three seasons. As a Bear, Phipps won 14 of 21 starts over five seasons.

2. 1984: DL Carl Hairston from Philadelphia for a 1985 ninth-round pick.

From Veterans Stadium to veteran stalwart, "Big Daddy" was already 31 when acquired. He continued as a very productive starter and team leader through the Browns' five-year playoff run. With Cleveland's late-round pick, the Eagles chose UTEP OL Dave Toub, whose playing career never took root. He's a longtime NFL special teams coordinator.

3. 1984: Three picks in the supplemental draft of USFL/CFL players from Chicago for ninth-, tenth-, 11th-, and 12th-round regular draft choices.

With the Bears' picks, Cleveland chose RB Kevin Mack, WR/KR Gerald "Ice Cube" McNeil, and LB Doug West. Mack and McNeil were instrumental additions to the late '80s playoff teams. Three of the four late picks (Mark Casale, Mark Butkus and Donald Jordan) didn't help the

Bears, but they did hit on the tenth-rounder, Ohio State DB Shaun Gayle, who lasted 11 years in the league.

4. 1964: DT Dick Modzelewski from the New York Giants for TE/WR Bobby Crespino.

The 33-year-old Modzewlewski was acquired as veteran depth, but injuries to Frank Parker and Bob Gain required him to step up. He earned his only career Pro Bowl selection for his work on the Browns' championship team. He remained with the Browns as a player, scout and coach through 1977. Crespino, the Browns' top pick in 1961, played five more unspectacular years in New York.

5. 1975: WR Reggie Rucker from New England for a fourth-round pick.

He had established himself with his third team, but after a broken wrist limited him in 1974, the Patriots dealt the 27-year-old to Cleveland. Rucker arrived to lead all NFL wide receivers in catches in 1975. He became a key veteran piece of the Kardiac Kids offense that developed under Sam Rutigliano and Brian Sipe, gaining over 5,000 yards in seven years. In return, the Patriots drafted USC RB/KR Allen Carter, who lasted just 15 games.

6. 1968: QB Bill Nelsen and DB Jim Bradshaw from Pittsburgh for QB Dick Shiner, DT Frank Parker and a 1969 second-round draft pick.

Nelsen overcame creaky knees to enjoy his best seasons as a Brown, winning 34 of 51 starts. While Bradshaw failed to make the Browns, neither of the new Steelers excelled either. Parker was on the down side of his career, and the journeyman Shiner went just 3-16-1 in two years as Pittsburgh's starting signal-caller. The pick was used on Warren Bankston, a backup RB/TE who played ten years for the Steelers and Raiders.

7. 1966: Third-round draft pick in 1967 from the New York Giants for DL Jim Garcia.

The Browns selected K/P Don Cockroft, who led the nation with a punting average of 48.1 as an Adams State senior. After a redshirt year, he replaced Lou Groza and Gary Collins as placekicker and punter, respectively, maintaining stability on special teams for another decade. Garcia was an underperforming second-round pick who never lasted more than a year with his four teams.

8. 1963: OT Monte Clark from Dallas for G Jim Ray Smith.

Smith was a tremendous lineman, but he would have retired had the Browns not sent him back home in this deal, which yielded an experienced, quality starter to hold down the right tackle position for the rest of the decade.

9. 1979: DE Lyle Alzado from Denver for second- and fifth-round picks in 1980 and third-round pick in 1981.

Offense got top billing in the Kardiac Kids era, but this fiery force of nature was the heart of the Browns' defense during their first division-winning season in eight years, He and league MVP Brian Sipe were the Browns' two first-team All-Pros in 1980. The Broncos made good use of the second-rounder, drafting Rulon Jones, who developed into an elite defensive end.

10. 1964: DB Lowell Caylor and second- and third-round draft choices from Chicago for WR Rich Kreitling. Picks used on DE Jim Garcia and RB Bo Scott.

Kreitling was a former first-round pick who would play only one more unremarkable season. Caylor was a bit player, Garcia was later salvaged for a third-rounder, and Scott went to the CFL. But the former Buckeye runner joined the Browns in 1969 and contributed over 4,000 all-purpose yards in six seasons, playoffs included.

14 Worst Trades of the Modell Era

1. 1970: WR Paul Warfield to Miami for a first-round draft pick. Pick used on Purdue QB Mike Phipps.

This infamous deal cost Cleveland a future Hall of Famer in his prime. The Browns' braintrust felt they needed a franchise quarterback to succeed 29-year-old Bill Nelsen and his suspect knees. Pittsburgh drafted Terry Bradshaw first, so the Browns took Phipps third overall. The fates of both trade partners effectively flipped that day, as encapsulated on Christmas Eve of 1972, when Phipps threw five interceptions in a playoff game in Miami. In the Dolphins' game-winning drive, Warfield caught two passes for 50 yards and drew a key interference penalty, preserving their perfect season. The Browns wouldn't sniff the postseason the rest of the decade.

2. 1989: RB Earnest Byner to Washington for RB Mike Oliphant.

Byner had established himself as a versatile, productive, high-motor back, but key mistakes late in two straight playoff losses loomed large. Keen on improving team speed, the Browns focused on another small-college runner, one with much less experience, a history of hamstring problems, and a listed weight of 183 pounds, tops. Injuries severely curtailed Oliphant's NFL career, while Byner re-established himself as a 1,000-yard back, earned his only two Pro Bowl berths, and helped Washington win Super Bowl XXVI.

3. 1963: First-round draft choice in 1965 to San Francisco for G Ted Connolly.

With fine linemen Gene Hickerson and John Wooten already in their primes, the 31-year-old former standout, acquired after a contract dispute with the 49ers, was relegated to a reserve role. He retired after one year. San Francisco used the Browns' 13th-overall pick on S George Donnelly, who played three seasons. LB Mike Curtis, who enjoyed a superb career with the Colts, was the next player taken.

4. 1988: C Mike Baab to New England for a fifth-round pick in 1989.

The Browns had drafted Gregg Rakoczy with a high second-rounder the year before and wanted him to be the starter, so the productive Baab was shipped out near the end of training camp. Cleveland packaged the Patriots' pick (127th overall) in the 1989 deal with Green Bay that led to the drafting of WR Lawyer Tillman.

5. 1970: RB Ron Johnson, DT Jim Kanicki and LB Wayne Meylan to the New York Giants for WR Homer Jones.

The Browns acquired the once-elite deep threat to backfill for the loss of Warfield, but Jones did little in his final season aside from a scoring kickoff return in the debut of Monday Night Football. Meanwhile Johnson emerged from Leroy Kelly's shadow to earn All-Pro honors that year. His numbers were even better in 1972, with a league-leading 14 touchdowns from scrimmage. The veteran Kanicki was a starter for the Giants for two seasons.

6. 1982: DE Lyle Alzado to Los Angeles Raiders for an eighth-round draft choice in 1982. RB Greg Pruitt to Los Angeles Raiders for an 11th-round draft choice in 1983.

Though technically separate transactions, they occurred on the same day between the same teams for essentially the same reason. Modell, despite his denials, was shedding veteran salaries. For a pittance, Al Davis got a pair of productive and popular players with more to prove. Alzado tallied 23 sacks in four years as a Raider and was the 1982 Comeback Player of the Year. Pruitt earned his fifth Pro Bowl berth in 1983 as a return specialist for the Super Bowl champs. Meanwhile, Cleveland's late draft picks, TE Van Heflin and LB Howard McAdoo, never played a down.

7. 1968: WR Clifton "Sticks" McNeil to San Francisco for a second-round draft choice.

Cleveland sent the pick to Pittsburgh as part of the trade that yielded QB Bill Nelsen. McNeil had just 12 catches in four years as a Brown, though five went for touchdowns. He immediately led the league with 71 receptions for the 49ers.

8. 1989: RB Herman Fontenot, 1989 third- and fifth-round picks, and 1990 first-rounder to Green Bay for 1989 second- and fifth-round picks.

In this draft day trade, the Browns essentially ceded a future first-rounder and a useful, 25-year-old backup skill player to move from the third to the top of the second round. Their big target was Auburn WR Lawyer Tillman, whose injury-riddled career produced just 38 receptions in 37 games. The Packers used the first-rounder on LB/DE Tony Bennett, who amassed 64.5 career sacks. Their other picks: Ohio State RB Vince Workman (4,011 career all-purpose yards) and QB Anthony Dilweg. With the higher fifth-rounder, Cleveland took Bowling Green DB Kyle Kramer, a reserve for one season.

9. 1973: **First-round pick in 1974 and second-round pick in 1975 to San Diego for MLB Bob Babich.**

Youngstown native Babich was the Chargers' top pick in 1969 but missed his rookie year with a knee injured against Cleveland in the preseason. He started four of his six years as a Brown but did not recoup the high cost in draft value. San Diego used those picks on LB Don Goode and DT Louie Kelcher, who both became fixtures, the latter an outsized star. Trading for veterans (including QB Don Horn and WR Gloster Richardson for three other 1974 draft picks) when the Browns needed to restock young talent proved fateful. The Steelers drafted four future Hall of Famers in 1974, including Kent State MLB Jack Lambert.

10. 1979: **First-round draft pick to San Diego for their first- and second-round picks.**

Cleveland traded down seven spots from 13th overall, where the Chargers selected TE Kellen Winslow, who earned Hall of Fame induction for his huge impact in the Air Coryell offense. The Browns in turn drafted another player to wear number 80, WR Willis Adams, a speedster who never developed into a regular starter, and T Sam Claphan, who was released after a back injury cost him his rookie year. He then joined the Chargers and played there through 1987.

11. 1982: **First-round draft choice in 1983, third-rounder in 1984 and fifth-rounder in 1985 to Buffalo for the rights to LB Tom Cousineau.**

The former Cleveland St. Ed's and Ohio State star had played three years in Canada after failing to agree on a contract with the Bills, who had drafted him first overall in 1979. The trade seemed like a good idea, and Cousineau signed a five-year deal for $2.5 million, a franchise record at the time. Though he did lead the Browns in tackles in three of his first four years, his play never quite justified the investment. He and his agent later blamed his 1986 release on unfounded rumors from jealous teammates that he was gay. He played his last two seasons in San Francisco. Meanwhile, Buffalo used the Browns' 14th overall pick on Miami QB Jim Kelly, a future Hall of Famer.

12. 1971: **LB Bob Matheson to Miami for a 1972 second-round draft choice. Pick used on Alabama DE Lester Sims.**

Though the former first-rounder didn't live up to expectations in four years as a Brown, he lasted nine more as an integral part of the Dolphins' "No-Name Defense." Sims, meanwhile, suffered a knee injury and never appeared in a pro game.

13. **1992**: Second- and fifth-round 1992 picks (36th and 121st overall) to Dallas for second-, third-, sixth-, eighth- and 12th-rounders in 1992 (52nd, 78th, 163rd, 222nd, and 329th overall).

The Cowboys, with a surfeit of picks due in part to the famous Herschel Walker trade, moved up to draft WR Jimmy Smith, who would eventually overcome injury and illness to have a tremendous career with Jacksonville. The rebuilding Browns were also looking for help at receiver, as they took San Diego State's Patrick Rowe with the lower second-rounder. Injury limited him to just three career receptions. The Cowboys' other pick was G Rod Milstead. Cleveland took LB Gerald Dixon, DT George Williams and G Tim Simpson and traded away the eighth-round pick. Only Dixon made much of a dent as a pro.

14. **1995**: RB Eric Metcalf and a first-round pick (26th overall) to Atlanta for their first-round pick (10th overall).

This trade came on the heels of the Browns signing ex-Falcon WR Andre Rison in free agency. One big problem with the deal was that it came almost a month before the draft. Penn State TE Kyle Brady was reportedly Bill Belichick's target, so when the Jets drafted him ninth and the Browns weren't quite sold on DT Warren Sapp, they traded back down with San Francisco and settled for Ohio State LB Craig Powell. Metcalf moved to receiver and caught 104 passes for 1,189 yards in 1995.

8 Best Trades of the New Browns Era

1. **2013**: A first-round pick in 2014 from Indianapolis for RB Trent Richardson.

Two games into his second season, a new Browns front office gave up on a feature back who'd scored 12 times as a rookie. That cemented the impression that Cleveland was gearing up for 2014 and beyond at the expense of their near-term chances. But the unusual move has since been vindicated by Richardson's struggles. Through 2014, no modern-era player with as many rushing attempts had a lower per-carry average than his 3.31. It proved prescient to salvage what turned out to be the 26th-overall pick, regardless of how it was used (i.e., traded in the move up for QB Johnny Manziel).

2. **2011**: OL John Greco from St. Louis for a 2012 conditional seventh-round pick.

The Ohio native, familiar to incoming head coach Pat Shurmur, remained a backup in 2011, so the Browns ultimately didn't cede a pick for him. But he started 40 games the next three years at three different interior line positions, earning a nice five-year contract in the process.

3. 2002: TE Steve Heiden from San Diego for a seventh-round pick in 2003.

The Chargers and head coach Marty Schottenheimer dumped their former third-round pick for negligible return days before the 2002 regular season. A dependable blocker and sturdy receiving target, Heiden lasted eight more seasons. By the time he was released, he had appeared in more games than any other new Browns offensive player.

4. 2007: Sixth-round pick in 2008 from Seattle for QB Charlie Frye.

After a poor Week 1 start dropped his career record to 6-13, the third-year Ohio native was sent westward, clearing the way for Derek Anderson's surprising emergence. The next spring, the Browns made their best pick of the draft with the 190th selection: Iowa State DT Ahtyba Rubin, who started 75 games for them through 2014. Frye appeared in only five games in two seasons after the trade.

5. 2006: C Hank Fraley from Philadelphia for a 2008 sixth-round pick.

Acquired eight days before the the season opener, this veteran ended an increasingly desperate search for a center. Cleveland had traded incumbent Jeff Faine after signing LeCharles Bentley in free agency, but Bentley's knee soon gave way. Potential fill-ins Bob Hallen, Alonzo Ephraim, Rob Smith, Ross Tucker, Todd Washington and Lennie Friedman all washed out for various reasons. Fraley solidified the position, starting every game for three seasons. The Browns later reacquired the same draft pick and chose unsuccessful WR Paul Hubbard.

6. 2010: RB Peyton Hillis, 2011 sixth-round and 2012 fifth-round picks from Denver for QB Brady Quinn.

Incoming team president Mike Holmgren cleaned house at quarterback, and the underachieving former first-rounder netted an interesting player in return. Hillis electrified the fan base with a combination of bullishness, leapfrogging, and catching ability, racking up 1,654 yards from scrimmage for his new team in 2010. Although his star power soon imploded, the one-year wonder shined brighter than Quinn ever did. Cleveland included one of the acquired draft choices to trade for the pick used on G Jason Pinkston. G Ryan Miller was selected with the other.

7. 2014: First-round pick (9th overall) in 2014 and 2015 first- and fourth-rounders (19th and 115th) from Buffalo for a 2014 first-round pick (4th).

Time will tell with the players selected, but on its face, the Browns accumulated good potential value with this deal. WR Sammy Watkins was the Bills' target, so many will judge this trade on whether the Cleveland would've been better off taking him instead. The Browns spent a third-rounder to move up one spot and select CB Justin Gilbert eighth overall. They invested the 2015 picks in OL Cameron Erving and S Ibraheim Campbell.

8. 2005: RB Reuben Droughns from Denver for DLs Ebenezer Ekuban and Michael Myers.

Droughns became the workhorse for a new regime, the first Browns back in 20 years to gain 1,000 yards. But a 309-carry season can affect longevity. Droughns lagged in 2006 and was traded the next off-season to the Giants for WR Tim Carter. Ekuban and Myers, part of a large contingent of former Browns on the Denver defensive line *(see page 47, "The 7 Browncos")*, combined for 60 starts and 19 sacks as Broncos.

7 Worst Trades of the New Browns Era

1. 2006: First-round draft pick (12th overall) to Baltimore for first- (13th overall) and sixth-round picks.

In the second year of their conversion to a 3-4 defense, the Browns needed both a stout nose tackle and a pass-rushing threat. The Phil Savage/Romeo Crennel braintrust prioritized the latter, letting fearsome Oregon DT Haloti Ngata go to a division rival. The Browns took Florida State tweener Kamerion Wimbley, who never improved on his 11-sack rookie year. The sixth-rounder they gained in the exchange went for naught, as Stanford DT Babatunde Oshinowo never panned out.

2. 2004: First- (7th overall) and second-round (37th) picks to Detroit for a first-rounder (6th overall).

Browns honcho Butch Davis, desperate for a quick turnaround from a letdown season, put all his chips on the table for his former University of Miami recruit Kellen Winslow II. The Lions used the Browns' picks on WR Roy Williams and LB Teddy Lehman. Cleveland's brash new 20-year-old playmaker proceeded to hold out and then break his leg in Week 2, and Davis' tenure didn't last the season. Meanwhile, the division rival Steelers plucked a franchise quarterback from the Buckeye state, Ben Roethlisberger, with the 11th pick and won two Super Bowls before the talented but troublesome Winslow was traded to Tampa.

3. 2012: First- (4th overall), fourth-, fifth- and seventh-round picks to Minnesota for a first-rounder (3rd overall).

The Browns again paid a steep premium to move up a single spot and get their guy, in this case Alabama RB Trent Richardson. While Minnesota was set at the position with Adrian Peterson, they might have traded the third pick elsewhere, so the Holmgren/Heckert team sacrificed three selections to swap spots near the top. In retrospect, the Browns are considered fortunate to have recouped a late first-rounder for Richardson via an in-season trade in 2013. The Vikings netted Pro Bowl OT Matt Kalil, WR Jarius Wright (1,332 yards in his first three seasons), starting safety Robert Blanton, and (via other trades) backups Michael Mauti and A.J. Jefferson.

4. **2014: First- (26th overall) and third-round picks to Philadelphia for their first-rounder (22nd).**

Rookie general manager Ray Farmer parted with the 83rd overall pick in a deep draft class to move up for QB Johnny Manziel. The Aggie hotshot may very well have stayed on the board for four more picks. Significantly, other highly-rated passers remained available, including Teddy Bridgewater, Derek Carr and Jimmy Garoppolo. Browns QB coach Lowell Doggains later wore a visor with "I'm a dummy" written on it as penance for reporting that owner Jimmy Haslam III had given word to "pull the trigger" on the trade, a touchy topic among the Browns brass.

5. **2008: Second-round pick to Green Bay for DL Corey Williams.**

Coming off consecutive seven-sack seasons, Williams was due for free agency but was slapped with the Packers' franchise tag, and they got a nibble from Browns GM Phil Savage. The Packers used the Browns' 56th overall pick on QB Brian Brohm. Cleveland signed Williams to a six-year deal including $16.3 million guaranteed. Never a good fit for the Browns' 3-4 scheme, he left two years later for Detroit in a swap of late-round picks. Savage's 2008 draft, his last, lacked picks in the first three rounds due to trades.

6. **2002: MLB Wali Rainer and third-round pick (79th overall) to Jacksonville for their third-rounder (76th overall).**

Rainer started 44 games in the first three expansion seasons and twice led the team in tackles. He was deemed expendable after Earl Holmes signed in free agency. Barely 25 at the time of the trade, Rainer would go on to play all 16 games in each of the next four seasons, though not always as a starter. The received value — moving up just three slots in the third round — was meager. Butch Davis used the pick on C Melvin Fowler, who failed to show enough promise to prevent the Browns from spending a first-round pick on another center, Jeff Faine, a year later. The Jaguars traded the pick to Washington, who selected DB Rashad Bauman. QB Josh McCown and RB Brian Westbrook were among those drafted later in that round.

7. **2007: Second-round pick (36th overall) in 2007 and first-round pick (22nd) in 2008 to Dallas for their 2007 first-round pick (22nd) in 2007. Pick used on QB Brady Quinn.**

The problem here was more with the draftee than the trade itself, but it's easy to see in retrospect that the Notre Dame signal-caller's long wait on draft day happened for a reason. Quinn essentially busted, compiling a 4-16 record as a starter and just 3,043 career passing yards. The Cowboys traded the high second-rounder to the Eagles, who chose QB Kevin Kolb. He had a similar but slightly more successful career arc. With the Browns' pick the next year, Dallas took Arkansas RB Felix Jones, who averaged 4.7 yards per carry mostly in a complementary role.

CHAPTER 3
MOMENTS AND MEMORIES

12 Superb Goal-Line Stands

1. November 21, 1954, versus Philadelphia

By narrowly avenging their 28-10 season-opening loss to the Eagles, the Browns gained the upper hand on their closest division rival. A pair of Lou Groza field goals would be all the scoring at the Muni this day, thanks to a goal-line stand in the last three minutes. A pass interference call on Tommy James put the ball at the Browns' one-yard line, but Philly failed to get the final yard. Rookie first-round fullback Neil Worden netted nothing in two carries, stopped both times by Mike McCormack, successor to the great Bill Willis at middle guard. A delay of game call pushed the ball back to the six. QB Bobby Thomason, who led the league in TD passes the previous year, couldn't connect on their two last tries. McCormack, who would become a Hall of Famer after switching back to offensive tackle, batted down the fourth-down pass, fracturing his ring finger. He didn't miss a game, though. The 6-0 win proved pivotal in the division standings, and the Browns, with the league's best defense, went on to reclaim the NFL championship.

2. December 17, 1950, versus New York Giants

This battle of 10-2 teams would decide who would play for the NFL title. The Browns' only losses had come at the Giants' hands. Though Cleveland had home-field advantage, inclement weather favored the Giants' run-heavy approach. Well into the fourth quarter, a Lou Groza field goal accounted for the only points. Browns middle guard Bill Willis chased down Choo Choo Roberts for a miraculous touchdown-saving stop, setting up the Giants with first-and-goal at the Browns four-yard-line. Willis then stoned Eddie Price on consecutive plays. Penalties on each team then nullified a touchdown and an interception in succession. Again the Giants had first-and-goal from the four. And again the great Willis shone, tackling runner Joe Scott five yards back on second down. A third-down pass failed, and New York settled for a tying field goal, their only points. The Browns retook the lead on another Groza field goal in the final minute and added a late safety to win the American Conference playoff, 8-3.

3. December 29, 2002, versus Atlanta

With their playoff lives on the line, the Browns treated the home fans to an unforgettable, back-and-forth season finale. They lost QB Tim Couch to a broken leg in the second quarter, then surrendered a ten-point lead. But they rallied for two fourth-quarter touchdowns, including rookie William Green's thrilling 64-yard sprint, which put the Browns up by eight points with less than four minutes to go. Needing a touchdown and two-point conversion to force overtime, Michael Vick led the Falcons downfield with three pass plays, setting up first-and-goal from the Browns' four with 83 seconds left and all three time-outs remaining. Earl Holmes lassoed Warrick Dunn by the leg on first down, leaving him a yard short of the goal line. Dwayne Rudd then made amends for the infamous helmet toss that had cost Cleveland a win back in Week 1. He covered TE Alge Crumpler on a second-down incompletion, then stuffed Dunn for no gain on third down. On fourth down, rather than utilizing Vick's multidimensional talents, Atlanta gave the ball to Dunn up the middle again. Holmes, the longtime Steeler linebacker playing his only year as a Brown, stopped him to seal the game that gave the "new" Browns their first winning season and a wild-card berth.

4. November 23, 1947, at New York Yankees

The Browns found themselves in a rare position, down 28-0 at halftime, as Yankee backs Spec Sanders and Buddy Young could not be contained. After intermission, they drove through the Browns defense again, reaching the one-yard line but no further. Rookie LB/FB Tony Adamle was instrumental in the Browns' resistance, repeatedly stuffing Cleveland native Eddie Prokop, and the home team came up empty. That turned the tide. The Browns scored four touchdowns of their own, and time expired with New York preparing for a last-second field goal. The Browns had escaped Yankee Stadium without losing to the AAFC's second-best team.

5. October 2, 1960, versus Pittsburgh

The Browns withstood a furious rally by Bobby Layne and the Steelers with the help of a key fourth-quarter goal-line stand. After leading 21-0 at halftime, the Browns gave up two scores before a short Jim Brown touchdown widened the lead to 15. On the next play from scrimmage, Layne found former Brown Preston Carpenter for a 70-yard gain down to the Browns' four. Rookie fullback Charley Scales (who would spend most of his career as a Brown) gained three yards in two tries. Tom Tracy, their leading rusher, was stopped cold, setting up a fourth down for coach Buddy Parker. Alliance, Ohio, native Tom Barnett got the rare call, but young DT Floyd Peters was up to the task. By denying Pittsburgh any points at that juncture, a late Steeler scoring throw to emerging star Buddy Dial did little but narrow the final margin to 28-20.

MOMENTS AND MEMORIES 65

6. September 16, 1950, at Philadelphia

After dominating the AAFC, the Browns had plenty prove in their first NFL game. Commissioner Bert Bell (who earlier founded, owned and coached the Eagles) scheduled this battle between the respective league champs to open the season. A questionable clipping call on Len Ford nullified an early Browns score. An Eagles field goal and Browns touchdown followed, but Marion Motley fumbled twice, and Philadelphia pounded the ball down to the Browns' six-yard line. The visitors then inserted Motley at middle linebacker. The supersized star stuffed three straight runs, and the Eagles came away empty. Rather than yielding the lead, Cleveland regained the momentum and rolled to a convincing 35-10 upset victory.

7. December 13, 1959, at Philadelphia

The Browns snapped a three-game losing streak with an inspired comeback in their season finale. Down a touchdown in the third quarter and backed up to their own four-yard line, Cleveland's defense saved the day by keeping the Eagles out of the end zone for seven straight plays, including a pass interference call that gave Philadelphia a first down at the one. Four different backs then failed to break the plane. The Browns methodically drove 99 yards for the tying score, keyed by Jim Brown and Bobby Mitchell, who combined for 279 rushing yards on the day. With the 28-21 win, the Browns matched their division rivals' record of 7-5, good for second place. They secured their 13th winning season in 14 years and narrowly preserved their decade-long streak of never finishing worse than another division rival, the Pittsburgh Steelers.

8. December 8, 2011, at Pittsburgh

An incredible goal-line stand spearheaded by linebacker Chris Gocong was overshadowed by events occurring later in that fateful fourth quarter. For a fleeting moment, the 4-8 Browns were in range to upset the 9-3 Steelers on Thursday night in Heinz Field. Down just 7-3 early in the fourth, they surrendered a catch-and-run by Mike Wallace that was called a touchdown but after review was spotted at the two-yard line. Four times, the hobbled Ben Roethlisberger handed it to RB Rashard Mendenhall, who had scored five times in his last four games. Gocong was in on all four tackles, including impressive solo stops on the first two downs. The Browns took over at their own one and went three-and-out, but then Mike Adams picked off Big Ben to renew hope. It was on the ensuing drive that Browns QB Colt McCoy took a wicked and illegal hit from James Harrison but returned to action two plays later. Browns' staff did not diagnose him with a concussion until after the game. McCoy was called for grounding, then threw an interception in the end zone. The Steelers found Antonio Brown, CB Joe Haden lost his footing, and the 79-yard touchdown secured their 14-3 win.

9. September 12, 1976, versus New York Jets

This home win launched the most-improved season in Browns history. The game would also prove fateful for the franchise's field generalship, as Mike Phipps started out stronger than ever, but a separated shoulder created an opening for understudy Brian Sipe. The Jets would also see a passing of the torch in '76, as Joe Namath and rookie Richard Todd, two first-round Alabama quarterbacks, both saw action in the opener. Cleveland overcome a 10-0 deficit with three Phipps TD passes to take a 21-10 halftime lead. A key goal-line stand came in the third quarter, as the Jets came away empty after six snaps within five yards of the Browns' end zone. Cleveland won going away, 38-17. Though they would drop their next three, the Browns were on their way to a 9-5 follow-up to their 3-11 record the previous year.

10. December 20, 1992, versus Houston

The 7-7 Browns were fighting for their playoff lives against the division rival Oilers. Cleveland led 14-3 in the fourth quarter, but QB Cody Carlson brought Houston down to the Browns' one. The home crowd was thrilled with the four-down denial that followed. It included Randy Hilliard's break-up of a third-down pass to ex-Brown Webster Slaughter. After another pass on fourth-down failed, the Browns took over and drove well into Oiler territory. But their commanding position turned into a collapse, as Cleveland allowed two touchdown in the game's final three minutes to kill any postseason aspirations.

11. October 7, 2001, versus San Diego

After two rough expansion seasons and a coaching change, the Butch Davis-led Browns were 2-1 and hopeful they were coming of age. It was a dogfight on the lakefront, as the Chargers drove deep into the Dawg Pound end of the stadium with the score tied at 10 in the fourth quarter. Star back LaDainian Tomlinson popped free for 17 yards down to the one. Then DT Gerard Warren, drafted ahead of Tomlinson the year before, smothered him on first down. QB Doug Flutie lost two yards on the next play. The 38-year-old then saw his tight end open in the end zone, but Keith McKenzie batted the third-down pass to the ground. San Diego settled for a field goal, a moral victory for the Browns that made a difference in the end. Tim Couch led a late touchdown drive for a most encouraging 20-16 comeback win.

12. September 5, 1993, versus Cincinnati

Hosting their season-opener against a Bengals team that would finish 3-13, the Browns found themselves down two touchdowns in the first quarter. But after getting burned on a few screen passes, Cleveland switched to zone coverage and allowed just 90 yards from the second quarter on, hounding QB David Klinger, who was sacked six times and intercepted twice. Safety Stevon Moore returned Klinger's third fumble for a touchdown and 27-14 lead. Any Bengal hopes for a late comeback of their own were quashed when Derrick Fenner was stopped three straight times from the Browns' one-yard line. In what would become a tumultuous third year for head coach Bill Belichick, the emerging team's foundation was its defensive front seven. The unit — ranked in the top ten in fewest yards per carry and per pass attempt — was solid throughout with Michael Dean Perry, Rob Burnett, Anthony Pleasant, Jerry Ball, James Jones, Pepper Johnson, Clay Matthews and Mike Johnson.

15 Non-Quarterbacks Who Threw for Touchdowns

1. **Greg Pruitt** — The sensational scatback completed eight of 18 passes as a Brown in the mid-1970s, six of them for scores. Touchdowns tosses of 55 and 60 yards went to Gloster Richardson in 1974. Two others — Brian Duncan's sole NFL touchdowns — each broke ties in winning efforts. The latter of these came in a Monday night matchup with the Patriots in 1977, a 30-27 thriller in which Pruitt also gained 202 yards from scrimmage.

2. **Jim Brown** — Great backs draw attention, so the option pass keeps defensive backs honest and while providing occasional big-play payoff. In addition to his 106 rushing and 20 receiving touchdowns, the legendary fullback threw for three scores and another 28-yard gain in a dozen career pass attempts. All three TDs, one to Ray Renfro and a pair to Gary Collins, extended the Browns' lead in games they won.

3. **Leroy Kelly** — Brown's successor as the workhorse runner completed just three of 16 career passes, but two of them went the distance, both to Paul Warfield. The connections of 34 and 36 yards came in 1968 and 1969, respectively.

4. **Brian Brennan** — The diminutive possession receiver completed all three of his career passes (regular- and post-season) for a combined 73 yards, including a 33-yard touchdown to Ozzie Newsome in a 24-20 win over New England in 1985. It was Brennan's first game of the season after missing four with a shoulder injury, and it was also the first of his three career 100-yard receiving games.

5. **Ray Renfro** — The three-time Pro Bowler completed just one of six career passes, a 36-yard touchdown to Pete Brewster in a 62-14 blowout of the Giants in 1953. In that game, Renfro also scored on a 58-yard run and a 60-yard reception from Otto Graham.

6. **Eric Metcalf** — The talented tailback used his gloved hand to loft a 32-yarder into the end zone for Reggie Langhorne, one of several gadget plays that turned a 10-0 halftime deficit into a 28-17 win over the Houston Oilers in 1989. It was the rookie Metcalf's first career pass and the only one of five he would ever complete.

7. **Bobby Mitchell** — The future Hall of Famer was perfect in three career passes. The only one as a Brown was also his only touchdown. He lobbed the ball over pursuing Washington defenders to Ray Renfro, who went in for a 23-yard score in a 1960 win over Mitchell's future team.

8. **Herman Fontenot** — The halfback got the Browns off to a good start by launching a 46-yard scoring strike to rookie Webster Slaughter early in the 1986 regular season finale, a 47-17 win over San Diego.

9. **Spencer Lanning** — The rookie punter earned AFC Special Teams Player of the Week honors for his contributions to a thrilling 31-27 win at Minnesota in 2013. As the holder on a fake field goal attempt, he hit Jordan Cameron for an 11-yard score. The role reversal was later completed when QB Brian Hoyer served as the holder on an extra point try, which Lanning converted in place of the injured Billy Cundiff.

10. **Kevin Johnson** — The Syracuse product switched to wide receiver after losing a college quarterback competition to Donovan McNabb. As a Brown, Johnson threw seven career passes, three in a 2000 game against McNabb's Eagles. His only touchdown throw came in the wild 2002 season opener against the Chiefs. He hit Quincy Morgan for a 33-yard score to give the Browns a 20-14 halftime lead in the game infamous for Dwayne Rudd's helmet toss, which led to a 40-39 heartbreaker.

11. **Chet "The Jet" Hanulak** — Two speedsters connected in 1957 when this little back found Ray "Rabbit" Renfro wide open for a 32-yard touchdown early in a 23-12 win in Pittsburgh.

12. **Brian Hansen** — Washington was riding a three-game streak of home shutouts until the Browns faked a field goal attempt in 1991. Hansen, the holder, lofted it to Webster Slaughter from 11 yards out to tie the score at seven. Slaughter was uncovered after not completely leaving the field following third down. The Browns lost 42-17 to the eventual Super Bowl champs.

13. **Dub Jones** — He'd thrown 17 times for the AAFC's Brooklyn Dodgers but none in his first four years as a Brown. Then, in 1952, his only career passing touchdown — a three-yarder to Dante Lavelli — came late in a 48-24 win at Washington. His son, Bert, was barely a year old then, but he'd eventually throw 124 TD passes in a ten-year NFL career.

14. **Mohamed Massaquoi** — On an end-around option pass, he found Brian Robiskie for a 29-yard touchdown to give the Browns an early 7-0

lead over Baltimore on December 26, 2010. The trickery featuring the two 2009 second-round receivers turned out to be the highlight of a bitterly cold 20-10 home loss.

15. Willie Miller — His only career pass came in garbage time of a 42-10 loss to Minnesota in 1975. Off a pitchout from Brian Sipe, the rookie receiver threw for TE Gary Parris, and the ball deflected off him and a defender into the arms of Reggie Rucker for a 26-yard touchdown.

8 Most Noteworthy Hits By and Upon Browns

From form tackles to flagrant fouls, here are some of moments of singular impact reverberating over the years.

1. Galen Fiss on Lenny Moore — The signature play of this Browns captain's linebacking career came in the first quarter of the 1964 NFL Championship game. The heavily-favored Colts had scored the most points that year and allowed the fewest. Hall of Fame halfback Lenny Moore had averaged 22.5 yards per reception on the season, and the screen pass from Johnny Unitas was all set up. Fiss sliced through the blockers and undercut the shifty Moore for a loss that would otherwise have gone for a big gainer and perhaps altered the course of what became a 27-0 Browns upset.

2. "Turkey" Joe Jones on Terry Bradshaw — No single play better encapsulates the intensity of the Browns-Steelers rivalry during its heydey of the 1970s. The big defensive end burst through the Steelers' line in the fourth quarter of a 1976 game for a sack that ended with a piledriving throw from behind. Bradshaw hit the turf helmet first, causing a sprained neck and concussion. He returned to action two weeks later. Jones was penalized for unnecessary roughness and fined $3,000 but would almost certainly have been assessed much more and perhaps suspended under today's rules. With Brian Sipe also lost to an in-game concussion, rookie quarterback Dave Mays helped Cleveland to a much-needed 18-16 win.

3. Bill Willis on Gene "Choo Choo" Roberts — The Giants' speedster had scored 17 times the year before and was headed for the biggest touchdown of his career in a 1950 playoff game. He'd escaped Marion Motley's reach and broken free down the right side in the fourth quarter, with a clear path to the goal line that no player would cross on that sloppy December day. But after a game-high gain of 32 yards, Roberts was somehow caught from behind by Cleveland's great middle guard, Bill

Willis, at the four-yard line. That tackle preserved what became an 8-3 Browns win, leading to their first NFL championship a week later.

4. Felix Wright on Don Beebe — Driving for points before halftime of a January 6, 1990, playoff game, the Bills' Jim Kelly threw a fourth-down pass high to Don Beebe. Browns' safety Felix Wright's shoulder tackle upended the airborne rookie, whose helmeted head bounced off the field like a pogo stick. The ball popped free from Beebe's grasp, and Wright gathered it in before it could hit the ground. The officials called the play incomplete based on a (phantom) blown whistle, but the Browns went on to win anyway. The dangerous play had long-term physical effects on Beebe, but it could've been much worse, as he went on to play eight more NFL seasons.

5. Kevin Mack on Greg Lloyd — The Steelers' Pro Bowl linebacker knifed into the backfield to tackle the Browns' big fullback, who had just taken a handoff from Mike Tomczak. Mack lowered his broad shoulders and withstood the head-on blow, sending a dazed Lloyd face-down on the Stadium turf and temporarily out of the 1992 game. With the home crowd pumped up, Mack rumbled on for a three-yard gain and soon scored the go-ahead touchdown, earning a game ball in the 17-9 win.

6. James Harrison on Mohamed Massaquoi — The Steelers' star linebacker leveled the Browns' young receiver with a shot to the head on a crossing route on October 17, 2010. Harrison had earlier that day concussed the Browns' Joshua Cribbs on another helmet-to-helmet hit. Neither play was flagged, but the league later fined Harrison $75,000 for the blow on Massaquoi, which was featured on the cover of *Sports Illustrated*. The second-year wideout never matched his rookie-year production, sustaining more concussions the next two seasons.

7. Harrison on Colt McCoy — Late on Thursday, December 8, 2011, Cleveland's second-year quarterback scrambled, flipped a pass to Montario Hardesty, and was decleated by Harrison's head-on, helmet-to-helmet shot. The repeat offender was penalized for roughing the passer and suspended by the league for one game. Controversially, McCoy returned to the game after two plays — throwing a weak, game-sealing interception — with a not-yet-diagnosed concussion that kept him out the rest of the season. It was his 21st and final Browns start. The league revised its concussion protocol in the wake of the episode.

8. Thom Darden on Pat McInally — The Kardiac Kids needed to beat Cincinnati in the 1980 season finale to break their long playoff drought. In the game-opening drive, the veteran Browns safety broke up a third-down pass with a hard, high shot on the Bengals' lanky receiver/punter. McInally hit the Astroturf hard and was knocked out, swallowing his tongue. Ten minutes later he left the field on a stretcher. Though Darden's style had always been more ball hawk than head hunter, the

scary moment did not play well less than three years removed from Jack Tatum's fateful hit on Darryl Stingley. He was penalized and fined $1,000. Amazingly, McInally returned in the second half and caught a career-long 59-yard touchdown to tie the score.

13 Once-in-a-Career Touchdowns

1. Late in a 1950 win in Washington, Hal Herring picked off Pro Bowler Harry Gilmer, but his scoring return was nullified by a blocking foul on Chubby Grigg. That merely set up a tackle-eligible toss from Otto Graham to **Lou Groza**, who ran it into the end zone to complete a 23-yard score, his only career touchdown.

2. What Groza accomplished in the Browns' first NFL season, kicker Phil **Dawson** repeated in the team's return season of 1999. That is, he became only the second Brown to kick the extra point for his own touchdown. Dawson's four-yard scoring scamper on a fake field goal was the first rushing touchdown of the new Browns era. It came in a narrow Week 5 loss to Cincinnati.

3. Hall of Fame center **Frank Gatski** also played some linebacker in his early years. The only touchdown of his 12-year career came in 1946, his rookie year. A 36-yard interception return off Bob Hoernschemeyer capped the scoring in a 51-14 rout of the Chicago Rockets.

4. If you could point to a single early sign that the mid-to-late-'80s Browns would turn into something special, it might be **Earnest Byner**'s first career touchdown in 1984. The 1-8 Browns were losing to the winless Bills when the rookie runner scooped up a fourth-quarter fumble by WR Willis Adams and ran 55 yards for the winning score. It was a rare break for a snakebit Browns squad and the first of Marty Schottenheimer's 200 career coaching victories. Byner would go on to score 71 more touchdowns, none via fumble recovery.

5. Longtime tight end **Johnny Brewer** switched to outside linebacker after the Browns drafted TE Milt Morin in the first round of 1966. The team's brass facilitated his sole career Pro Bowl selection after that season as a reward. Late in 1967, Brewer scored his only defensive touchdown, returning a Sonny Jurgensen pass tipped by Jim Houston 70 yards in a wild 42-37 win over Otto Graham's Washington squad.

6. Linebacker **Van Waiters**' only career score ended a crucial game late in 1989. The 7-6-1 Browns were 0-2-1 that season in overtime games, including a loss the previous week that ended with the Colts returning a

Bernie Kosar interception. They found themselves again in sudden death against a good Vikings team. Setting up for a 32-yard Matt Bahr field goal on third down, holder and backup quarterback Mike Pagel sensed an all-out effort to block the kick, so he rolled right and found wingman Waiters uncovered to end the four-hour battle in the home team's favor.

7. Cornerback **Anthony Henry** had 17 interceptions in his four years with Cleveland. The sole score was a 97-yard interception return against Jacksonville in 2001, the Browns' only touchdown in the game better known for "Bottlegate."

8. Henry's pick-six tied a team record for length (since surpassed) set by **Najee Mustafaa**, whose only Browns touchdown came against Miami in 1993. Strangely enough, his previous scoring interception return, achieved as a Minnesota Viking known as Reggie Rutland in 1991, also went for 97 yards.

9. **Doug Dieken**, the jocular offensive tackle who played tight end in college, finally struck paydirt against the Oilers in 1983, his 13th season. Down seven points as halftime approached, the Browns faked a field goal, and holder/quarterback Paul McDonald found Dieken at the five. He rumbled in for a 14-yard score on his only career reception. The Browns won in overtime to drop Houston to 0-9.

10. Linebacker **Billy Andrews** played 100 games for the Browns and 142 in his 11-year career. His sole scoring play gave him some well-timed limelight. In the first Monday Night Football game, as Joe Namath tried to erase the Jets' three-point deficit, Andrews intercepted a last-minute pass and returned it 25 yards to seal a historic 31-21 win.

11. Given the memorable comeback that ensued, rookie DT **Michael Dean Perry**'s only career touchdown risks being overshadowed. In a wintry season finale to decide the winner of the 1988 AFC Central Division, Don Strock rallied the Browns back from a 23-7 third-quarter deficit. It would've been tougher had LB David Grayson not popped the ball loose from the Oilers' Warren Moon, resulting in Perry's ten-yard fumble return.

12. A defensive lineman returning an interception for a touchdown is fairly unusual. But two different Browns once accomplished this feat in the same quarter of play. Down 13 points to the Giants in the fourth quarter of a 1960 game, the Browns exploded for 27 points, including two Jim Brown touchdowns and two on turnovers. DE **Paul Wiggin** picked off a Charlie Conerly flare pass and found the Yankee Stadium end zone 20 yards later to even the score. DT **Bob Gain** then lumbered 22 yards with a ball yielded by besieged backup Lee Grosscup, the veteran's only career touchdown.

13. A year after trading away the great Paul Warfield, the Browns were still on the hunt for receivers and drafted another Paul in the third round. Paul Staroba from Michigan had just one reception for the Browns. It was a 19-yard touchdown from Mike Phipps to give Cleveland a fourth-quarter lead over the Broncos in 1972. He had entered the game to give starter Frank Pitts a breather. The 27-20 comeback would be the Browns' last win in Denver until 1990.

6 Significant Two-Point Conversions

The post-touchdown choice to "go for two" first came to the NFL in 1994, and the Browns have converted them 16 times through 2014. Their overall success rate is 42%. Browns opponents are 13 for 35 (37%). Here are the most noteworthy of the Browns' two-pointers.

1. Rallying from a 21-3 deficit in their first game after the death of owner Al Lerner in 2002, the Browns managed a miraculous two-point conversion to tie the game. Jets DT Josh Evans was in the process of planting Tim Couch, who tossed the ball skyward while horizontal. Smallish receiver Dennis Northcutt snatched the ball in the crowded end zone. The Browns evened their record at 4-4 with a crucial 24-21 win, saving what would become a playoff season.

2. The NFL's first two-point conversion followed Leroy Hoard's 11-yard touchdown reception in the first quarter of opening day in 1994. Holder Tom Tupa surprised the Bengals by charging up the middle and over the goal line. The Browns later scored on kickoff and punt returns, winning 28-20 in Cincinnati. Tupa, also the punter and emergency quarterback, scored twice more that season on two-point runs.

3. In an important 2007 game, Braylon Edwards had just completed a 67-yard score to bring the Browns to within five points of the Cardinals at the end of the third quarter. Cleveland lined up to go for two, with Josh Cribbs taking the shotgun snap and charging toward the line. He then stopped suddenly and sent the ball to Kellen Winslow, who had helped sell the run and was alone in the back of the end zone.

4. Against Seattle also in 2007, Phil Dawson's rare missed extra point forced the Browns to try for two to knot the score in the fourth quarter. Derek Anderson's pass to Edwards failed, and the Seahawks drove for a field goal and a five-point lead. Jamal Lewis then banged through for his second short touchdown of the quarter, and this time the conversion to

Joe Jurevicius worked, putting the Browns up three points in a game they would eventually win in overtime.

5. Edwards scored his first two-point conversion to complete the scoring in a satisfying 35-14 Monday night win over the defending Super Bowl champion Giants. It followed Eric Wright's 94-yard interception return.

6. The next week, Edwards again caught a pass from Anderson for two points. This narrowed the Browns' deficit to three points in the final three minutes in front of a Washington crowd of 90,487. But Phil Dawson's last-ditch field goal try from 54 yards went wide right, and a tough season got worse from there. With four career two-point conversions in all, Edwards is tied for 14th on the league's all-time list.

The 12 Browns Who Scored Touchdowns on Offense and Defense

This list illustrates the end of the era of two-way players. Only one Brown since 1968 has found the end zone on both offensive and defensive plays. With expanded rosters and increasing specialization, it will take another oddity of some sort for this list to ever lengthen.

QB/DB **Otto Graham:** 44 rushing (plus one fumbled handoff he recovered and ran into the end zone in 1951) and one interception return of 37 yards vs. Miami Seahawks, Dec. 3, 1946.

FB/LB **Marion Motley:** 31 rushing, seven receiving and one interception return of 48 yards vs. the old Buffalo Bills, Sept. 5, 1947.

HB/P **Tom Colella:** four rushing, six receiving and one interception return of 23 yards vs. the original Baltimore Colts, Sept. 21, 1947.

HB **Les Horvath:** one rushing, one receiving and one fumble return of 84 yards vs. New York Yankees, Sept. 18, 1949.

DB **Warren Lahr:** one rushing (2 yards vs. Los Angeles Dons, Oct. 14, 1949) and five interception returns.

HB **Bill Lund:** two rushing, three receiving and one interception return of 38 yards vs. Brooklyn Dodgers, Sept. 12, 1947.

E/P **Horace Gillom:** three receiving and one return of a recovered fumble vs. Pittsburgh, Oct. 21, 1951. A Steeler punt from their 38 was low and caromed off a lineman's back. Gillom scooped up the ball at the three-yard line and finished off the unique play in stride.

DB Bobby Franklin: two interception returns and one rushing (12 yards around left end as the holder on a fake field goal) vs. St. Louis Cardinals, Oct. 29, 1961.

RB Charley Scales: four rushing and one 23-yard return of a fumbled kickoff return vs. New York Giants, Oct. 25, 1964.

LB/DE Jim Houston: three interception returns and one 10-yard reception from Jim Ninowski on a fake field goal vs. Philadelphia Eagles, Dec. 11, 1966.

TE/LB Johnny Brewer: six receiving and one interception return of 70 yards vs. Washington, Nov. 26, 1967.

DT James Jones: one interception return (20 yards vs. Indianapolis Colts, December 1, 1991), one receiving (1 yard from Bernie Kosar vs. Houston Oilers, December 20, 1992) and one rushing (1 yard vs. San Francisco 49ers, September 13, 1993).

21 Browns Safeties

The two-point safety is the most uncommon type of score in football, occurring about once in every 14 NFL games. No one has been credited with more than one safety as a Brown, so here's a rundown of all the players tied for the top spot in the category.

DT John Kissell at Pittsburgh, October 7, 1950
The Browns' first defensive score in the NFL came when the Steelers' first-down snap from the 20 rolled all the way into their end zone. Back Lynn Chandnois tracked it down but couldn't escape Kissell.

MG Bill Willis versus New York Giants, December 17, 1950 (playoffs)
The Giants' last possession in this American Conference title game ended with a sack of QB Charley Conerly. Willis, who had earlier made a season-saving tackle, got credit for the safety, but other accounts refer to game film that shows rookie Jim Martin making the tackle.

DE George Young versus Pittsburgh, November 16, 1952
A first-quarter safety proved important in what became a wild 29-28 Browns win. Young and Len Ford combined on the sack of Steelers QB Jim Finks (a future Hall of Famer for his work as a team executive). One could make a case that Ford and Young should each have been awarded

one point, much as sacks today are often shared between players. That would put Ford above all others for most safeties scored as a Brown.

DE Len Ford at Chicago Bears, November 14, 1954
The all-time great pass rusher's career predated sacks as an official statistic, but he did get credit for a safety when he decked backup QB Zeke Bratkowski during a 39-10 Browns win at Wrigley Field.

LB Chuck Noll at Chicago Cardinals, October 30, 1955
On a wet day at Comiskey Park, the future coaching legend blocked a Dave Mann punt out of the end zone to help the defending champion Browns recapture first place in their division.

DB Junior Wren versus New York Giants, October 14, 1956
Officially, he tackled QB Charley Conerly in the end zone, but really the Giants took the safety on purpose near the end of their 21-9 victory after the Browns surrendered the ball on downs at the one.

DE Ron Snidow versus Pittsburgh, October 3, 1970
Browns quarterbacks this Saturday night completed just four of 21 passes, but they won, 15-7, by making fewer mistakes than rookie Terry Bradshaw, who was intercepted three times and sacked seven others, including an early safety by the Browns' All-Pro.

DT Walter Johnson versus Cincinnati, October 11, 1970
The Browns' very first regular season points against the Bengals came when the big lineman broke through blockers to sack Virgil Carter in the end zone, the start of turning a 10-0 deficit into a 30-27 win.

OL Chuck Reynolds versus Dallas, December 12, 1970
Hall of Famer Bob Hayes fielded a deep Don Cockroft punt and crossed into his own end zone, where Reynolds was credited with bringing him down. Those were the home team's only points in a 6-2 loss.

LB Jim Houston at Pittsburgh, November 7, 1971
The veteran tackled Steelers punter Bob Walden, who had bobbled a long snap in the end zone.

DE Ron East versus Kansas City, December 14, 1975
In a muddy Browns romp, a fumble by Chiefs rookie QB Tony Adams was recovered by tackle Charlie Getty in the end zone. East, in his only season with the Browns, fell on him to score the only points of his 137-game NFL career.

DE Mack Mitchell at Houston, November 7, 1976
Less than two minutes into this division contest, Oilers quarterback Dan Pastorini lost the ball and cracked his ribs on a sack. With Joe Jones, Jerry Sherk and Walter Johnson converged on the quarterback, lineman Elbert Drungo recovered the fumble in the end zone, where Mitchell got credit for the two-point tackle.

DT Jerry Sherk versus Houston, December 11, 1977
Cleveland committed eight turnovers in Forrest Gregg's last game as the Browns' coach. One bright spot was the play of the star defensive lineman, who felled rookie RB Rob Carpenter for a third-quarter safety.

DB D.D. Hoggard at Denver, January 17, 1988 (playoffs)
The special-teamer was the closest player to punter Mike Horan when he intentionally ran out of the end zone after the play known as "The Fumble" sealed the Browns' fate in this epic AFC Championship game.

DE Charles Buchanan at Phoenix, October 23, 1988
The one-and-done lineman sacked QB Cliff Stoudt to complete the scoring in a 29-21 Browns win.

DT James Jones versus Cincinnati, September 15, 1991
After three straight penalties backed them up to their own one-yard line, Bengals RB James Brooks couldn't elude the Browns' rookie third-round pick in the end zone. Cleveland won, 14-13, on the safety and four Matt Stover field goals.

DB Louis Riddick at Los Angeles Raiders, September 19, 1993
As with Hoggard's safety, this was more proximity than performance. Ex-Browns punter Jeff Gossett stepped out of the end zone on purpose as the Raiders nursed a late lead. But Eric Metcalf returned the free kick 37 yards and scored the winning touchdown in the game's final seconds.

DE Anthony Pleasant at Seattle, November 14, 1993
In a sloppy 22-5 loss following the sudden release of popular QB Bernie Kosar, one of their few good plays came after Brian Hansen's punt pinned the Seahawks at their one. Pleasant captured Rick Mirer behind the goal line, notching one of his career-high 11 sacks on the season.

DL Orpheus Roye versus Pittsburgh, November 11, 2001
The former and future Steeler gave the Browns an early lead by tackling RB Jerome Bettis in the end zone. But Butch Davis' club would go on to lose in overtime for the second straight week.

Team, at Detroit, November 22, 2009
While Hoggard and Riddick may not deserve the points for their roles in intentional safeties, LB Jason Trusnik merits some credit for pressuring Lions' QB Matthew Stafford into committing intentional grounding in the end zone.

LB Tank Carder at Tennessee, October 5, 2014
He blocked a punt back through the Titans' end zone, a key part of the largest comeback win by any road team in NFL history. For his work in the Browns' 29-28 victory, Carder earned AFC Special Teams Player of the Week honors.

9 Notable Browns-Related Pro Bowl Moments

1951: Three weeks after the Browns won the championship in their first NFL season with a thrilling 30-28 home win over the Rams, the inaugural Pro Bowl was held at the Los Angeles Coliseum. Paul Brown and Joe Stydahar were rematched as the opposing coaches. Unlike the modern pattycake affairs, this game was hard-hitting and closely contested. Browns legend Otto Graham went most of the way at quarterback, scoring two touchdowns on sneaks and throwing for another. Six other Browns played that day, but the great Graham was named Player of the Game in the East's 28-27 comeback win.

1953: Graham scored the only touchdown for the Eastern Conference "Americans" coached by Paul Brown, but he was also intercepted five times and lost a fumble in the 27-7 loss.

1962: Cleveland's phenomenal fullback Jim Brown shed four tacklers for a Pro Bowl record 70-yard scoring run, giving his side a late 30-24 lead. Moments after being announced as the game's MVP, as the East milked the clock, Brown fumbled deep in his own end. The Bears' Bill George made the hit and recovery, giving Johnny Unitas a last-ditch chance to work his magic, which he did. Rams back Jon Arnett made the game-winning catch on his knees as time expired.

1963: Four days following the stunning dismissal of longtime coach Paul Brown, Jim Brown broke his year-old game record with 141 rushing yards, including first-quarter scoring runs of one and 50 yards in the East's 30-20 win.

1965: Two weeks after leading the Browns to a 27-0 title game triumph over Baltimore, quarterback Frank Ryan felt the brunt of Colts' end Gino Marchetti's anger. Reportedly still seething from Ryan's choice to pass to Johnny Brewer in the dying seconds of the championship game, Marchetti sacked Ryan with a vengeance in the second quarter, knocking him out of the exhibition with a separated shoulder that required surgery and ultimately shortened his career.

1966: In what would turn out to be his last game, Jim Brown scored three times in a 36-7 romp at the Los Angeles Coliseum. Coach Blanton Collier led the East squad, which included Browns QB Frank Ryan, WR Gary Collins, guards Gene Hickerson and John Wooten, OT Dick Schafrath, LB Jim Houston and DE Paul Wiggin.

1990: Browns coach Bud Carson coached the AFC in Honolulu, and Cleveland was represented by five players. Defensive starters Michael Dean Perry, Clay Matthews and Frank Minnifield were joined by WR

Webster Slaughter and LB Mike Johnson. Johnson picked off Mark Rypien midway through the fourth quarter, the 22-yard touchdown return narrowing their deficit to six points. With five seconds left Dave Krieg of Seattle (then in the AFC) found teammate Brian Blades in the end zone for the apparent winning touchdown. But the officials flagged a lineman for illegal formation, a technicality that sealed a 27-21 NFC win.

2008: This game served as a consolation prize of sorts for the Browns, deprived of a playoff appearance despite a 10-6 record. The previous eight years had seen only one Brown in the Pro Bowl (Jamir Miller in 2002), so six solid orange helmets in Hawaii seemed remarkable. Derek Anderson played more than any quarterback, but he was atrocious, going 10-for-26 for 103 yards and one interception, with a passer rating of just 34.6. The best Browns moments in the 42-30 AFC loss were Braylon Edwards' 31-yard catch from Peyton Manning to set up an early score and Josh Cribbs' 41-yard kickoff return.

2011: With the Pro Bowl devolved into something of a farce, and only two offensive lineman, Joe Thomas and Alex Mack, to represent the Browns, Cleveland fans had little reason to tune in. But most of them eventually saw one bizarre highlight that embodied what this exhibition had become. With the AFC down 20 points in the final minute, QB Matt Cassel found teammate Dwayne Bowe deep over the middle. He lateraled to Montell Owens, who eventually flipped the ball back to the waiting Mack. The Browns' center rumbled down the left sideline 40 yards to complete an absurdly amusing 67-yard scoring play.

CHAPTER 4
FRANCHISE FACETS AND FEATURES

17 Browns Who Made the Pro Bowl At Least Half the Time

These players proved to be the likeliest to earn Pro Bowl honors during their Browns careers since the inaugural Pro Bowl, which followed the 1950 season. Though the methods for Pro Bowl selection have changed over the years, it remains a useful, if subjective, general measure of player quality in that it encompasses all positions across eras.

1. Jim Brown — 100% (nine Pro Bowls in nine Browns seasons played)
2. Joe Thomas — 100% (eight of eight*)
3. Donte Whitner — 100% (one of one*)
4. Otto Graham — 83% (five of six)
5. Chip Banks — 80% (four of five)
6. (tie) Michael Dean Perry — 71% (five of seven)
   Jim Ray Smith — 71% (five of seven)
8. Leroy Kelly — 60% (six of ten)
9. Don Paul — 60% (three of five)
10. (tie) Abe Gibron — 57% (four of seven)
    Bill Glass — 57% (four of seven)
12. Mike McCormack — 56% (five of nine)
13. Lou Groza — 53% (nine of 17)
14. Walt Michaels — 50% (five of ten)
15. Len Ford — 50% (four of eight)
16. Don Colo — 50% (three of six)
17. Tommy O'Connell — 50% (one of two)

14 Seasons, 14 Browns Players of the Year

The disappointing fate of most Browns first-round draft picks in the new era is well-known. But no less depressing is what happened to players who were actually productive. Each year since 2001, the Cleveland chapter of the Pro Football Writers Association identifies a Player of the Year. Almost every honoree suffered a significant career setback within the next year, and there have been no repeat winners.

2001: **Jamir Miller** — The first-team All-Pro linebacker ruptured his Achilles tendon in the first exhibition game in 2002 and never played again. He was the Browns' only Pro Bowler between 1999 and 2006.

2002: **William Green** — After rushing for 887 yards as a rookie, this first-rounder ran into trouble with an arrest, suspension and domestic discord in 2003, playing just seven games. He was out of the league at age 26.

2003: **Andra Davis** — A knee injury caused the emerging middle linebacker to miss the last five games of 2004, the only one of his seven Browns seasons in which he played fewer than 14 games.

2004: **Robert Griffith** — The veteran strong safety was the team's leading tackler but was released the next February to net the Browns nearly $3 million in salary cap savings.

2005: **Reuben Droughns** — After a career-high 309 carries and the Browns' first 1,000-yard rushing season in 20 years, Droughns was arrested following a domestic disturbance the next May. His per-carry average plummeted to 3.4 yards in 2006, his last year as a Brown and as an NFL starter.

2006: **Kamerion Wimbley** — He shined with an 11-sack rookie year, but though he remained a healthy contributor he never again reached that level of pass-rush production.

2007: **Derek Anderson** — Rewarded with a $24 million contract after a Cinderella season, the strong-armed quarterback suffered a pre-season concussion, a midseason benching and a season-ending MCL injury in the disastrous 2008 campaign.

2008: **Shaun Rogers** — The longtime Lion was an immediate force at nose tackle, earning Pro Bowl honors, but it would be the last season he'd start 16 games. He broke his leg the next November in Cincinnati.

2009: **Joshua Cribbs** — The stellar special teamer renegotiated his ill-advised contract after another spectacular season, but in 2010 he failed to find the end zone on a return for the first time in his six-year career. His kickoff return and rushing averages also hit personal lows.

2010: **Peyton Hillis** — Seldom has a fan favorite fallen so far and fast. Voted onto the Madden NFL 12 cover, the big back followed his fine season with a bizarre swirl of contract controversy, questionable scratches and diminished performance.

2011: **D'Qwell Jackson** — Here's the exception that proves the rule. The inside linebacker returned from two straight season-ending pectoral injuries to lead the team with 158 combined tackles. He continued to play all 16 games for several seasons to follow and earned his first Pro Bowl berth as a new member of the Indianapolis Colts in 2014.

2012: **Phil Dawson** — This kicker's 14th season as a Brown was his best, as he went seven-for-seven on field goals of at least 50 yards. It was also his last. After two seasons playing under the franchise tag, the free agent signed with San Francisco.

2013: **Josh Gordon** — After blowing away the Browns' single-season record with 1,646 receiving yards, he got caught up in the league's drug policy. News of a year-long suspension was leaked during the 2014 draft. The policy was revised and he missed the first ten games, but his season was ultimately a washout. Another lengthy suspension ensued.

2014: **Joe Thomas** — If anyone can break this nearly perpetual pattern of post-award problems, it's this eight-time Pro Bowl tackle who's never missed a snap, perhaps because he didn't win this honor earlier.

8 Heisman Trophy Winners Who Became Browns

The Heisman Trophy is college football's premiere individual award, granted each season to the most outstanding player in the country. Eight Heisman winners eventually earned enshrinement in the Pro Football Hall of Fame. And eight Heisman winners (listed here chronologically) became Cleveland Browns. But a Venn diagram would show no overlap.

1. **Les Horvath** — A graduate of Cleveland's Rhodes High School by way of Parma, Horvath became Ohio State's first Heisman Trophy winner in 1944. The single-wing halfback was slight but quick and strong-armed. After the Buckeyes won the national title his senior year in 1942, he earned his bachelor's degree and enrolled in OSU's dental school. Taking advantage of a wartime exception, he returned after a year away from football and excelled as a play-calling quasi-coach on a team of

mostly freshmen. He threw for three touchdowns and rushed for 12 more, including the game-winner against Michigan. He played two years for the Los Angeles Rams and rejoined Paul Brown as a two-way reserve and special-teamer for the 1949 Browns.

2. **Howard Cassady** — Nicknamed "Hopalong" after the fictional cowboy hero, the star Ohio State halfback was named not only the best college football player of 1955, but also the Associated Press Athlete of the Year. He rushed for 964 yards and 15 touchdowns for the Buckeyes as a senior and also excelled at baseball, the field where he'd later spend decades as an assistant in George Steinbrenner's Yankee organization. Drafted third overall by the Detroit Lions, Cassady never had pro success commensurate with his college exploits. He played five games with the 1962 Browns as a returner before being released mid-season.

3. **Ernie Davis** — Cassady might not have suited up for the Browns had this top pick not tragically fallen ill. The story of the Elmira Express, the first African American Heisman winner, has been well documented in print and on film. From a school with legendary rushing talent, including Jim Brown, Davis to this day owns Syracuse's top two seasonal marks in yards per carry. A blockbuster trade made him Brown's teammate in Cleveland, but leukemia prevented him from ever playing as a pro, and he passed away in 1963 at age 23.

4. **Charles White** — The Los Angeles native won the 1979 Heisman Trophy by rushing for 2,050 yards and 19 scores for Southern Cal, capping a superb college career with his second Rose Bowl MVP award, as he gained 247 yards in the Trojans' 17-16 win over undefeated Ohio State. The Browns drafted him in the first round and his quarterback, Paul McDonald, in the fourth. Cocaine did him no favors as a pro, and he underperformed in his five years as a Brown, never rushing for 100 yards in a game. His career eventually rebounded as an L.A. Ram, where he topped his Browns career totals in attempts, yards and touchdowns in 1987 alone, when he led the league in all three categories.

5. **Vinny Testaverde** — Beaten out by Boardman, Ohio's Bernie Kosar for the starting quarterback job of the Miami Hurricanes, the much more athletic Testaverde got his chance two years later when Kosar (actually 12 days younger) turned pro. Flanked by such stars as Michael Irvin, Alonzo Highsmith and Brett Perriman, Testaverde threw for 26 scores against just nine interceptions in winning the Heisman as a senior for Jimmy Johnson's second-ranked squad. The top pick of the 1987 draft, he came to Cleveland in free agency following six rough years in Tampa (including 1988, when he threw an NFL record 35 picks). Eventually supplanting Kosar, Testaverde in his three years here had his first positive TD/INT ratio and first winning season. He played until age 44 for five more teams after the Browns left town.

6. Ty Detmer — Despite an incredibly productive college career at Brigham Young, his slight 6' frame made him just a ninth-round draft pick in 1992. He had thrown for 16,206 yards and 127 TDs at BYU, winning the Heisman as a junior, when his exploits included spearheading an upset of top-ranked Miami, amassing 406 yards against the defending national champs. His journeyman pro career included starting the first and last games of the reborn Browns' 1999 season. He missed all of 2000 after tearing his Achilles in pre-season. He next emerged as a Lion in 2001, and in his first game the Browns intercepted him seven times to tie a league record.

7. Rashaan Salaam — This Colorado Buffalo also won the Heisman after his junior season, which included four straight games rushing for over 200 yards. The first Colorado player so honored, he led the nation in rushing, scoring and all-purpose yards for an 11-1 team that included Kordell Stewart, Michael Westbrook, Rae Carruth and Detmer's brother Koy. Forgoing his senior year, he gained over 1,000 yards as a rookie for the Chicago Bears, who drafted him 21st overall. But he wore out his welcome after three declining seasons, lazy and immature by his own later admission. His last NFL appearance came with the talent-starved 1999 Browns, for whom he had one carry for two yards before being waived in October.

8. Johnny Manziel — In 2012, this Texas A&M quarterback became the only freshman to throw for 3,000 yards and rush for 1,000 more, and the first to win the Heisman. In a season that included 21 rushing touchdowns, he led the Aggies to a road win over top-ranked Alabama and a rout of #12 Oklahoma in the Cotton Bowl. Their final poll ranking of #5 was the school's best finish since Bear Bryant's 1956 squad. After a 2013 season that was good enough to place him fifth in the Heisman voting, Johnny Football entered the draft as one of the more polarizing prospects in history. Trading up to the 21st overall pick, Cleveland made him the second QB taken from a deep draft class. A rocky rookie year lent support to many who had doubted his maturity and NFL readiness.

11 Best Rookie Seasons

It's one of those inherently subjective words, but in this case "best" means most noteworthy, most accomplished, greatest contribution to the team, comparing favorably to later seasons, or some combination of these. Many of the original 1946 Browns were technically rookies but older than usual due to their service in World War II. Since they'd dominate here as they did the league, they're omitted from this list.

1. Paul Warfield, 1964 — Fellow receiver Gary Collins' three touchdowns in the title game triumph are indelible Browns moments, but they wouldn't have happened without the season-long sensational play of the rookie from Warren and Ohio State. Strong from the start with scores in each of his first three games, the converted running back led the prolific Browns offense in all major receiving categories. It was the first of eight Pro Bowl seasons for the future Hall of Famer, and his 52 receptions turned out to be a career high. His Browns rookie record of nine touchdown receptions remains on the books half a century later.

2. Kevin Mack, 1985 — Whether you consider him a rookie or first-year player (he rushed for 330 yards with the USFL's Los Angeles Express in 1984) the broad-shouldered fullback was an impact player for Cleveland from the outset. He earned Pro Bowl honors by gaining 1,104 yards on the ground at 5.0 yards per carry, both career highs. The team's second-round pick that year, RB Greg Allen, soon became an afterthought. Along with fellow 1,000-yard rusher Earnest Byner and a stout defense, the Browns won the AFC Central with an 8-8 mark in 1985, sparking a memorable era of resurgence.

3. Jim Brown, 1957 — The legendary fullback may have rushed for "only" a career-low 942 yards as a rookie, but it still led the league, as did his nine rushing touchdowns in the 12-game season. Coach Paul Brown had needed a franchise quarterback, but San Francisco drafted John Brodie third overall. The Steelers won a coin flip with the Browns for the fifth pick and took Len Dawson. So the Syracuse star, selected sixth, proved quite a consolation prize. The Browns swiftly recovered from their first losing record in 1956, returning to the title game with a 9-2-1 record and the league's best point and yardage differential. The Browns wouldn't suffer their second sub-.500 season until 1974.

4. Joe Thomas, 2007 — He went fishing on draft day, but the third-overall pick has shown up as reliably as any Browns player ever. The unassuming, 6'6", 313-pounder from Wisconsin became Cleveland's immediate fixture at the crucial position of left tackle. He never sat out so much as a single snap that season and several subsequent. The much-improved offensive line was a big reason the 2007 Browns won six more games than the previous year and sent journeyman quarterback Derek Anderson to his sole Pro Bowl. As a team, they allowed only 19 sacks, third-best in the league. In yards per rush, they ranked sixth. Thomas, who was called for holding just once all year, started a long string of Pro Bowl appearances as a rookie.

5. **Kevin Johnson, 1999** — Eleven rookies started games for the Browns' re-emergence in 1999, but only this Syracuse second-rounder started all 16 of them. His Hail Mary catch in New Orleans provided their first win and the season's signature moment for an otherwise overwhelmed organization with the NFL's most anemic offense. KJ's 986 receiving yards and eight touchdowns were more than the team's other wide receivers combined. Though cut midway through his fifth season in Cleveland, he remains the new Browns' leader in receptions and receiving yards.

6. **Bobby Mitchell, 1958** — The steal of the draft in the seventh round, the fleet Illinois product was brilliant from the beginning, scoring the Browns' first touchdown of a season that saw him reach paydirt four different ways: rushing, receiving, punt return and kickoff return. He gained 500 yards on the ground in just 80 carries at a 6.3 clip, providing the perfect lightning to Jim Brown's thunder.

7. **Kamerion Wimbley, 2006** — The story goes that general manager Phil Savage acceded to head coach Romeo Crennel's preference for a pash rusher over a stout interior defender. That's why Savage traded down one spot in the draft, let the Baltimore Ravens have Haloti Ngata, and touted the "Gumby-like" skills of the DE/LB tweener from Florida State. Wimbley notched a Browns rookie record 11 sacks in 2006 along with three fumble recoveries, numbers he never achieved again.

8. **Jabaal Sheard, 2011** — The pass rusher out of Pitt started all 16 games as a rookie, leading the team by a wide margin with 8.5 sacks and five forced fumbles. The Browns finished just 4-12, but their defense improved to rank among the league's top ten in both fewest points and yards allowed.

9. **Don Fleming, 1960** — College teammate Bernie Parrish helped coordinate Fleming's return to Ohio, as the Shadyside native became an instant starter in a talented young defensive backfield. The two-sport star at Florida solidified a safety spot and recorded five interceptions, including two of Hall of Famer Norm Van Brocklin in a season-opening win at Philadelphia.

10. **Bobby Franklin, 1960** — This 11th-round pick from Ole Miss was another new starter in the Browns' 1960 secondary. He racked up eight of his 13 career interceptions in his 12-game rookie season. In a 42-0 romp over the Bears, Franklin had three of the team's seven interceptions, returning two for touchdowns.

11. **Anthony Henry, 2001** — The fourth-round rookie from South Florida was the Browns' third cornerback, starting only two games, but he led the league with ten interceptions, tying Thom Darden's team record. Four of them came in two games against the defending Super Bowl champion Ravens, Cleveland's first wins over the original Browns'

successor franchise. He returned another pick 97 yards for the only Browns touchdown in the notorious "Bottlegate" loss to Jacksonville.

Honorable mention:

- LB Chip Banks, strike-shortened 1982
- S Larry Benz, 1963
- G Joel Bitonio, 2014
- RB William Green, 2002
- DT James Jones, 1991
- RB Eric Metcalf, 1989
- CB Bernie Parrish, 1959

17 Ways the Browns' Record Book Would Improve by Including the AAFC Years

Unlike the American Football League of the 1960s, the Browns' original league, the All-America Football Conference, was not fully accepted into the NFL when it ceased operations after four seasons in 1949. Only three of its teams were absorbed into the NFL, and none of its statistics are included in the league's records. Conversely, the NFL retroactively made all of the AFL's pre-merger activity official.

Whether due to politics or documentation issues, the exclusion of AAFC exploits is especially detrimental to the Browns. Although plenty of reliable statistics from the league exist and are recognized by the Pro Football Hall of Fame, even the Browns' own team records published in its media guide largely ignore AAFC contributions.

What if the team changed its practice and decided to fully honor the work done by its earliest championship squads? Here are some ways that the Browns record book would — and really should — be different.

1. Lou Groza would be first all-time with 268 games played as a Brown. Their media guide now shows him 16 games behind Clay Matthews, who played 232.

2. Groza's leading career point total would increase from 1,349 to 1,608. (Had Phil Dawson, second with 1,271 points, stayed one more year, he likely would have topped Groza's NFL-only total.)

3. Marion Motley's 4,712 total rushing yards would be fifth on the team's all-time list, his 31 rushing TDs would be sixth, and his 6,941 all-purpose yards would be eighth. As it stands, he's out of the top ten.

4. Including his AAFC seasons, Motley averaged 5.7 yards per career rushing attempt, higher than any other pro running back, including Jim Brown, whose 5.2 per-carry average is now topped by the Chiefs' Jamaal Charles with 5.5.

5. Motley's 6.14 yards per carry in 1948 would rank second in Browns history, behind only Jim Brown's 1963 season.

6. Otto Graham would rank first, not fourth, in career touchdown passes if he got credit for all 174 he actually threw. His 23,584 passing yards, officially upgraded from 13,499, would place him just 129 behind leader Brian Sipe.

7. Graham's rushing touchdown total would increase from 33 to 44, which is more than any other NFL quarterback, including Steve Young, Randall Cunningham, Michael Vick, Fran Tarkenton, or John Elway.

8. Dante Lavelli and Mac Speedie would rank behind only Ozzie Newsome in career receptions with 386 and 349, respectively. They don't show up in the team's top ten as it stands. They would also be second and third in receiving yards. The Browns record book now puts Lavelli tenth with an asterisk.

9. Two of Speedie's 1,000-yard receiving seasons would appear on the team's top ten list. His average of 23.5 yards per reception in 1946 would be recognized as the third-highest season by any Brown.

10. A 1947 screen pass from Graham to Speedie that went 99 yards for a touchdown would forever remain a record that could only be tied, as it was in 2004 by a Jeff Garcia-to-André Davis connection.

11. Graham and Lavelli connected for 29 NFL passing touchdowns, but 57 if their AAFC feats are included. That would top the listed team record of 49 by Frank Ryan and Gary Collins.

12. For most career interceptions, Tommy James would move up four spots to fourth with 34 in all, and Cliff Lewis would rise from 61st to sixth for his 30 picks.

13. Tom Colella would top the single-season leader board for interceptions, joining Thom Darden and Anthony Henry, who also had ten apiece, though they played two more games than Colella did in 1946.

14. Legendary punter Horace Gillom would pass Chris Gardocki to rank second behind Don Cockroft in career punts and yardage.

15. Team records in the games won category would be quite different. For example, "most games won, one season (including postseason)" would be 15 for the undefeated title season of 1948, rather than 13 in 1986. "Most consecutive games won (regular season)" would be 16 rather

than 13 from 1951-52. "Most consecutive home games won (regular season)" would be 15 rather than 12 from 1950-52.

16. The 1946 team would be credited both for scoring the most points in a season and for allowing the fewest.

17. The 41 interceptions snared by that inaugural team — nearly three per game — should be first in team history, well above the 33 picks gathered by the Browns defense in 2001. No fewer than 16 different players out of 36 contributed to that tally.

39 Starting Guards Since 1999

The quarterback position rightly gets the headlines, and it's remarkable that the new Browns featured 22 different starters behind center through 2014. But the sheer length of this list of guards explains much of the new Browns' struggles. Chronic instability on either side of the center helped shorten Tim Couch's career and limited the Browns' offense to a yardage ranking of 23rd or worse for 14 of 16 seasons.

Each player below started at least one regular season game at left or right guard during the expansion era. The average starter at guard lasted fewer than 13 games, though several also played at center or tackle.

- Orlando Bobo (1999)
- Scott Rehberg (1999)
- Jim Pyne (1999-2000)
- Jim Bundren (1999-2000)
- Steve Zahursky (1999-2000)
- Everett Lindsay (2000)
- Shaun O'Hara (2000-03)
- Ross Verba (2001)
- Tre' Johnson (2001)
- Jeremy McKinney (2001)
- Brad Bedell (2001)
- Barry Stokes (2002)
- Paul Zukauskas (2002-04)
- Melvin Fowler (2003)
- Chad Beasley (2003)
- Enoch DeMar (2003-04)
- Kelvin Garmon (2004)
- Damion Cook (2004)
- Joaquin Gonzalez (2004)
- Mike Pucillo (2005)

- Dave Yovanovits (2005)
- Joe Andruzzi (2005-06)
- Cosey Coleman (2005-06)
- Lennie Friedman (2006)
- Rob Smith (2006)
- Seth McKinney (2007)
- Ryan Tucker (2007)
- Eric Steinbach (2007-10)
- Rex Hadnot (2008-09)
- Hank Fraley (2009)
- Floyd "Pork Chop" Womack (2009-10)
- Billy Yates (2010)
- Shawn Lauvao (2010-13)
- Jason Pinkston (2011-13)
- John Greco (2012-14*)
- Oniel Cousins (2013)
- Garrett Gilkey (2013)
- Joel Bitonio (2014*)
- Paul McQuistan (2014)

9 NFL Rule Changes Inspired by Browns

1. **The Lou Groza rule** — Early in his pro career, the legendary straight-on placekicker would keep a two-yard piece of tape, stuck together back to back, tucked in his helmet. In lining up for a kick, he would lay it on the ground, aimed at the center of the crossbar, in order to optimize his alignment on approach. He later used a tee with a long tail for this purpose. In 1956, the league outlawed any artificial medium to assist in executing a placekick.

2. **Helmet radio receiver** — Ohio inventors John Campbell and George Sarles approached coach Paul Brown in 1956 about their radio receiver, thinking it could aid in sideline-to-field communications. Brown recognized the opportunity to gain an edge and had the device installed in quarterback George Ratterman's helmet, with orders to keep it secret and test it before using it in a game. The scheme didn't stay secret long, as the sideline transmitter was spotted in its first game, an exhibition against Detroit. Ratterman, for his part, wanted opponents to know that the unit was plenty durable: "I'm not in favor of losing any teeth while the opposition is trying to get me off the air." The Browns used the system in just four games before NFL commissioner Bert Bell outlawed

it. In 1994, 38 years later, the league finally legitimized the limited use of radio helmets.

3. **Taxi squads** — Now formalized into ten-man practice squads, the retention of extra players for added depth and development beyond the active roster originated in Cleveland. Paul Brown collaborated with the team's original owner, Mickey McBride, who put reserve personnel on the payroll of his taxicab company. It was one of many Brown innovations that became standard practice league-wide.

4. **Tearaway jerseys** — The elusive Greg Pruitt often left would-be tacklers grasping at cotton while he continued scooting downfield. "For it to be effective, you couldn't wear anything under it, or they'd just grab that shirt," Pruitt told *Cleveland Magazine* in 2007, "It got pretty cold playing on the lakefront." While others including the Oilers' Earl Campbell also wore the flimsy fabric, the prohibition of tearaway jerseys in 1979 became known as the Greg Pruitt rule.

5. **Eliminating the "force-out"** — The 2007 Browns finished 10-6 but missed the playoffs. The difference may have come down to one judgment call. On the last play of a December game in Arizona, Kellen Winslow II snagged a 37-yard Derek Anderson pass in the left corner of the end zone. It would've set up a winning extra point try, but he was pushed out of bounds, and the officials didn't rule that both feet would have landed in-bounds had the defender not forced him out. The league soon changed its rules to end the need for such judgment calls, so now a force-out can never be ruled a completion.

6. **Replay review of placekicks** — An unforgettably bizarre Phil Dawson field goal led to another rule change after the 2007 season. Dawson's game-tying, 51-yard attempt hit an upright, then caromed off the support post and back onto the field. Initially called no-good, the kick by rule was not subject to video review. Nonetheless, it was ultimately deemed good because it did pass over the crossbar. Dawson kicked another field goal in overtime to beat the Ravens in a critical road win. The subsequent rule allows video review of whether a kick passes over the crossbar, but only for those within the height of the uprights.

7. **The Dwayne Rudd rule** — The Browns linebacker's famous gaffe cost his team a win in their 2002 season opener against Kansas City. Thinking he'd ended the game with a sack of QB Trent Green, Rudd pulled off his own helmet and threw it in celebration. Green had actually lateraled the ball to tackle John Tait to keep the play alive. Though time had expired, Rudd's penalty resulted in an untimed down, letting the Chiefs kick a field goal to win, 40-39. The off-season rule change was to reclassify removing the helmet as a dead-ball foul even if it occurs during a play. That would have prevented the extra down, and the Browns would have won that memorable game.

8. Hitting quarterbacks after turnovers — After Orpheus Roye intercepted a Jaguars pass early in a 2001 game, rookie defensive tackle Gerard Warren decked QB Mark Brunell with a helmet-to-helmet hit away from the play. Brunell was knocked woozy and later left the game. Warren (he of the self-proclaimed nickname "Big Money") escaped an on-field penalty but was later fined $35,000. Although already illegal, the play prompted the league to specifically ban any helmet-to-helmet contact on a quarterback after a change of possession.

9. The crown rule — Warren was not the only Browns rookie drafted third overall to cause the NFL's competition committee to act. In running back Trent Richardson's regular-season debut in 2012, he charged hard and head first into the Eagles' Kurt Coleman, knocking the safety backwards and popping his helmet skyward. The rule approved the following off-season made it a 15-yard penalty to lower the head and use the crown of the helmet on an opponent outside the tackle box.

6 Browns Coaching Careers Hurt by Losing to Cincinnati

The division rivalry between the Browns and the Cincinnati Bengals isn't just the Battle of Ohio. It started with a most personal grudge. In January 1963, 37-year-old owner Art Modell unceremoniously fired legendary coach and franchise namesake Paul Brown.

After 17 years establishing one of football's most respected and successful organizations, Brown was crushed, but he rebounded with a franchise of his own, founding the Bengals, who began play in 1968 sporting uniforms similar in their plain design and orange helmets to those of his original pro team. He served as head coach through 1975, and his son, Mike, runs the organization to this day.

Meanwhile, many of the coaches who followed Brown in Cleveland (presented here in succession) suffered losses to their cross-state counterparts that proved disproportionately detrimental — in some cases decisive — to their coaching careers.

1. Blanton Collier's progressive hearing loss would make 1970 his final season as Browns coach, so it's not fair to say that losing both pre- and regular-season games at Cincinnati affected his career longevity, except in this respect: the 7-7 Browns missed the playoffs because they finished one game behind the young Bengals, who won the first AFC Central title in the now-merged NFL. Paul Brown avenged a 30-27 October loss at

Cleveland with a 14-10 triumph on November 15 that left him both exhilarated and tearful. Browns QB Mike Phipps made his first career start in place of the injured Bill Nelsen, and he failed to generate any second-half points. The Browns' record (4-5) slipped below .500 for the first time that year. Cleveland hadn't had a losing record that late in the season since 1956.

2. **Nick Skorich** remains the only Browns head coach hired with previous experience as a pro head coach. He took the Browns to the playoffs his first two seasons, but the aging club slipped to 7-5-2 in 1973. The following year yielded a 4-10 record, worst in the franchise's 29-year history. And it started with what would be their worst loss of the season, a 33-7 rout at Riverfront Stadium in which the Browns mustered just three net yards passing. A month later, a defeat at home in the rematch with the Bengals dropped Skorich's career coaching record to .500 and sinking. As the team stumbled to a last-place finish for the first time, Modell concluded that the rebuilding effort would continue with a new coach. Skorich, age 53, was fired and his coaching career was over.

3. **Sam Rutigliano** had rightfully earned lots of good will over the years on the strength of his personality. And his high-flying offense had lifted the Browns back to respectability after the disappointing mid-1970s. But by 1984 many of the Kardiac Kids had left the scene, including Brian Sipe, Reggie Rucker, Dave Logan and Greg Pruitt. When right tackle Cody Risien, the blind-side blocker for lefty QB Paul McDonald, went down for the year with a pre-season injury, tragedy's stage was set. The last straw was a battle of field goals that Sam Wyche's Bengals won, 12-9, on the game's last play. Despite McDonald's 300 passing yards, their only points came on kicks of 50, 60 and 47 yards, and the Browns fell to 1-7. Modell announced the coaching switch to defensive coordinator Marty Schottenheimer the next day.

4. **Jim Shofner** was a Browns defensive back who retired at age 28 just prior to the championship season of 1964. His multi-stop journey through the coaching ranks included serving as Brian Sipe's quarterback coach during the Kardiac Kids era. As offensive coordinator in 1990, he was promoted to interim head coach when Bud Carson was fired during the bye week. Taking over a 2-7 team, Shofner couldn't right the ship, winning just one of the final seven games. The finale was a 21-14 loss at Cincinnati in which backup QB Mike Pagel helped keep the game close, but his third interception proved fateful. The Bengals clinched the division title that had belonged to the Browns four of the prior five years. Shofner's third tour of duty in Cleveland ended after a year as the director of player personnel.

5. **Butch Davis** had grasped all the reins of the Browns' football operations, but his team continued faltering in 2004, his fourth year.

After a 3-3 start, they lost four straight headed into Cincinnati. The heat was on, and starting QB Jeff Garcia, the big-ticket free agent Davis had signed to stabilize the position, was out with a shoulder injury. Kelly Holcomb, known for big games in losing efforts as a fill-in, threw for 413 yards and five touchdowns. But in one of the wildest games ever, the Bengals prevailed 58-48, sealing it with a Deltha O'Neal pick-six with less than two minutes left. *Sports Illustrated* later reported that Davis said he had suffered a panic attack hours before the game. Soon thereafter, Davis and the Browns negotiated the terms of his departure, which was called a resignation and included a buyout settlement of the three years remaining on his contract.

6. Rookie coach Rob Chudzinski was the toast of the town after a home win over the defending Super Bowl champion Ravens put the retooling Browns at 4-5 at the bye week in 2013. "I'd be hard-pressed to think that in nine weeks a first-time head coach can do any better or any more than he's doing. All of the measurables that you'd look to come up with ... I just think he's doing an outstanding job," gushed CEO Joe Banner. But after the Browns took a 13-0 lead in Cincinnati, the roof collapsed. The Bengals scored 31 points in the second quarter en route to a 41-20 blowout. The debacle included a touchdown pass from a wide receiver, a blocked punt and fumble each returned for touchdowns, another deflected punt, and three interceptions. It was the first of seven straight losses to end the season, after which Chud, a lifelong Browns fan in his dream job, was summarily fired.

7 Uniform and Equipment Oddities

1. Lee Johnson was the only barefoot player in Browns history. He punted for Cleveland in six regular-season and two playoff games in 1987 and 1988.

2. Scott Player, who ended his ten-year career as the Browns' fill-in punter in 2007, was the last player to use the now-outlawed single-bar face mask, a design credited to none other than Paul Brown.

3. Tommy McDonald was the last non-kicker to play without a face mask as he finished his Hall of Fame career with the Browns in 1968.

4. Peyton Hillis adopted a unique face mask design during his time in Cleveland in 2010-11. The addition of an inverted "U" bar created the impression of a bulldog, which seemed appropriate for a Brown.

5. David Boss of NFL Properties designed a helmet logo for the Browns in 1965. The stylized monogram, in which the bottom of the "C" flows into the top of the "B," appeared in various collectibles, artwork and ads of the period. But despite urban legend, the insignia was never worn in a game, pre-season or otherwise.

6. The only thing ever to infringe on the solid sides of the Browns' iconic helmets were the players' numbers, which were a regular part of the uniform in 1957-60. They returned with the team's "throwback" uniforms for one home game each in 2006-08. The Browns went 2-1 in those games, a winning percentage nearly identical to the combined results of those four earlier years.

7. No Brown wore a single-digit jersey number for the team's first 31 years. That string ended in 1977. A quarterback named Terry Luck wore number 7 and threw seven interceptions (versus one touchdown) in his only NFL season.

10 Ownership Changes in Browns History

1. Arthur B. (Mickey) McBride founded the Browns in 1945 as a charter member of the All-America Football Conference, with support from minority owner Robert H. Gries, a former May Company executive who had earlier kicked in $1,000 to help start the Cleveland Rams in 1936. McBride paid $50,000.

2. As part of the merger agreement with the NFL in 1950, James Brueil, owner of the Buffalo Bills AAFC franchise, gained a 25% ownership stake in the Browns as three players transferred in from the disbanded Bills. Other stockholders during the Browns' early years included McBride's sons Edward and Arthur (the former eventually buying the latter's shares), the father and son Harry and Dan Sherby, Patrick Dunne, Gries, and coach Paul Brown.

3. In 1953, McBride sold his majority stake in the Browns for $600,000 to a group of investors headed by local industrialist Dave R. Jones, who became club president. Parties included Rams founder Homer Marshman, who initiated the deal; insurance man Ellis Ryan; Randall Park race track owner Saul Silberman; and Silberman's associate Ralph DeChairo, a Baltimore real estate developer.

4. Silberman, a flamboyant figure known more for his horse racing interests, sold his stake to the Jones-led syndicate after the Browns repeated as NFL champions in 1955. Accounts of the sale price range

from $575,000 to $1.3 million, a very tidy profit in any event. The ownership during the subsequent period was Nationwide Insurance Company, 30%; Gries, 20%; Marshman, 14%; Jones, Ryan, and Paul Brown, 12% each.

5. In 1961, young New York advertising executive Arthur B. Modell led a syndicate that bought the Browns for $3.925 million. Using mostly borrowed money, Modell acquired 25% of the shares plus voting control of an equivalent amount held by brewing magnate R.J. (Rudy) Schaefer. Gries increased his share to 28% to help Modell swing the deal. Several minority partners, including Brown, split the remaining 22%.

6. Modell leveraged the Browns to buy out Schaefer's share in 1965 for $1.5 million. By 1971, he owned 53% of the team. Gries died in 1966, and his son, also named Robert, inherited responsibility for representing the family's large minority ownership stake. The uneasy Modell-Gries relationship descended into several lawsuits in the 1980s.

7. Modell infamously moved the Browns to Baltimore after the 1995 season, sparking a furor in Cleveland that led to an unprecedented deal: the league would treat Modell's transplanted team as an expansion franchise known as the Ravens. Modell surrendered the cultural legacy of the Browns — name, colors, history, records, awards and archives — so it would continue in Cleveland with a team to begin play in 1999 in a new stadium.

8. In September 1998, Alfred Lerner, CEO of credit card firm MBNA Corp., was awarded the new Cleveland Browns by offering, at the time, the highest price ever paid for a sports franchise: $530 million. He had owned less than 10% of the original Browns when he assisted Modell in negotiating the deal with Baltimore. Lerner outbid several groups including those led by Charles and Larry Dolan, Howard Milstein, and Bart Wolstein. Modell, as the Ravens' owner, originally voted for the Dolans over his formerly close friend, but he then ended a potential standoff by urging league owners to show unanimous support for Lerner. Carmen Policy became team president/CEO and a 10% partner.

9. Lerner died of brain cancer in 2002, so his son, Randy, at age 40, became the controlling owner as chair of the family's trust. Randy Lerner bought back Policy's 10% stake in 2003.

10. Ten years after his father's passing, Lerner sold the Browns to Jimmy Haslam III for $1.05 billion, including 70% up front, with the rest of the transfer set for 2016. The CEO of truck stop chain Pilot Flying J was in the process of divesting his 12.5% share of the Pittsburgh Steelers as the Browns deal closed.

The 21 Best Brief Browns Careers

Football glory can be fleeting, so here we recognize those players who made the most difference for the Browns in the least amount of time. The cutoff of 30 games, including playoffs, is admittedly arbitrary, representing something shy of two full seasons in the modern age or three for the old-timers. It also excludes Browns under contract for 2015.

1. **Tommy O'Connell (1956-57)** — Not many Pro Bowl quarterbacks retire at age 27 to pursue coaching, but that's what this former Illinois star did. Piloting the Browns' 7-1-1 start in 1957, he suffered an ankle sprain and hairline fractures on a sack by the Rams' Larry Morris. He returned, limping, five weeks later for the NFL championship game, which did not go well. Still, his 11.2 yards per pass attempt is higher than any player who's ever thrown 100 or more times in a season.

2. **Peyton Hillis (2010-11)** — The former fullback was an instant hit, winning Browns' Player of the Year honors in 2010. His 1,654 yards from scrimmage and 13 touchdowns were both career bests by more than double.

3. **Antonio Bryant (2004-05)** — Acquired midseason for Quincy Morgan in a straight-up swap of second-round receivers, the talented but temperamental Bryant averaged 60 receiving yards per game as a Brown, third highest in franchise history among qualifiers, behind only Josh Gordon and Mac Speedie.

4. **Brian Hoyer (2013-14)** — Of the 22 Browns quarterbacks since 1999, he's the only one to win most of his starts (10-6). The former St. Ignatius star's 232 passing yards per game is the most for Browns QBs of any era.

5. **Reuben Droughns (2005-06)** — Like Hillis, a converted fullback acquired from Denver by trade, he too was named the Browns' Player of the Year. In 2005, Droughns gained 1,240 yards rushing for Cleveland's first 1,000-yard season since 1985. His team record 309 carries comprised 78.2% of the Browns' rushing attempts that year, the highest share of the workload in franchise history.

6. **Joe Jurevicius (2006-07)** — A Clevelander who came home after Super Bowl appearances with three other teams, this rangy, sure-handed vet was the perfect complement to the Braylon Edwards/Kellen Winslow receiving corps.

7. **Kelly Holcomb (2001-04)** — A Cinderella story with four 300-yard passing games in 12 starts, Peyton Manning's former backup earned the Browns' starting job but couldn't keep it.

FRANCHISE FACETS AND FEATURES 99

8. Trent Richardson (2012-13) — Overdrafted in retrospect, he gained 1,317 yards from scrimmage and scored 12 touchdowns as a workhorse rookie running back.

9. Keith McKenzie (2000-01) — In 23 games, the defensive end amassed 11 sacks, five pass break-ups, two forced fumbles and a 29-yard fumble return.

10. Jason Pinkston (2011-13) — This fifth-round pick started all 16 games as a rookie right guard, with only two penalties marked off against him. He was released with an injury settlement in 2014 after a recurrence of a blood clot in his lung.

11. Daven Holly (2006-07) — The street free agent became a surprise starter at cornerback, registering five interceptions and two defensive touchdowns in 2006. A serious knee injury sustained in a May 2008 practice shortened his career.

12. Barry Stokes (2002-03) — An energetic free spirit, he held down the left guard position for the Browns' playoff year and slid to left tackle in 2003. In a well-traveled career, he was at his best in Cleveland.

13. Gary Danielson (1985-88) — Mike Phipps' successor as Purdue's quarterback become the epitome of the veteran mentor for the Bernie-era Browns. In his first game in brown and orange, he rushed for 60 yards, the most for any Browns QB since 1962.

14. Ebenezer Ekuban (2004) — One of four former first-round draft picks on the team's defensive line, he led the Browns with eight sacks but was traded upon regime change.

15. Ray Ellis (1986-87) — The starting strong safety for the Eagles until purged by Buddy Ryan, he quickly filled a vacancy on his hometown team and contributed 115 tackles to a playoff squad. Playing through a career-ending neck injury in 1987, he scored his only NFL touchdown on a fumble return against Buffalo.

16. Don Greenwood (1946-47) — The NFL's sixth-leading rusher on the champion Cleveland Rams of 1945, he chose to stay when the Rams moved west. He led the AAFC with six rushing touchdowns for the 1946 Browns, but a severe facial injury ended his playing career the next year. He later became the head coach at Toledo but quickly resigned in protest of inadequate player safety and excessive roughness.

17. Brian Russell (2005-06) — He provided a veteran presence at safety, starting two seasons. His most memorable moment as a Brown was a then-legal hit on the Bengals' Chad Johnson that knocked his helmet off and resulted in a concussion.

18. Don Strock (1988) — Retired after 14 years in Miami, the 38-year-old career backup answered the Browns' call during a bizarre season in

which injuries knocked Bernie Kosar and two other quarterbacks out of action. He outplayed Randall Cunningham in a 19-3 win over the eventual NFC East champion Eagles. He nearly beat his old team in December, tying the game with two fourth-quarter touchdown passes, until Dan Marino worked some late Monday night magic. Then, with the playoffs at stake in a snowy season finale, trailing the Oilers by 16 in the third quarter, Strock rallied the team to an improbable 28-23 win in a 326-yard effort. In the next week's wild-card rematch, a sprained wrist forced him to the sidelines, and the Browns fell a point short.

19. Bob Cowan (1947-48) — A starting halfback on the perfect 1948 team, the Fort Wayne native scored eight touchdowns in his brief Browns career.

20. Marcus Benard (2009-11) — This pass-rush specialist notched 11.5 sacks in 25 games, including a team high 7.5 in 2010.

21. Robert Banks (1989-90) — One of four Browns Plan B free agent signees with B surnames (along with Bubba Baker, Ted Banker and Tom Baugh), the former Oiler started 15 games at defensive end in 1989, registering 1.5 of his four sacks in the division-clinching season finale against his old team.

Browns Who Wore Each Jersey Number the Most

This list of jersey numbers includes Browns players and their team-leading total of regular season games played in that uniform.

- 1 — WR Michael Jackson, 32 games (later wore 81)
- 2 — QB Tim Couch, 62
- 3 — K Matt Stover, 80
- 4 — K Phil Dawson, 215
- 5 — P Spencer Lanning, 32
- 6 — QB Brian Hoyer, 17
- 7 — P Jeff Gossett, 53
- 8 — P Johnny Evans, 48
- 9 — K Matt Bahr, 115
- 10 — QB Mike Pagel, 42
- 11 — WR Mohamed Massaquoi, 54
- 12 — K/P Don Cockroft, 188
- 13 — QB Frank Ryan, 84
- 14 — QB Otto Graham, 48 (number retired in his honor; earlier wore 60)

FRANCHISE FACETS AND FEATURES 101

- 15 — QB Mike Phipps, 88
- 16 — WR Joshua Cribbs, 124
- 17 — QB Brian Sipe, 125
- 18 — DB Bobby Freeman, 21
- 19 — QB Bernie Kosar, 108
- 20 — S Ross Fichtner, 102
- 21 — RB Eric Metcalf, 88
- 22 — DB Clarence Scott, 186
- 23 — CB Joe Haden, 72*
- 24 — DB Warren Lahr, 90 (earlier wore 80)
- 25 — RB Charles White, 49
- 26 — WR/HB Ray Renfro, 142
- 27 — S Thom Darden, 128
- 28 — CB Ron Bolton, 90
- 29 — CB Hanford Dixon, 131
- 30 — CB Bernie Parrish, 94
- 31 — CB Frank Minnifield, 122
- 32 — RB Jim Brown, 118 (number retired in his honor)
- 33 — WR Reggie Rucker and CB Daylon McCutcheon, 103
- 34 — LB Walt Michaels, 120
- 35 — LB Galen Fiss, 139
- 36 — CB Stephen Braggs, 66
- 37 — CB Anthony Henry, 61
- 38 — FB Johnny Davis, 57
- 39 — CB Randy Hilliard, 57
- 40 — CB Erich Barnes, 85
- 41 — TE Ralph "Catfish" Smith and DB Ray "Bubba" Ventrone, 56
- 42 — WR Paul Warfield, 97
- 43 — RB Mike Pruitt, 124
- 44 — RB Leroy Kelly, 136
- 45 — RB Leroy Bolden, 23 (number retired in honor of Ernie Davis)
- 46 — T/K Lou Groza, 74 (later wore 76; number retired in honor of Don Fleming)
- 47 — FB Lawrence Vickers, 76
- 48 — RB Ernie Green, 89
- 49 — DB Clinton Burrell, 67
- 50 — LB Vince Costello, 130
- 51 — LB Eddie Johnson, 148
- 52 — LB Dick Ambrose, 116
- 53 — LB Craig Robertson, 46*
- 54 — C Tom DeLeone, 149
- 55 — C Alex Mack, 85*
- 56 — C John Morrow, 90
- 57 — LB Clay Matthews, 232

- 58 — WR Mac Speedie, 74 (later wore 88)
- 59 — LB Charlie Hall, 146
- 60 — G John Wooten, 122
- 61 — C Mike Baab, 114
- 62 — S/QB Cliff Lewis, 71
- 63 — OL Cody Risien, 146
- 64 — LS Ryan Pontbriand, 134
- 65 — OL John Demarie, 109 (earlier wore 55)
- 66 — G Gene Hickerson, 202
- 67 — LB Sidney Williams, 41
- 68 — G Robert E. Jackson, 160
- 69 — OL Dan Fike, 112
- 70 — DT Don Colo, 72
- 71 — DT Walter Johnson, 168
- 72 — DT Jerry Sherk, 147
- 73 — T Doug Dieken, 203
- 74 — OL Paul Farren, 132
- 75 — DT Pio Sagapolutele, 63
- 76 — T/K Lou Groza, 194 (number retired in his honor; earlier wore 46)
- 77 — T Dick Schafrath, 164 (earlier wore 80)
- 78 — DL Carl Hairston, 92
- 79 — DT Bob Gain (earlier wore 74) and OL Gerry Sullivan, 119
- 80 — DE Bill Glass, 94
- 81 — DE Jack Gregory, 86
- 82 — TE Ozzie Newsome, 198
- 83 — WR Ricky Feacher, 122
- 84 — DE Paul Wiggin, 122 (earlier wore 86)
- 85 — WR Dave Logan, 115
- 86 — WR/P Gary Collins, 127
- 87 — TE Darnell Dinkins, 43
- 88 — WR Reggie Langhorne, 102
- 89 — TE Milt Morin, 129
- 90 — DE Rob Burnett, 93
- 91 — DE Sam Clancy, 59
- 92 — DT Michael Dean Perry, 109
- 93 — DL John Hughes, 36*
- 94 — DE Elvis Franks, 73
- 95 — LB Kamerion Wimbley, 63
- 96 — DE Reggie Camp, 70
- 97 — LS Ryan Kuehl, 64
- 98 — DE Anthony Pleasant, 94
- 99 — DL Orpheus Roye, 113

CHAPTER 5
THE BEST OF THE BROWNS

Determining the best Browns players at each position is an inherently subjective task. Given the profound differences in the game over the years, it's challenging to compare different styles of athletes competing under different rules, schemes and conditions.

Rather than speculating about how an old-timer might fare in today's NFL, these rankings consider the demands of each position and determine who best met them while wearing Browns colors. Who made the strongest, deepest positive impact, during his own time, in helping the team succeed? Who most closely embodied the vision of an ideal Cleveland Brown?

In stacking up the backs, tackling the tackles, and so forth, these lists of varying length provide rankings and reasoning within brief narrative portraits of over 150 of the Browns' greatest on-field contributors.

8 Best Quarterbacks in Browns History

1. Otto Graham (1946-1955) — If not for three factors beyond his control, he'd undeniably be at the forefront of any discussion of the best quarterback of all time. But World War II delayed his pro career. His first four seasons were in a league whose statistics the NFL ignores. And he retired before the dawn of the Golden Age of televised football and NFL Films. But Graham's greatness endures, encapsulated in one pithy point of fact: ten seasons, ten title games. His record as leader of the Browns' great dynasty was 105-17-4, plus 9-3 post-season. He wrote the book on quarterbacking from the T formation, and he also rushed for 44 touchdowns, which would be an NFL record for QBs even today. The former pro basketball player was an all-around contributor, returning 23 punts at an 11-yard average and making seven interceptions on defense. A true leader who set an enviable standard as a quarterback, teammate, and man, "Ottomatic" was "the greatest player in the game's history," according to his coach, Paul Brown, who presented Graham at his 1965 Hall of Fame induction. Graham returned the favor two years later.

2. Bernie Kosar (1985-93) — A savvy sidearm slinger as intelligent as he was unorthodox, Kosar was especially beloved as a hometown product who wanted to play for the Browns and managed to make it happen. After just two playoff games in 12 years, the Browns made post-season

appearances in each of Kosar's first five seasons. At age 23, he threw for 489 yards in the classic playoff win over the Jets in 1987. Gangly and slow, he dared defenses to blitz and often found the right receiver for a big play. His streak of 308 consecutive passes without an interception was an NFL record for 19 years.

3. **Frank Ryan** (1962-68) — This three-time Pro Bowler is the only man since Graham to quarterback the Browns to the league championship. Relying more on guile and grit than physical gifts, Ryan didn't rack up the gaudiest stats, though he maintains three of the top nine spots in Browns annals for touchdown passes in a season. As courageous in the pocket as anyone, he had the patience to wait for routes to develop from the likes of Paul Warfield and Gary Collins. Under the man with a doctoral degree in mathematics, the Browns always figured to have a winning record.

4. **Brian Sipe** (1974-83) — Another fan favorite, this 13th-round draft pick eventually replaced underachieving first-rounder Mike Phipps to became the Browns' official leader in completions, yards and touchdown passes. In his prime, the cool San Diego native led a high-flying offense, throwing for 3,500-plus yards four times. He and Graham are the only Browns quarterbacks to start games in ten straight seasons. Named NFL MVP for the magical Kardiac Kids season of 1980, Sipe led numerous thrilling comeback wins while throwing for 4,132 yards and 30 TDs.

5. **Milt Plum** (1957-61) — His 110.4 passer rating for 1960 stood as an NFL record for 29 years on the strength of 21 touchdowns with only five interceptions. With Jim Brown, Bobby Mitchell and Ray Renfro at skill positions, Plum's ball-control style led to two Pro Bowl seasons and kept future Hall of Famer Len Dawson on the bench. But the ideas and inclinations of Plum and Coach Brown crossed, so off to Detroit he went in a six-player deal that brought DE Bill Glass to town. Plum's career had already reached its peak ripeness.

6. **Bill Nelsen** (1968-72) — Acquired from the Steelers and soon succeeding Ryan, he led a potent Browns offense that averaged 36 points per game during an eight-game winning streak. Nelsen's Browns twice corralled the Cowboys in the playoffs but failed to win a Super Bowl berth in the NFL title game. The 1969 win in Dallas remains their last playoff win on the road. The Browns traded away Hall of Fame receiver Paul Warfield for the first-round pick used to draft Nelsen's eventual successor, Phipps, in 1970. In a battle of the balky-kneed quarterbacks, he outdueled Joe Namath in the debut of Monday Night Football. Retired at age 31, Nelsen is one of only three full-time Browns quarterbacks to have won two-thirds of his starts.

7. **Tim Couch** (1999-2003) — Though he failed to live up to being the first overall pick of the reborn franchise, The Deuce had a few coups: a

pair of Hail Mary wins, a pair of Titanic comebacks over Tennessee, and a sweep of the defending Super Bowl champion Ravens in 2001. Ill-served by two coaching regimes and plagued by injuries, he still ranks fifth all-time in passing yards for the Browns. Though maddeningly inconsistent, Couch deserves credit for being a game competitor during trying times and squeaking the team into the playoffs in the exciting 2002 season.

8. Vinny Testaverde (1993-95) — After an error-prone era in Tampa Bay, this top-shelf physical specimen displaced hometown hero and college teammate Kosar within a year of his free-agency signing. It was the first year this top pick's touchdowns outnumbered his interceptions, a maturation milestone that helped him play through age 44. Behind center for the Browns' only playoff win in the last quarter century, Testaverde would later play for the coach he defeated that day, New England's Bill Parcells, with the Jets and Cowboys.

Honorable mention:

- Derek Anderson (2006-09)
- Gary Danielson (1985-88)
- Kelly Holcomb (2001-04)
- Brian Hoyer (2013-14)
- Tommy O'Connell (1956-57)
- Mike Phipps (1970-76)
- George Ratterman (1952-56)

17 Best Running Backs in Browns History

Once the marquee skill position in football, it predates the emergence of the quarterback as we know it. And the Browns are known for their tradition of excellence at running back, from big bruisers to shifty scatbacks. Over the years, the team has used its first draft pick on a runner about one year in four.

This list contains a few key measurables for each back: rushing yards, yards per carry, receiving yards, yards per reception and total touchdowns. They include all Browns regular season games in the NFL and AAFC.

1. Jim Brown (1957-65) — Syracuse; 6'2" 228; 12,312 rush yds.; 5.2 ave.; 2499 rec. yds.; 9.5 ave.; 126 TDs

This must be the least surprising entry in this book. He's also topped lists on ESPN for best all-around athlete of all time, best rookie running back in NFL history and greatest all-time NFL player. That says plenty. Yes, we can wish he had played longer than his nine Pro Bowl seasons. Yes, we can wish his off-the-field reputation were purer, while still honoring his positive contributions to society and to the Browns. Fifty years after his surprising retirement to pursue a movie career, old-time Cleveland fans still marvel at Brown's unsurpassed greatness. He left the game on top, dominating the league's record book in many yardage and touchdown categories. His eight seasons leading the league in rushing are still double the total of anyone else. Nobody else has averaged 100 rushing yards per game (his mark is 104.3). He was smart enough to find the right avenue of attack, strong enough to punish defenders, swift enough to break away from the pack, and durable enough to have never missed a game.

2. **Marion Motley** (1946-53) — Nevada; 6'1" 232; 4720 rush yds.; 5.7 ave.; 1107 rec. yds.; 13.0 ave.; 39 TDs

Is it possible for a Hall of Famer and member of the NFL's 75th Anniversary All-Time Team to be underrated? Not here, at least. Motley was, quite simply, an amazing player. He had a much higher career rushing average than Brown and was a far superior blocker. Whereas Brown called it quits at age 29, Motley's career was just starting at 26. And while Brown is rightfully proud of his record on behalf of racial equality, it was Motley, along with three others, who broke pro football's color barrier a year before Jackie Robinson did it in baseball. The first black player enshrined in Canton, he's second only to Otto Graham as the most vital player on the Browns' early dynasty. A powerful fullback who also made an impact at linebacker, he'd be considered a big back even today. As heavy as his offensive linemen but with a sprinter's speed, it's easy to see how intimidating he was to potential tacklers.

3. **Leroy Kelly** (1964-73) — Morgan State; 6' 199; 7274 rush yds.; 4.2 ave.; 2281 rec. yds.; 12.0 ave.; 90 TDs

If there was one beneficiary of Jim Brown's sudden retirement, it was this former eighth-round draft pick who was largely relegated to special teams his first two seasons. Upon Brown's departure, Kelly immediately produced three straight phenomenal seasons, leading the league in rushing touchdowns each year, in rushing yards twice, and in yards per carry twice. He was a different breed than Brown and Motley, a fine all-purpose back with great acceleration, the ability to avoid direct hits, and the balance to excel on muddy fields. By the time he retired, he ranked fourth on the NFL's all-time rushing list. The six-time Pro Bowler was inducted into the Hall of Fame in 1994.

4. **Greg Pruitt** (1973-81) — Oklahoma; 5'10" 190; 5496 rush yds.; 4.7 ave.; 3022 rec. yds.; 9.4 ave.; 43 TDs

This exciting scatback helped make Browns football fun to watch during some otherwise mediocre years. The second-round pick led the team in rushing five straight seasons, including 1,000-yard totals in '75, '76 and '77. Speedy and elusive, he was also fine receiver and returner. He gained 304 all-purpose yards in a 1975 upset of the Bengals, the last of just three times that a Brown has topped 100 yards both rushing and receiving in a game. He was also quite a weapon with the option pass, throwing for six touchdowns. A knee injury, the emergence of fullback Mike Pruitt (no relation), and the drafting of Charles White combined to reduce his role in later years (he had more receptions than carries in both 1980 and 1981). Though later traded to the Raiders, the four-time Pro Bowler lives in the Cleveland area and was among the first players inducted into the team's Legends program.

5. **Mike Pruitt (1976-84)** — Purdue; 6' 225; 6540 rush yds.; 4.1 ave.; 1761 rec. yds.; 6.9 ave.; 52 TDs

The Browns laid several seeds for their prolific Kardiac Kids offense in the 1976 draft, choosing Pruitt first, WR Dave Logan in the third round, and OL Henry Sheppard in the fifth. At first, Pruitt underwhelmed, with little to show for his first two seasons. But upon Sam Rutigliano's arrival, he began proving himself as a rugged workhorse who kept defenses honest up the middle while Brian Sipe scanned the field for the likes of Rucker, Logan, Newsome, and Greg Pruitt. And his hands improved too: he caught more passes than any other Brown during Sipe's MVP season of 1980. Pruitt remains third in team history in both rushing yards and rushing touchdowns.

6. **Bobby Mitchell (1958-61)** — Illinois; 6' 192; 2297 rush yds.; 5.4 ave.; 1462 rec. yds.; 11.4 ave.; 38 TDs

Before Crowell and West, before Mack and Byner, before the Pruitts, the Browns actually had two future Hall of Famers in the same backfield. Mitchell, a college track star, was an absolute steal in the seventh round. While Jim Brown's power game wore defenses out, Mitchell faked them out. He had at least 500 rushing yards each of his four seasons here, with eight 100-yard games, including 232 at Washington in 1958. He had more receptions than any other Brown during his time in Cleveland, and he was a superb kick returner to boot. But the Pro Bowler and Sporting News Rookie of the Year was traded to Washington, thus integrating the last all-white NFL team. He moved from halfback to flanker and led the league in receiving in the first of many great seasons in D.C.

7. **Kevin Mack (1985-93)** — Clemson; 6' 224; 5123 rush yds.; 4.0 ave.; 1602 rec. yds.; 8.1 ave.; 54 TDs

This two-time Pro Bowler was a hard-charging fullback with a nose for the goal line. He ranks third among all Browns backs in total touchdowns. Acquired in the same supplemental draft of USFL players that netted linebacker Mike Johnson and kick returner Gerald "Ice Cube" McNeil, Mack made a sudden impact in '85, running for 1,104 yards at five yards per carry. The Browns won the division for three straight years, with Mack as the leading rusher in each. In November of '86, the Browns won two straight overtime games against division foes, and Mack topped 100 yards each time. But his most important contribution may have been his 1989 comeback from injury and a cocaine conviction. In three straight games, Mack was absolutely crucial: an overtime win against Minnesota, a successful comeback at Houston, and a 34-30 playoff victory over the Bills. He went on to lead the team in rushing the next three seasons and now works for the Browns in alumni relations.

8. **Ernie Green** (1962-68) — Louisville; 6'2" 205; 3204 rush yds.; 4.8 ave.; 2036 rec. yds.; 10.4 ave.; 35 TDs

When rookie trade target Ernie Davis got sick, Paul Brown turned to Green Bay to acquire a different Ernie, a 14th-round draft pick. The founding coach lasted just one more year, but Green thrived as the unselfish, versatile backfield partner of Brown and Kelly. His rushing and receiving stats are impressive, but his excellent blocking was no less instrumental. The Browns had nothing but winning records during Green's injury-shortened seven-year career, which included two Pro Bowl appearances. The ultimate team player, Green now presides over a successful Ohio-based manufacturer, EGI.

9. **Earnest Byner** (1984-88, 1994-95) — East Carolina; 5'10" 215; 3364 rush yds.; 3.9 ave.; 2630 rec. yds.; 9.5 ave.; 38 TDs

This tenth-round draft pick was an instant keeper, averaging 5.9 yards per carry as a rookie, while neither Boyce Green, Mike Pruitt nor Charles White exceeded 3.3. Only Byner remained with the Browns the next year, when they began their five-year playoff run. He and Mack each posted 1,000-yard seasons in '85, as rookie QB Bernie Kosar was kept on a short leash. Hurt much of 1986, Byner returned with a fine 1987 season, scoring 10 times and leading the team with 52 receptions. On January 17, 1988, he was inches from greatness. After two touchdowns and a team playoff record 187 yards from scrimmage, Byner nearly culminated a epic comeback in pursuit of the Browns' first Super Bowl berth when Denver's Jeremiah Castille stripped the ball just short of the goal line in the game's final moments, a fateful moment known simply as "The Fumble." After a trade to Washington, Byner amassed two more 1,000-yard seasons and earned his Super Bowl ring. He then returned to the Browns for two more years, the best game of which was his 157-yard performance in the Browns' bittersweet win to close Cleveland Municipal Stadium. A productive, personable and versatile back, Byner left a most compelling story as his career legacy.

10. **Eric Metcalf** (1989-94) — Texas; 5'10" 187; 2229 rush yds.; 3.8 ave.; 2732 rec. yds.; 9.2 ave.; 33 TDs

The Browns traded up with Denver to draft this son of another NFL great with the 13th overall pick. The slight speedster stunned defenders with some electrifying elusiveness, beginning with his first career touchdown, which sent Bengal defenders sprawling in a memorable Monday night moment. But he was often misused by the coaching staff. The phrase "Metcalf up the middle" springs to mind. Nonetheless, he ranks second among all Browns backs in career receiving yards and is among the franchise's very best returners. He scored all four Browns touchdowns in a road win over the Raiders in 1992. After the 1994 playoff season, the Browns traded him to Atlanta, where he switched to wide receiver and caught 104 passes for 1,189 yards in '95.

11. **Edgar "Special Delivery" Jones** (1946-49) — Pittsburgh; 5'10" 193; 1509 rush yds.; 5.2 ave.; 635 rec. yds.; 19.8 ave.; 29 TDs

An excellent overall athlete, Jones was overshadowed by the great Motley, but he was no minor contributor to the Browns' dominance of the All-America Football Conference. He scored ten touchdowns in the team's perfect 1948 season, plus two more in the title game. He also led the league with 6.4 yards per carry in 1947. Only Byner has scored more playoff touchdowns in a Browns uniform. Paul Brown called the Navy veteran "one of the finest clutch players we ever had."

12. **Leroy Hoard** (1990-95) — Michigan; 5'11" 223; 2203 rush yds.; 4.0 ave.; 1849 rec. yds.; 10.4 ave.; 24 TDs

Upon trading Byner in 1989, the Browns used their first draft pick on a running back three times in four years. In 1990 they got this rugged but rough-edged rambler, one who gave great second effort but was also prone to concentration lapses (27 fumbles). Surprisingly for a big back, he scored more often as a receiver, including nine of his 11 touchdowns in 1991. Hoard continued to develop, and he led the team in rushing in both '94 and '95. He scored the go-ahead touchdown in his only Pro Bowl following the '94 season.

13. **Cleo Miller** (1975-82) — Arkansas-Pine Bluff; 5'11" 207; 2286 rush yds.; 4.2 ave.; 1026 rec. yds.; 8.1 ave.; 17 TDs

Not as spectacular as Greg Pruitt nor as powerful as Mike, Miller nonetheless enjoyed a fairly lengthy career with the Browns, starting for two of the years that Greg Pruitt gained 1,000 yards, then filling in effectively when needed. Though primarily a blocking back, his per-carry average ranks fifth in team annals among runners with at least 500 carries. In 1980, he came up with both Browns touchdowns and a key 50-yard run in the Kardiac Kids' crucial 17-14 division triumph over the Oilers in the Astrodome.

14. **Jamal Lewis** (2007-09) — Tennessee; 5'11" 240; 2806 rush yds.; 3.9 ave.; 514 rec. yds.; 8.4 ave.; 15 TDs

After running Reuben Droughns roughshod for two years, the Browns signed this longtime nemesis from GM Phil Savage's former employer, the Baltimore Ravens. Lewis' tenacity helped power the Browns to six more wins than they had the year before. His 1,304 rushing yards in 2007 are the most in team history by anyone not named Jim Brown.

After another 1,000-yard season in '08, Lewis ran out of gas in '09, gaining precisely 500 rushing yards, the exact total he put up against the Browns in just two games in 2003.

15. Calvin Hill (1978-81) — Yale; 6'3" 228; 516 rush yds.; 3.7 ave.; 1248 rec. yds.; 11.7 ave.; 18 TDs

The father of hoops great Grant Hill was himself a fantastic pro athlete. His career included some superb years with the Cowboys and ended with four seasons in Cleveland, where he had an uncanny knack as a third-down pass receiving back. A big target with a veteran's savvy, he helped keep many a drive alive for Brian Sipe and the Kardiac Kids.

16. Bo Scott (1969-74) — Ohio State; 6'3" 213; 2124 rush yds.; 3.8 ave.; 826 rec. yds.; 7.4 ave.; 24 TDs

The Browns drafted him in the third round of the 1965 draft, despite a backfield already stocked with Brown, Green and Kelly. So Scott signed with Ottawa and won all-CFL honors twice before coming to Cleveland. Mainly a blocker for Kelly during several playoff seasons, his best year was 1970, when he scored 11 times, led the team with 40 catches, and averaged 4.1 yards per carry on a team that otherwise averaged just 3.1.

17. Ken Carpenter (1950-53) — Oregon State; 6' 195; 1186 rush yds.; 5.0 ave.; 473 rec. yds.; 11.3 ave.; 17 TDs

The Browns' first NFL draft pick, Carpenter was overshadowed by other great stars on those prolific Browns offenses, but he earned Pro Bowl honors for the 1951 season, in which he gained 954 all-purpose yards. He later starred for the CFL's Saskatchewan Roughriders and finished with a stint on the 1960 Denver Broncos.

Honorable mention:

- Maurice "Mo" Bassett (1954-56) — Langston; 891 rush yds.; 4.0 ave.; 317 rec. yds.; 9.6 ave.; 11 TDs
- Ken Brown (1970-75) — no college; 1193; 3.4; 468; 8.1; 9
- Reuben Droughns (2005-06) — Oregon; 1990; 3.8; 538; 8.2; 6
- Boyce Green (1983-85) — Carson-Newman; 1170; 3.8; 291; 7.9; 5
- William Green (2002-2005) — Boston College; 2109; 3.7; 277; 6.2; 9
- Jerome Harrison (2006-10) — Washington State; 1401; 4.6; 444; 7.3; 9
- Peyton Hillis (2010-11) — Arkansas; 1764; 4.1; 607; 7.3; 16
- Harry "Chick" Jagade (1951-53) — Indiana; 747; 5.0; 396; 13.7; 7
- Dub Jones (1948-55) — mainly used as a flanker, often in motion at the snap, he had more receiving than rushing yards and is thus listed with the wide receivers.
- Ed "Big Mo" Modzelewski (1955-59) — Maryland; 1097; 3.5; 168; 6.2; 11

- Fred "Curley" Morrison (1954-56) — Ohio State; 1395; 4.8; 295; 10.9; 7
- Trent Richardson (2012-13) — Alabama; 1055; 3.5; 418; 7.2; 12.
- Jamel White (2000-03) — South Dakota; 1324; 3.8; 1273; 7.7; 11

7 Best Tight Ends in Browns History

1. Ozzie Newsome (1978-90) — A Hall of Fame combination of talent, durability and character, this Alabama wideout had superb hands and a big enough rear end to convert to tight end, as a pre-draft scouting trip by Browns assistant Rich Kotite confirmed. The first-round pick was among the earliest tight ends to emerge as a primary receiving threat. His 662 catches amount to exactly double the next highest total on the Browns' official career list. Newsome spanned the Kardiac Kids through the Kosar era and caught passes in 150 straight games. He stayed with the organization after retirement through its infamous move to Baltimore, where he became the NFL's first African American general manager. He remains among the most successful executives in pro sports.

2. Milt Morin (1966-75) — In the unmistakable vernacular of a late-'60s NFL Films team yearbook, "Once he's loose in the secondary, he has the awesome force of an irate hippopotamus." The first-rounder from Massachusetts averaged 15.5 yards per catch during his decade as a Brown, a remarkable figure for a 6'4" 236-pounder who could and did block with the best of them. Though the two-time Pro Bowler's salary topped out at $65,000, he earned the all-around respect of his teammates. With 4,208 receiving yards, Morin remains in the Browns' all-time top ten.

3. Johnny Brewer (1961-67) — Here's another case of how pro football has changed over time. The Browns' championship team of 1964 led the league in passing touchdowns but had just five players with five or more receptions. This former All American from Ole Miss was among them. A very capable blocker on those run-oriented teams, he added 1,256 receiving yards an average of 14.1 yards at a time. Brewer didn't miss a game in his seven seasons as a Brown, the last two of which he played at linebacker upon Morin's arrival.

4. Kellen Winslow II (2004-2008) — His father rivaled Newsome as the game's best tight end of the 1980s, and this Miami Hurricane blew into town as the most highly-touted prospect ever at the position. For a variety of reasons, he failed to live up to the hype or to the Browns'

investment in him. He started just half of their 80 games over five seasons and committed 27 penalties. On the bright side, he gained 56 yards per game, best of any Browns tight end. His hands were outstanding, and his 1,107-yard receiving total in 2007 also is tops at the position in team history.

5. **Jordan Cameron (2011-14)** — After catching only 16 passes in college and playing sparingly his first two years as a Brown, this fourth-round former basketball player blossomed in 2013 with 80 receptions in 118 targets for 917 yards. Three of his seven touchdowns — including the last-minute game-winner — came in Brian Hoyer's first Browns start at Minnesota. His 2014 season was limited by a concussion, but he still led all NFL tight ends with four plays of at least 40 yards.

6. **Ben Watson (2010-12)** — A former first-rounder who arrived in free agency after six years in New England, he led the Browns in receptions and receiving yards his first season here. His 1,674 yards are the fourth-highest career total among Browns tight ends.

7. **Steve Heiden (2002-09)** — Only Newsome and Morin suited up for more games as a Browns tight end. A reliable role player during some tumultuous times, the 6'5" 265-pounder started 70 of 106 games after arriving in a trade with San Diego. He scored three touchdowns against the Bengals in a wild 2004 game, a team record for tight ends since matched by Cameron.

Honorable mention:

- Darrel "Pete" Brewster (1952-58) — listed with wide receivers
- Chip Glass (1969-73) — 20 yards per reception, including a 78-yard TD in 1970
- Harry Holt (1983-86) — 48-yard overtime TD beat the Chargers in 1983
- Brian Kinchen (1991-95) — also a long-snapper, he had 73 receptions as TE
- Oscar Roan (1975-78) — 41-catch rookie season
- Aaron Shea (2000-05) — When healthy, he was tough to tackle.

15 Best Wide Receivers in Browns History

Wide receivers, also known as offensive ends or flankers, depending on the era and formation, used to have a harder go of it. Back when the rules permitted defenders much more contact — both before and after the ball's arrival — than is allowed today, successful pass catchers had to be

THE BEST OF THE BROWNS

nifty enough to find free range, tough enough to shake off head-rattling hits, or preferably both. From the beginning, the Browns revolutionized the passing attack in pro football, and every period of their success hinged upon extraordinary contributions from receivers such as these.

1. **Dante Lavelli (1946-56)** — "Glue Fingers" was Otto Graham's favorite target on some of the best football rosters ever assembled. Including AAFC stats, this Buckeye from Hudson caught more passes (386) for more yards (6,488) than any other Brown save TE Ozzie Newsome, despite playing in a more run-oriented era. Fresh from a three-year Army hitch that included the Omaha Beach landing and the Battle of the Bulge, he beat out more heralded players and became the top AAFC receiver as a rookie. In the Browns' first NFL championship game, the epic 30-28 comeback over the Rams in 1950, he caught 11 passes for 128 yards and two scores. An early practitioner of the now-common comeback route, Lavelli proved a worthy Hall of Famer, a life-long Brown, and an affable community fixture until his death in Cleveland at age 85.

2. **Mac Speedie (1946-52)** — He overcame a crippling childhood disability to become the AAFC's all-time leading receiver and appear in seven championship games in seven seasons as a Brown. With more receiving yards than any other Brown except Lavelli and Newsome, the aptly-named Speedie figured prominently in many great Browns accomplishments, including scoring the first touchdown in AAFC history, setting a Browns' single-season reception record that lasted 34 years, and rambling 99 yards to score on a screen pass. Twice a finalist for the Hall of Fame, he compares favorably to his inducted contemporaries but suffered for having played only three NFL seasons, leaving Paul Brown embittered when he took a huge raise to play in Canada.

3. **Gary Collins (1962-71)** — This reliable 6'5" target is the all-time team leader in receiving touchdowns (70), many coming on his trademark post pattern. He's best known for scoring the 1964 championship game's only three touchdowns after publicly predicting a win over the favored Colts, four years before Joe Namath did something similar. Less known: he beat out future Boston Celtics legend John Havlicek to make the team after the Browns drafted both in 1962. Also the regular punter for six seasons, Collins spent his entire NFL career as a Brown, scoring ten or more TDs four times and twice earning Pro Bowl honors. His sustained excellence far surpassed a single game, no matter how momentous.

4. **Paul Warfield (1964-69, 1976-77)** — If not for the infamous trade that sent him to Miami for many of his prime years, this local star (Warren native and OSU) and Hall of Famer likely would have topped this list. Still, he ranks second in franchise history in receiving touchdowns and yards per catch, and he gained more receiving yards in

NFL playoff games than any other Brown. A rare combination of athletic talents, Warfield was a smooth, gliding deep threat with dependable hands and excellent blocking skills. He led a championship team in receiving as a rookie and was later the first Browns receiver to notch a 1,000-yard season in the NFL.

5. **Ray Renfro (1952-63)** — In 12 NFL seasons, all as a Brown, this fleet flanker known as "Rabbit" averaged a team-record 19.6 yards per catch. He ranks second in receiving yards (5,508) and third in receiving touchdowns (50) in official Browns annals. Add in two scores in the 1954 title game win over Detroit, three Pro Bowl seasons and 682 rushing yards, and that's pretty good value from a fourth-round draft pick. Upon retiring he helped train his successor, Warfield, a converted running back, in the nuances of the craft.

6. **Dub Jones (1948-55)** — A 6'4" flanker whose talents helped revolutionize the modern passing game by putting three receiving threats on the field, Jones amassed 4,665 yards from scrimmage as part of the Browns' powerhouse offense. He scored the team's first NFL touchdown on a 59-yard pass from Otto Graham in the 1950 trouncing of the league champion Eagles. Jones is best known for scoring six touchdowns in a 1951 game against the only team, the Bears, to equal that feat, in the persons of Ernie Nevers and Gale Sayers. Neither of them sired an NFL quarterback though. Bert's father remains the only player in team history other than Jim Brown to score 20 or more times both rushing and receiving, an accomplishment only 22 men have managed.

7. **Reggie Rucker (1975-81)** — He combined with Ozzie Newsome and Dave Logan to give Brian Sipe plenty of potent options in the Kardiac Kids' offense. After starting for Dallas in a Super Bowl as a rookie and playing several years as a Patriot, Rucker led all NFL wide receivers in receptions in his first year in Cleveland. Sam Rutigliano, his former receivers coach in New England, said Rucker was the first to recommend that Art Modell hire him as head coach. The team leader in catches three years and in yardage four times, he was a solid veteran pass-catcher with a knack for getting open even without blazing speed.

8. **Webster Slaughter (1986-91)** — This nifty little speedster led the Kosar-era Browns in receptions and yards three straight years. Slaughter gained 1,236 receiving yards (including consecutive 180-yard-plus games) in his Pro Bowl 1989 season, a franchise record that lasted until 2007. The sole 1986 Browns draftee to make even the slightest impact on the NFL, Slaughter as a rookie scored a 36-yard touchdown in overtime to seal the Browns' first season sweep over the Steelers since 1969. Always a big-play threat, he racked up 114 yards on just three catches — two of them for scores — in the dramatic 34-30 playoff win over Buffalo in 1990. Unable to come to terms on a contract with the Bill Belichick-led

Browns, he left as a Plan B free agent in 1992. He tallied a career-high 11 catches against Pittsburgh in his last game for Cleveland.

9. **Darrel "Pete" Brewster (1952-58)** — This strong and sure-handed contributor led the Browns in receptions and yards three straight years. His breakout game came in a 62-14 win over the Giants in 1953, when he hauled in seven passes for 182 yards and three touchdowns. Later in his career, the two-time Pro Bowler became something of an early version of what we now recognize as a tight end. Though no speedster, he averaged an impressive 18.1 yards per reception.

10. **Dave Logan (1976-83)** — Athletic enough to be drafted in three sports, Logan used his 6'4" height to great effect. In fact, in the classic song "12 Days of a Cleveland Browns Christmas," Logan's leaping was the eleventh gift. A peak thrill of Kardiac Kids era was his 46-yard score on a 3rd-and-20 play with just 16 seconds left to beat the Packers, 26-21, in 1980. The Browns otherwise would've fallen to 3-4. The next week, Logan caught a career-high eight passes for 131 yards in a 27-26 comeback win over the two-time defending Super Bowl champion Steelers. Good times.

11. **Brian Brennan (1984-91)** — A steady, professional receiver, he excelled as the third-down/possession complement to Slaughter and Reggie Langhorne. Like Logan, his good hands made him the holder for placekicks. What he lacked in size he made up in cleverness, character, and courage in the clutch. His 48-yard tiebreaking touchdown late in the '86 season's AFC championship game would've sent the Browns to the Super Bowl if not for "The Drive." Incidental to his 315 career receptions — sixth in team history — he was two-for-two in career passing for 68 yards and a touchdown.

12. **Reggie Langhorne (1985-91)** — Bernie Kosar once wrote, "Webster could stretch the field; Brian had the guts to catch the ball over the middle; and Reggie could do both." A seventh-round small school selection, Langhorne was a solid starter for the standout squads of the late '80s, racking up 261 catches for 3,597 yards and 15 touchdowns. His decades of community service in the area earned him the 2015 Dino Lucarelli Lifetime Achievement Award.

13. **Kevin Johnson (1999-2003)** — The most reliable receiver on an expansion roster that otherwise could barely budge the ball, KJ put up some positive statistics in his brief time in Browns Town. Not particularly big or fast, he nonetheless provided some of the best highlights for the reborn Browns: the Hail Mary catch in the Superdome for their first win, the entertaining experiment behind center against the Eagles for the QB-depleted 2000 team, the go-ahead score in the crucial 2002 win against the Falcons, and the 83-yard catch and run that opened their wild playoff game the next week. Released midseason in 2003, Johnson

stands sixth on the Browns' career receptions list (tied with Brennan) and remains the new era's leader in catches and receiving yards.

14. Michael Jackson (1991-95) — The Browns found a playmaker in the sixth round with his combination of size and speed. Eighth in Browns history with 26 receiving touchdowns, he caught seven passes for 122 yards to help Bill Belichick beat his mentor, Bill Parcells, in the 1994 playoffs. Jackson wore the number 1 jersey early in his career, the most recent Brown to do so in the regular season.

15. Braylon Edwards (2005-09) — While ultimately a letdown as a third-overall draft pick, the Michigander managed to hang on to 238 passes before being traded midway through his fifth season. Edwards was key to the winning season of 2007, scoring a team-record 16 receiving touchdowns and setting a franchise yardage mark (since surpassed by Josh Gordon). Only three other Browns have averaged more receiving yards per game than his 59.6.

Honorable mention:

- Ricky Feacher (1976-84)
- Josh Gordon (2012-14*)
- Fair Hooker (1969-74)
- Rich Kreitling (1959-63)
- Dennis Northcutt (2000-06)
- Frank Pitts (1971-73)

11 Best Offensive Tackles in Browns History

1. Lou Groza (1946-59, 1961-67) — 6'3" 240, Ohio State.
"The Toe" didn't just fill a spot on the line to keep busy in between placekicking duties. In the era of 33-man rosters, he was a great left tackle too, earning All-Pro honors at that position six times and being named the 1954 NFL Player of the Year. He wasn't a nasty mauler type, but his superior technique more than got the job done for the bulk of 14 straight seasons. (A back injury cost him the 1960 season, and he focused on kicking thereafter.) He and Chuck Noll were the only Browns to block for both Marion Motley and Jim Brown. Groza proved in the trenches that his enshrinement in Canton wasn't just for kicks.

2. Mike McCormack (1954-62) — 6'4" 246, Kansas.
After a Pro Bowl rookie year with the old New York Yanks and a two-year hitch in the Army, McCormack's Hall of Fame career developed in Cleveland due to his inclusion in a 15-player trade with the Colts. First he

succeeded the great Bill Willis as the middle guard on defense, and the Browns resumed their championship reign, as McCormack snatched the ball from Bobby Layne's grasp to set the tone in the title game. In '55, he settled in at right tackle, and the Browns repeated as champs. With no real weakness in his game, McCormack became, in Paul Brown's words, "the finest offensive lineman I've ever coached," earning Pro Bowl honors five more times. He later moved to the sidelines as an NFL coach and to the front office, where he found more success as president of the Seahawks and Panthers.

   3. Dick Schafrath (1959-71) — 6'3" 253, Ohio State.

If anyone could begin to fill Groza's big shoes, it was this Canton native who was raised in Wooster, played for Woody Hayes in Columbus, and then suited up for 176 pro games, all for the Browns. Ordered by Paul Brown to gain weight, he entered eating contests all over Ohio, then tried to sneak by wearing an iron jockstrap to his weigh-in. Schafrath made six straight Pro Bowls blocking for four Pro Bowl backs. This Cleveland Browns Legend ought to be in the Hall of Fame along with the man who played next to him, Gene Hickerson. At least Schafrath — a four-term state senator — already has plenty of experience being elected.

   4. Joe Thomas (2007-14*) — 6'7" 311, Wisconsin.

A higher ranking would be justified for this fixture at left tackle, the best player of the Browns' new generation, if only his excellence had led to more offensive consistency and winning seasons. He's certainly done his part, playing every one of the Browns' 8,196 offensive snaps since being drafted third overall. A fine tactician in both run support and pass protection, he's the only offensive tackle to earn Pro Bowl honors in his first eight seasons. Those offended by his placement behind three Browns legends on this list may be comforted by the bottom line: with career earnings of nearly $90 million so far, nobody has made more money playing football for the Browns than Joe Thomas.

   5. Doug Dieken (1971-84) — 6'6" 250, Illinois.

A converted tight end, this sixth-round pick amazingly had even more longevity at left tackle than the two greats he succeeded. He played 203 games in a row, starting 194 of them, both franchise records. One of three Browns offensive lineman to make the Pro Bowl in the Kardiac Kids season of 1980, Diek was a stalwart Steeler-hater during some tough times. (He recovered four of his teammates fumbles during the horrid 1975 season.) His resilience was a function of toughness, yes, but also of a great sense of humor, which he continues to impress (or inflict) on Browns fans as their radio color man.

   6. Lou Rymkus (1946-51) — 6'4" 231, Notre Dame.

A rough-edged Chicagoan and Frank Leahy protege, Rymkus spent a year protecting Sammy Baugh and a few more protecting America in the Navy. A two-way player until 1948, he was best known for his textbook pass blocking, keeping defenders out of Otto Graham's face from the outset of the Browns' dynasty. He started for six strong seasons at right tackle, retiring after the first title game that the Browns couldn't capture, having never missed a game or practice. The 1988 "old-timer" Hall of Fame nominee — the route that got Bill Willis, Frank Gatski, and Leroy Kelly enshrined — Rymkus was passed over, as his old friend Mac Speedie was five years before. The first coach of the Houston Oilers, he won the AFL title in 1960 but was fired midway through 1961 and never got another chance at that level.

7. **Cody Risien** (1979-83, 1985-89) — 6'7" 269, Texas A&M.

His fine Browns career started and ended in pain. His father died during his rookie training camp, and coach Sam Rutigliano had to talk him back into football. The seventh-round pick started at left guard as a rookie, then moved to right tackle during a remarkably consistent career, considering he underwent surgery ten times. When he missed the 1984 season due to a knee injury sustained in the fourth quarter of an exhibition game, it was the beginning of the end for Rutigliano, as lefty QB Paul McDonald was sacked 53 times. A two-time Pro Bowler, Risien joined Clay Matthews and Ozzie Newsome as the only 1980 Kardiac Kids to play in all three Kosar-era AFC championship games. He deferred knee surgery to play through 1989, and when he was done, so was a long string of playoff seasons.

8. **Tony Jones** (1988-95) — 6'5" 291, Western Carolina.

A raw undrafted talent, he eventually won Bill Belichick's respect as one of the league's best pass blockers. Jones started 96 straight games for the Browns, mostly at left tackle, and was a team captain by the time the franchise was uprooted. The Ravens' first draft pick was his eventual replacement, Jonathan Ogden. Jones was later traded to Denver, where he won two Super Bowls, but he retained a fondness for Cleveland. He briefly pursued a comeback with the 2001 Browns but retired soon after the start of training camp.

9. **Monte Clark** (1963-69) — 6'6" 260, USC.

A savvy competitor on some excellent offensive units, Clark played mostly right tackle after arriving from Dallas in exchange for All-Pro guard Jim Ray Smith. He blocked for the NFL rushing leader in five of his seven seasons as a Brown. Clark kept Hall of Famer Gino Marchetti at bay during the Browns' 1964 title game win. His post-retirement career included eight years as head coach of the 49ers and Lions.

10. **Paul Farren** (1983-91) — 6'5" 280, Boston U.

The downfall of the Kosar era, perhaps more than anything, was the lack of a cohesive offensive line. Farren did all he could to fill in the breach. The 12th-round pick was certainly a great value. He played every line spot except center, but most of his action came at the critical left tackle position. The athletic Rickey Bolden was a better fit for that job, but he got hurt year after year. Over would slide the determined Farren, and the Browns' record was actually better with him at LT than without.

11. John Sandusky (1950-55) — 6'1" 251, Villanova.
The first offensive tackle taken in the 1950 draft, he bridged the years between Rymkus and McCormack on the right side and, as was common of players in that era, also played defense. He was one of six starters on the 1954 Browns who would eventually become pro head coaches.

Honorable mention:

- Bob McKay (1970-75)
- Barry Darrow (1974-78)
- Ryan Tucker (2002-08)
- Mitchell Schwartz (2012-14*)

8 Best Offensive Guards in Browns History

1. Gene Hickerson (1958-60, 1962-73) — 6'3", 248, Mississippi.
Thrice nominated for the Hall of Fame in the early '80s, he was finally inducted in 2007, when he was suffering from dementia and unable to speak for himself. Poignantly, he was wheeled onto the stage by the three enshrined Browns backs he blocked for: Jim Brown, Leroy Kelly and Bobby Mitchell. The six-time Pro Bowler made the NFL's All-Decade Team for the 1960s. Aside from a year missed with a broken leg, the career-long Brown never missed a game, playing in 212, including postseason. A ferocious force leading a power sweep, Hickerson was known for his mobility, durability and individuality. He was a longtime friend of Elvis Presley, who became a Browns fan as a result.

2. Jim Ray Smith (1956-62) — 6'3", 241, Baylor.
Selected as a sophomore in the sixth round of the 1954 draft, he served in the Army and then reported to Cleveland as a defensive end. But he built himself into a top-flight guard just in time for Jim Brown's arrival. In the inimitable parlance of Topps sports cards, "Jim has surprising speed for a fellow of his tonnage." His five straight Pro Bowl seasons are more than any other '54 draftee and included three first-team All-Pro selections. Wanting to retire to Texas for family and business reasons, he stayed for one more season and then netted the Browns tackle Monte Clark in a trade with Dallas.

3. Abe Gibron (1950-56) — 5'11", 243, Purdue.

The roly-poly "messenger guard" was eventually deemed too valuable to play part-time. He stayed on the field, flanked by fellow "G men" — Lou Groza and Frank Gatski — while other Browns guards shuttled play calls in from the sideline. Acquired from the disbanding AAFC Buffalo Bills for a Browns ownership stake, Gibron earned Pro Bowl honors four straight years for Paul Brown's dynasty. Otto Graham later recalled that Gibron was often erroneously flagged because he'd get such a quick jump off the ball. George Halas later hired him to coach the Chicago Bears. The World War II Marine veteran was inducted posthumously as a Cleveland Browns Legend in 2013.

4. John Wooten (1959-67) — 6'2", 235, Colorado.

His emergence helped prompt Chuck Noll to pursue coaching at age 27. He later subbed for the injured Hickerson and succeeded Smith at left guard. Wooten never missed a game playing for nothing but winning Browns teams, including the 1964 champs. His two Pro Bowls followed Jim Brown's strong final year and Leroy Kelly's breakout campaign. Wooten's peak seasons matched those of quarterback Frank Ryan, no mere coincidence. A very solid all-around blocker, he remains the best African American offensive lineman the Browns have ever had. The Cleveland Browns Legend chairs the Fritz Pollard Alliance, which promotes diversity in the NFL.

5. Joe DeLamielleure (1980-84) — 6'3", 254, Michigan State.

In exchange for second- and third-round draft picks, the Browns received a big-time Bill: a future Hall of Fame right guard. Coach Sam Rutigliano called his acquisition "like hitting an inside straight." Coming off five straight Pro Bowls as leader of "The Electric Company," he kept the streak alive in the Kardiac Kids' playoff season. Upon Joe D.'s arrival, quarterback Brian Sipe went from 26 interceptions down to 14, and from being sacked 43 times down to 23. A fine combination of strength, athleticism and veteran savvy, he never missed a game as a Brown and was instrumental in the up-the-gut success of fullback Mike Pruitt.

6. Robert E. Jackson (1975-85) — 6'5", 255, Duke.

This undrafted free agent needed to beef up on arrival, but with the makings of a good pulling guard, he cracked the starting lineup as a rookie. He was pretty much a fixture for a decade, switching from the right to the left side to make way for DeLamielleure and helping each of the Pruitts become multiple-time 1,000-yard backs. The blocker to his left, fellow Cleveland Browns Legend Doug Dieken, would become his longtime partner in their Westlake insurance business.

7. John Demarie (1967-75) — 6'3", 246, LSU.

This solid sixth-round find played several positions along the offensive line. He succeeded Wooten at left guard, where he contributed to the prolific offenses of the late '60s playoff teams. He later switched sides with the aging Hickerson. He also saw significant playing time at right tackle and center.

8. Lin Houston (1946-53) — 6', 213, Ohio State.
One of Paul Brown's favorites dating back to their Massillon days, Houston doubled as a defensive lineman in those five-man fronts and was the first Brown to wear the now-retired number 32. Not especially beefy, even for linemen of his era, this messenger guard was more of a technician who survived with tenacity and toughness.

Honorable mention:

- Bob Dahl (1992-95)
- Dan Fike (1985-92)
- Chuck Noll (1953-59), also a linebacker and long-snapper
- Shaun O'Hara (2000-03)
- Henry Sheppard (1976-81)
- Eric Steinbach (2007-11)
- Ed Ulinski (1946-49), who later became a Browns assistant coach and the team's film director
- Bill Willis (1946-53), a Hall of Famer mostly for his defense

8 Best Centers in Browns History

1. Frank Gatski (1946-56) — 6'3", 233, Marshall/Auburn.
Choosing the list-topper here is a snap: go for the only Hall of Famer in the category. Gunner, the strong, silent type, was a four-time All-NFL selection. Among the remarkable facts from his Canton bio: he never missed a game or practice in high school, college or pro football. He left the West Virginia coal mines to hitchhike to Bowling Green and try out for Paul Brown's first pro team. Rock solid, he earned the starting job in 1948, and Brown eventually had no need to keep a backup center on the roster. In 1957, rather than granting him a raise, Brown traded Gatski to Detroit for a third-rounder, and the great center's last game was the Lions' most recent NFL championship, a 59-14 win over the Browns.

2. Tom DeLeone (1974-84) — 6'2", 248, Ohio State.
This Kent native and first-team All-American started as a Bengal but was signed as a street free agent during his third pro season. He soon settled into the middle of the line that gave Brian Sipe time to throw and the Pruitts room to go for most of a decade. No center has played more games as a Brown. Strong and athletic, he did not rest on those gifts; he

came to battle prepared, and his toughness and leadership radiated outward. The two-time Pro Bowler had a lengthy second career as a federal law enforcement agent. He lost his first wife to cancer in 1976 and was himself diagnosed with an operable brain tumor in 2011.

3. John Morrow (1960-66) — 6'3", 244, Michigan.

Paul Brown traded away Pro Bowl center Art Hunter to get this former 28th-round draft pick from the Rams. Mostly a tackle in college and a guard in L.A., Morrow developed into a two-time Pro Bowler at the pivot, starting seven seasons on an exceptional Browns offense.

4. Mike Baab (1982-87, 1990-91) — 6'4", 270, Texas.

This beefy Texan was a popular teammate and a real tough guy in the trenches, once coming back to practice two days after a knee scope. By his second year he relegated DeLeone to the bench and was instrumental in the emerging playoff teams of the mid-'80s. The Browns unwisely traded him New England, but he returned as a Plan B free agent. Bill Belichick eventually cut him but said at the time, "You couldn't ask for more than what he gave." He's one of the best Browns never selected to the Pro Bowl.

5. Alex Mack — (2009-2014*) — 6'4", 312, California.

A starter from Day 1, he never missed a snap — despite an in-season appendectomy — until a broken leg sidelined him in 2014. He was penalized just once as a rookie, then garnered Pro Bowl recognition in 2010 and 2013. A stout run blocker, Mack is known for his intelligent approach to the game, a helpful quality for a position tasked with synchronizing the line's efforts on every play — doubly so when he gets a new offensive coordinator almost every year.

6. Fred Hoaglin (1966-72) — 6'4", 250, Pittsburgh.

The Alliance, Ohio, native was picked in the sixth round of the 1966 draft and soon proved valuable, as Morrow broke his leg that year and never returned. Hoaglin made 69 straight starts for those playoff teams of the late '60s, winning Pro Bowl honors in 1969. He lettered twice in golf at Pitt but didn't retire to the links after his 11-year career. He served as an assistant coach for several NFL teams, including two championship Giant squads under Bill Parcells.

7. Art Hunter (1956-59) — 6'4", 245, Notre Dame.

The third-overall pick in the 1954 draft by Green Bay, the northeast Ohio native was traded in 1955. After missing a year due to military service, he succeeded the great Gatski and had one Pro Bowl season under Paul Brown before going to the Rams in exchange for Morrow.

8. Steve Everitt (1993-95) — 6'5", 300, Michigan.

Bill Belichick drafted this long-haired artist 14th overall and immediately plugged him into the middle of an offense in transition. A free spirit who combined brawn and brains, Everitt earned the eternal admiration of Browns fans. When the team left town, Everitt could tolerate only one season in Baltimore, drawing a fine for sporting a Browns bandana during the Ravens' inaugural game.

Honorable mention:

- Bob DeMarco (1972-74)
- Jeff Faine (2003-2005)
- Hank Fraley (2006-2009)
- Jay Hilgenberg (1992)
- Mike "Mo" Scarry (1946-47)
- Dave Wohlabaugh (1999-2002)

9 Best Defensive Tackles in Browns History

1. Jerry Sherk (1970-81) — This second-round pick from Oklahoma State brought a wrestler's sensibility to the line. A conference champion heavyweight for Cowboys' renowned wrestling program, he became the Browns' best player during the franchise's first prolonged slump. He made four consecutive Pro Bowl appearances starting in 1973 and was named the NFL's Defensive Player of the Year by the Newspaper Enterprise Association in 1976. His great leverage, agility and persistence made Sherk an excellent pass rusher and tackler in pursuit. His 69 career sacks trail only Clay Matthews on the Browns' career list. His four sacks in a 1976 win over the Eagles set a Browns' single-game record later tied by Mack Mitchell and Andra Davis. Unfortunately, the next time those two teams met, in 1979, Sherk scraped his arm across Astroturf, and a resulting staph infection endangered life and limb and shortened his career. This career-long Brown's contributions include some excellent photography of his fellow players.

2. Bob Gain (1952, 1954-64) — Before Bear Bryant began his legendary coaching run at Alabama, his successful program at Kentucky included this Akron-born mainstay, winner of the 1950 Outland Trophy. The Browns traded for him after he won a Grey Cup in Canada rather than sign with Green Bay, which had drafted him fifth overall. Following military service in Korea, Gain established himself as an athletic 255-pound force, rowdy, durable and versatile. Paul Brown moved him around to end, middle guard and linebacker to field his best set of defenders. Still, Gain made five Pro Bowls and recovered 15 fumbles in his career, which ended with a broken leg early in the championship

season of 1964. His teammates remembered his robust on-field presence and a personality at turns crusty and eccentric. He was known for keeping his practice pants unwashed and for pranking rookies in the shower with a warm stream of his own.

3. Michael Dean Perry (1988-94) — His big brother, The Fridge, may have been more famous, but Michael Dean was by far the better player. Very quick off the ball, Perry had many Browns fans half-expecting that one day he'd beat the quarterback to the snap and gallop past the surprised backfield into the end zone. As it was, frequently facing double-team blocking, the 6'1", 290-pound Clemson product racked up 51.5 sacks as a Brown, including 11.5 among his 107 tackles in his second All-Pro season of 1990. Among his many highlights was a strip sack of John Elway to help the Browns break a 15-year drought against their nemesis Denver in 1989. A Pro Bowler in five of his seven years in Cleveland, Perry was inducted into the first class of Browns Legends in 2001.

4. Walter Johnson (1965-76) — If 2015 first-round pick Danny Shelton can accomplish anything close to what Johnson did wearing number 71, his selection will be amply vindicated. Strong, durable and explosive, this three-time Pro Bowler teamed with Jim Kanicki and then Sherk to form some of the toughest tackle tandems in football. He was hardy enough to take part in all 176 games the Browns played during his career, persisting in the 1969 title game loss at Minnesota despite severe frostbite in his fingers. Though sack stats weren't well-kept before his time and didn't become standard until 1982, he is credited with 58, officially third among all Browns. Johnson dabbled in pro wrestling after his playing career and died of a heart attack at age 56 in 1999, just two days after the passing of another Browns great, Marion Motley.

5. Bob Golic (1982-88) — The Browns played a 3-4 defense from 1980 to 1988, and Golic plugged the middle as a very effective nose tackle for most of that time. The Notre Damer brought an intense spirit to the interior of the Browns' defense. Preceded by three years as a New England linebacker and succeeded by four seasons as a Raider, Golic's prime years came in Cleveland, his hometown. He made the Pro Bowl three straight seasons beginning in 1985, coinciding with the team's playoff run. As a heavyweight wrestler at St. Joseph's, Golic defeated future Browns roommate Tom Cousineau en route to the 1975 state championship. He has largely stayed in the public eye (and ear) since his playing career on television and radio.

6. Don Colo (1953-58) — The only Brown to play at Brown University (where he was a teammate of Joe Paterno), the decorated WWII vet came to Cleveland in a 15-player swap with the Colts because Paul Brown recognized how much his players hated to face off with him. A team captain and the Browns' first player representative, Colo was a rough,

tough, unsentimental force inside who earned post-season accolades each year of his Browns career.

7. John Kissell (1950-52, 1954-56) — Paul Brown had seen enough of him as a Buffalo Bill standout to buy him, along with guard Abe Gibron and halfback Rex Baumgartner, in time for the Browns' entry to the NFL. Kissell was a stout and rowdy New Englander who served as a solid starter on some dominant defenses. He played 1953 in Canada but returned to contribute to teams that won consecutive NFL titles.

8. Jim Kanicki (1963-69) — One of 12 siblings, he played sparingly at Michigan State but was drafted in the second round nonetheless. He tipped the scales at over 280 pounds as a rookie and got early experience due to injuries to Gain. His size, strength and now-outlawed head-slap helped him stick around for 95 games on the consistently winning Browns teams of the Blanton Collier era, including the 1964 champs. His success against Colts great Jim Parker in the Browns' shutout upset was his career's crowning glory. Traded to the Giants for his final two seasons, Kanicki later returned to northeast Ohio and purchased a steel company in Ashtabula.

9. Orpheus Roye (2000-07) — One of the Browns' best unrestricted free agent signings, the former Steeler from Florida State was one of the most dependable defenders of new Browns era. He moved well for a 320-pounder and often chased down runners long after other linemen would've given up. He also showed a knack for deflecting footballs at the line, as he's credited with 27 pass break-ups during his Browns career.

Honorable mention:

- Henry Bradley (1979-82)
- Forrest "Chubby" Grigg (1948-51)
- James Jones (1991-94)
- Dick Modzelewski (1964-66)
- Derrell Palmer (1949-53)
- Floyd Peters (1959-62)
- Dave Puzzuoli (1983-87)
- Shaun Rogers (2008-10)
- Ahtyba Rubin (2008-14)
- Lou Rymkus (1946-51), listed with offensive tackles
- Gerard Warren (2001-04)

11 Best Defensive Ends in Browns History

1. **Len Ford (1950-57)** — The former Michigan Wolverine and Los Angeles Don (AAFC) end beefed up to focus on defense upon his arrival in Cleveland. Recovering from a wicked facial injury just in time for the famous 1950 title game, he became a dominant pass rusher, a ferocious focal point on the league's stingiest defense, and the reason the 4-3 defense was invented. With talent so supreme it caused hard-nosed Paul Brown to turn a blind eye to his alcohol issues, Ford was a first-team All-Pro four straight years. He recovered 20 fumbles in his career, an NFL record at the time. If only they'd kept statistics on sacks back then! He intercepted two passes in the 56-10 championship game romp over the Lions in 1954. Ford was inducted into the Hall of Fame four years after his death at age 46.

2. **Bill Glass (1962-68)** — The next end after Ford to wear number 80 was Jim Marshall, one of several defenders Paul Brown traded before they realized their full greatness. To the rescue came Glass, the former Baylor All-American, in a trade with Detroit involving quarterback Milt Plum. The clean-cut Christian became a key member of the defense that held Johnny Unitas to 95 passing yards in the 1964 championship game shutout. The durable Glass earned Pro Bowl honors in four of his seven years in Cleveland, primarily for his blind-side pass rushing. He still owns the Browns' single-season sack record with 14.5 in 1965. In 1966, he had sacks in seven straight games. One friend recalled, "Quarterbacks told the story on Bill that he would come charging in on you, knock you down, then reach down to pick you up and say, 'Bless you, brother.'" Off-season seminary studies led to writing several books during his playing career and later founding his own successful prison ministry.

3. **Paul Wiggin (1957-67)** — Can you imagine an active player today earning an advanced degree from Stanford during the off-season and teaching at the high school and college levels? That's what Wiggin did off the field. On it, he played in 146 straight games, recovering 19 fumbles (second most in Browns history) and earning two Pro Bowl starts. Drafted in the sixth round a year early based on potential, he eventually eclipsed future Hall of Famer Willie Davis, racking up three sacks in his first start. Durable, agile, strong and Phi Beta Kappa smart, Wiggin could both harass the passer and defuse the power sweep. He'd be a rock-solid choice for a hypothetical but impressive Mount Rushmore of Cleveland Browns Pauls.

4. **Carl Hairston (1984-89)** — His nickname "Big Daddy" says exactly what he meant to the Browns defenses of the '80s. He brought leadership, an easy confidence and Super Bowl experience with him from Phil-

adelphia, where he was a seventh-round steal for Dick Vermeil. The Browns got him for just a ninth rounder, as he was 31 and coming off knee surgery. A fine tackler with a nose for the ball carrier, Hairston tallied 1,141 tackles and 94 sacks in his 15-year career. During the legendary double-overtime playoff win over the Jets, Hairston led a stout defense with three sacks and seven solo tackles. His total of 42.5 sacks as a Brown is particularly impressive for a 3-4 defensive end who later moved inside to tackle.

5. **Jack Gregory** (1967-71, 1979) — An outstanding combination of size (6'5", 250 pounds) and speed, this Mississippian made the Pro Bowl in the successful 1969 season. His 14 sacks (including one of Joe Namath, the first in Monday Night Football history) in 1970 is tied for second on the Browns' single season list. He was equally adept against the run. Son of a former Cleveland Ram, Gregory had even more outstanding years in New York before returning for one last hurrah in 1979.

6. **John Yonakor** (1946-49) — The leading receiver on Frank Leahy's 1943 national champion Notre Dame team, he won All-American recognition. He eschewed the NFL's Eagles, who had drafted him ninth overall, to sign with the new Cleveland team. The Browns featured Dante Lavelli and Mac Speedie on offense, so the 6'4", 225-pounder saw most of his action at defensive end. He is considered among the best AAFC players at his position. The Boston native later settled in the Cleveland area and worked in industry.

7. **Rob Burnett** (1990-95) — The Browns drafted two defensive ends in 1990 that would play a combined 28 years in the league. Burnett was an especially good value in the fifth round. The Syracuse product had 40.5 sacks and seven fumble recoveries as a Brown. He was one of six Browns to make the Pro Bowl in 1994, as the league's stingiest scoring defense led Cleveland back into the playoffs after four losing seasons. Burnett had ten sacks that year, more than double the total of Anthony Pleasant or their other teammates.

8. **George Young** (1946-53) — Not to be confused with the Giants' legendary executive of the same name, this George Young grew up in poverty in eastern Pennsylvania but grew into a state champion wrestler. A Rose Bowl champion with Georgia, he first played for Paul Brown as a Navy cadet in Illinois. A solid, longtime starter (until future Hall of Famer Doug Atkins arrived), Young registered one safety and two defensive touchdowns, including one in the undefeated 1948 team's title game. During Young's tenure, only once did the Browns allow over 200 points in a season, while always tallying at least 300 of their own.

9. **"Turkey" Joe Jones** (1970-71, 1973, 1975-78) — Tall and talented, Jones was a fleet pass-rushing phenom taken 11 slots before Jerry Sherk in the second round of the 1970 draft. His memorable nickname

followed him from college and was based on his physique, but Jones as a rookie fell victim to the team's traditional practical joke before Thanksgiving. He was neither the first nor last Brown to go driving around rural Ohio for a non-existent free turkey, but he supposedly was the only player ever to go on the wild-turkey chase again the next year. A likable personality whose productivity never fully matched his potential, he is best remembered for a particularly punishing piledriving sack of the Steelers' Terry Bradshaw in 1976.

10. **Lyle Alzado (1979-81)** — His time in Cleveland was brief, but this tenacious wild man thrived when the Browns switched to the 3-4 defense he knew from his Denver days. Among six Browns Pro Bowlers in the Kardiac Kids year of 1980, Alzado, a first-team All-Pro, was the only defender. He twice led the team in sacks and had 24.5 in three years here.

11. **Anthony Pleasant (1990-95)** — Like "Turkey" Joe, he hailed from Tennessee State, as did several other fine defensive ends, including Richard Dent, Ed "Too Tall" Jones and Claude Humphrey. He was in on 297 tackles in Cleveland and amassed 33.5 of his 58 career sacks in the brown and orange. His six forced fumbles in 1995 is the most for a Brown on record.

Honorable mention:

- Al "Bubba" Baker (1987, 1989-90) — Great pass rusher turned barbecuer.
- Courtney Brown (2000-04) — Beset by injuries, former top pick made an impact at times.
- Reggie Camp (1983-87) — A bright spot for the '84 Browns with 14 sacks.
- Kenard Lang (2002-05) — Consistent performer once rambled 71 yards with an interception.
- Orpheus Roye (2000-07) — Started 102 games at either DE or DT.
- Jabaal Sheard (2011-14) — Led Browns in sacks in each of his first three years.
- Ron Snidow (1968-72) — Added a veteran presence to playoff teams and made All-Pro.

13 Best Linebackers in Browns History

1. **Bill Willis (1946-53)** — Every Browns fan should know about this extraordinary Hall of Famer. Graham, Motley, Lavelli and Groza scored

more points, but this 210-pound middle guard was every bit as important to Cleveland's early winning ways. The first African American signed by the Browns, he helped reintegrate pro football and handled that tough predicament with great class. Lining up in the center of the five-man defensive lines of that era, Willis had a sprinter's speed, lightning reflexes and a strong upper body. Precursor of the modern-day middle linebacker, he was renowned for bursting into the backfield before the center could react, but he would also drop into pass coverage effectively or chase down runners from sideline to sideline. Willis was a first-team all-league honoree seven of his eight seasons and second-team once. The only Ohio State Buckeye known mostly for defense to have his number retired, the Columbus native later served as director of the Ohio Department of Youth Services.

2. Clay Matthews (1978-93) — The son, brother, father and uncle of NFL players, the first-round pick arrived as a long-haired rookie from Southern Cal. By the time economics led him to Atlanta 16 seasons later, he had established franchise records for NFL games played (232), consecutive seasons (16), and sacks (76.5). He knocked quarterbacks backwards nearly a third of a mile over the course of his Browns career. The four-time Pro Bowler was a Hall of Fame semifinalist in 2012. He deserves more consideration, not just for his longevity, but for his solid all-around play at outside linebacker, peaking during the playoff run of the mid-to-late 1980s. Though neither a freakish speedster nor a physical specimen, his off-season workout regimen, winning personality and blue-collar dedication to duty made him one of the most beloved and successful Browns ever. Few fans will forget his infamous flub — lateraling away a recovered fumble during a crucial season finale at Houston in 1989 — followed by his playoff game-saving interception at the goal line to thwart Buffalo's furious rally the next week.

3. Jim Houston (1960-72) — The Massillon and Ohio State star was a first-round selection who certainly lived up to that billing, making the Pro Bowl four times. Everyone knows that Jim Brown was the best offensive player on the '64 championship team. This other Jim was probably their best defender, playing the left linebacker position after starting out as a defensive end. Listed at 6'3" and 240 pounds, his agility allowed him to thrive as one of the league's biggest linebackers. His three touchdowns on interception returns are more than any other linebacker in Browns history. As durable as they come, Houston was a team captain who later served as president of a Browns alumni group.

4. Walt Michaels (1952-61) — One of the toughest tacklers on a team loaded with them, Michaels started ten straight seasons on Paul Brown's defenses, earning Pro Bowl honors from 1955-59. Brown drafted him in the seventh round out of Washington & Lee (which hasn't produced a pro player since), then traded him to Green Bay, rectifying

his mistake a year later. Though not blessed with outstanding physical gifts, the outside linebacker had no real holes in his game. He had 11 interceptions and eight fumble recoveries as a Brown, plus three more turnovers in championship game wins. A heads-up player who called the defensive signals for several seasons, Michaels retired at 32 and began a long coaching career.

5. **Galen Fiss (1956-66)** — A 13th-round draft pick nearly four years removed from his last football game, Fiss seemed unlikely to stick with the defending league champion Browns. But the 6', 227-pound former Indians farmhand took advantage of Chuck Noll's preseason injury to earn a job he wouldn't relinquish for a decade. Along the way, his low-key leadership shone through, never brighter than in his biggest game, the 1964 championship game shutout of Johnny Unitas' Colts. The captain from Kansas retired as a career-long Brown with 13 interceptions, 18 fumble recoveries, two Pro Bowl selections and innumerable admirers, including Paul Brown himself.

6. **Chip Banks (1982-86)** — His athletic talent was on a par with Willis', but he was two inches and 25 pounds bigger. Career highlights included a 65-yard touchdown on an interception return at New England in 1983 (the last time the Browns registered consecutive shutouts) and an 11-sack season in 1985, when the defense led the Browns to the division title. The third overall pick of the 1982 draft, he is the only Brown to win AP Rookie of the Year honors on either offense or defense. But Banks never fully "clicked" as a teammate, as holdouts and conflict with coach Marty Schottenheimer helped earn him a ticket out of town, despite making four Pro Bowls in five seasons and never missing a game.

7. **Vince Costello (1957-66)** — This small-school find from Ohio was — like Fiss — a multi-sport athlete who joined the Browns after a brief minor league baseball career and military service. He too was a very productive starter for a decade. A tough-tackling middle linebacker with good speed, he intercepted 18 passes, most of any Browns LB, plus two more in post-season play. Though he only played six-man football in high school, he developed a thorough understanding of the game and later joined Paul Brown's staff in Cincinnati.

8. **Mike Johnson (1986-93)** — This Virginia Tech product started in the USFL and was one of three key contributors Cleveland gained in the 1984 supplemental draft. A very solid force as an inside linebacker in the 3-4 or in the middle of the 4-3, he led the team in tackles for six seasons. He made the Pro Bowl for the first of two times in 1990 as a late addition by his own coach, Bud Carson, a decision vindicated by his 22-yard score on an interception return in that game. He came back from a broken foot in 1991 to recover a league-high five opponents' fumbles in 1992. Like

Matthews and most Browns stars of the '80s, Johnson was eventually replaced by Belichick draftees and Giant imports.

9. **Tony Adamle** (1947-51, 1954) — Another Greatest Generation veteran from Ohio State, Adamle saw plenty of action as a fullback but made his mark on defense. A combination of toughness and smarts led to Paul Brown naming him team captain in 1950, the first of his two Pro Bowl seasons. He quit after the Browns' first title game loss and focused on medical school. In 1954, Adamle returned to fill a need on defense and to replenish his bank account. Practicing just once a week, he improved the Browns' defense, and they resumed their position as league champs. He spent the bulk of the next four decades practicing medicine in the area.

10. **Lou Saban** (1946-49) — Captain for three of the four AAFC championship seasons, Saban is better known for his long coaching career, but football historians consider him the best of all the upstart league's linebackers. Intense and intelligent, he picked off 13 passes in just 54 games. In title games he blocked a punt and had two more interceptions, returning one for a score. He also served as Lou Groza's kicking understudy, converting 21 of 22 extra points.

11. **Tommy Thompson** (1949-53) — Although he hailed from the East Coast and was the 16th overall selection by Washington out of William & Mary, this blond center/linebacker chose Cleveland, where he excelled as a rugged run stuffer. He also had a fourth-quarter interception in the epic 1950 title game to help the Browns overcome an eight-point deficit. Team captain and twice a second-team All-Pro, he was having an ever better season in 1953 until he dislocated his knee tackling a Steeler runner. He was named first-team All-Pro anyway, but the injury effectively ended his career at age 26.

12. **Dick Ambrose** (1975-83) — A 12th-round draftee in 1975, he had by far the best Browns career of any of their 19 picks that year. A solid middle and inside linebacker, "Bam Bam" led the team in tackles for five years running. He tried to come back from a broken ankle and its complications but eventually retired to begin his legal career in the Cleveland area.

13. **Charlie Hall** (1971-80) — One of two Charlie Halls taken in the third round of the 1971 draft, this Houston standout never missed a game in his decade of service. The outside linebacker was a bastion of consistency during some turbulent times. He and Clarence Scott led the lamentable 1975 squad with two interceptions. Hall was one of only five Browns (Cockroft, Darden, Dieken and Scott) to bridge the gap and appear in both the 1972 and 1980 playoffs. He was named the Cleveland Touchdown Club's 1979 defensive player of the year.

Honorable mention:

- Alex Agase (1948-51)
- Billy Andrews (1967-74)
- Bob Babich (1973-78)
- Johnny Brewer (1961-67) — He converted from TE in 1966.
- Tom Catlin (1953-54, 1957-58)
- Tom Cousineau (1982-85)
- Andra Davis (2002-08)
- John Garlington (1968-77)
- Weldon Humble (1947-50)
- D'Qwell Jackson (2006-09, 2011-13)
- Eddie Johnson (1981-90)
- Pepper Johnson (1993-95)
- Dale Lindsey (1965-72)
- Jamir Miller (1999-2001) — He was the reborn Browns' only Pro Bowl honoree in their first eight seasons.
- Marion Motley (1946-53) — The Hall of Fame fullback excelled at linebacker in goal line and short yardage circumstances.
- Chuck Noll (1953-59)
- Kamerion Wimbley (2006-09)

14 Best Cornerbacks in Browns History

1. **Hanford Dixon (1981-89)** — A first-round draft pick, a three-time Pro Bowler, a Cleveland Browns Legend: Dixon is all of those. But make no bones about it, his best appellation is Top Dawg, originator of a classic nickname and an attacking attitude that defined the Browns' stout defense of the '80s and inspired a new breed of fan loyalty. Dixon and his fellow corner, Frank Minnifield, didn't just cover receivers, they mauled them, getting the most out of the five-yard chuck rule. In Week 15 of the 1986 season, the 10-4 Browns went to Cincinnati (9-5) seeking to avenge an earlier 30-13 defeat. Dixon picked off a Boomer Esiason pass and limited star receiver Cris Collinsworth to one short catch, as the Browns routed the Bengals and their league-leading offense, 34-3, to win the division. Another of his many career highlights: intercepting Terry Bradshaw three times in a 1982 win.

2. **Frank Minnifield** (1984-92) — With his arrival from Louisville by way of the USFL, the Browns' defense improved to rank second overall, third against the pass. Rather than a dominant middle linebacker or a fierce pass rushing end, Cleveland's excellent defenses of the '80s began with the gritty bump-and-run coverage of Minnifield and Dixon. It's hard to find much space between the two in terms of their abilities. Minnifield was super speedy but just 5'9" and 180 pounds. He had "only" 20 interceptions, but then again teams knew better than to pick on him. The four-time Pro Bowler was selected to the NFL's All-Decade second team for the 1980s. His 48-yard scoring return of a Sean Salisbury pass put the finishing touches on a playoff win over the Colts in early 1988.

3. **Warren Lahr** (1948-59) — Not many gridiron stars played their college football in Cleveland, but this Western Reserve grad sure made good taking his act locally. Picked by the Steelers in the final round of the 1947 draft, Lahr spent his entire pro career as a Brown, racking up 44 interceptions (second in team history to Thom Darden). His fifth career touchdown via INT return set an NFL record that lasted 13 years. His team record five playoff picks include the last play of the epic 1950 championship game. One of his eight interceptions in 1950 came against the defending champion Eagles. The Browns and their offensive juggernaut won their NFL debut in Philly, 35-10, but the rematch in Cleveland was a wet and muddy affair. On the third play from scrimmage, Lahr dashed 30 yards down the sideline with a Tommy Thompson pass for the Browns' only TD. They won without benefit of a single forward pass. After his long playing career, Lahr partnered with Ken Coleman as the team's TV announcer from '63 to '67.

4. **Bernie Parrish** (1959-66) — This hard-nosed two-sport star from Florida intercepted 29 passes as a Brown, fifth on their all-time list. His 557 interception return yards are third, 92 of them coming on one play in a 42-0 rout of the Bears in 1960, the first of his two Pro Bowl seasons. In 1964, the Browns were down 16-13 in the fourth quarter in Dallas. Parrish returned an overthrown Don Meredith pass 54 yards for a touchdown that helped spur a five-game winning streak in that championship season. An outspoken sort who was active in the NFL Players Association, he later penned a controversial best-seller, *They Call It a Game: Shoulders the NFL Stands On*, that took dead aim at the league's establishment.

5. **Clarence Scott** (1971-83) — This first-round pick played his first eight years at cornerback and garnered 39 career interceptions. He teamed with Jerry Sherk, Thom Darden and Charlie Hall as fixtures on the Browns defense of the 1970s. Between 1969 and 1985, he was the only Browns CB to represent the team in the Pro Bowl. With his last five years at safety, Scott played 178 consecutive games, the longest string of any Browns defender.

6. **Don Paul** (1954-58) — Acquired after four years with the Chicago Cardinals, where he played in all three phases, this playmaker from Washington State made the Pro Bowl three of his five seasons as a Brown. He intercepted 22 passes, including seven for 190 yards and a touchdown in 1956. Career highlights include a 65-yard return of a Norm Van Brocklin pass for a score in the 1955 championship game win over the Rams, a 60-yard punt return TD against his former team earlier that year, and a team record 89-yard TD after scooping up a Steeler fumble in a 24-0 shutout in 1957. An engaging personality who countered the notion that Paul Brown only liked straight-laced conformists, Paul later self-published a memoir entitled *I Went Both Ways: The Adventures of the NFL's Joyboy During the Fabulous Fifties*.

7. **Tommy James** (1948-55) — Another one of Paul Brown's favorites from Massillon and Ohio State, James was a fleet defender on those legendary Browns teams. Though just 5'9" and 178 pounds, he wasn't afraid to lay some licks. James was selected to the Pro Bowl for his 1953 season, then switched to play safety his last two years here. He also got his share of picks, 34 in all, including nine in 1950. Twice he intercepted three passes in a game, the only Brown to do so until Anthony Henry in 2001.

8. **Joe Haden** (2010-2014*) — The highest-drafted cornerback ever to play for the Browns, the Florida Gator's pro play has largely justified the seventh overall pick used to bring him to Cleveland. The two-time Pro Bowler is a confident cover corner and popular personality within the team and the community. In four of his first five seasons, he's ranked in the top six in passes defensed. An effective tackler in run support with elite ball skills for a defensive back, Haden could rise much higher on future editions of this list if he plays up to his $67.5 million contract extension that runs through 2019.

9. **Erich Barnes** (1965-71) — At Purdue, he battled Illinois' Bobby Mitchell in track events, presaging their many NFL duels. He also caught a 95-yard touchdown pass from another one-time Brown, Len Dawson. Long, lean and graceful — but plenty aggressive — Barnes was traded to Cleveland at age 30 after outstanding years with the Bears and Giants. Eighteen of his 45 career interceptions came as a Brown. More important, though, was the veteran leadership he provided to the Browns' young secondary of the late '60s.

10. **Daylon McCutcheon** (1999-2005) — The son of a fine Ram runner of the '70s, McCutcheon was a solid starter for seven seasons. Though just 190 pounds (maybe), his tackling technique was textbook. A stabilizing force on a franchise in flux, he was one reason Browns' pass defense ranked an average of ninth during his tenure. McCutcheon intercepted two passes in the January 2003 playoff game at Pittsburgh

and scored on a 75-yard interception return in a win over the Steelers the next season.

11. Ben Davis (1967-68; 1970-73) — The 439th player drafted in 1967, Davis emerged from Defiance College in northwest Ohio to lead the league in punt return average as a rookie. His duties on defense soon increased, and he intercepted passes in seven straight 1968 games. After a knee injury cost him most of two years, he recovered to start three straight seasons at cornerback, earning Pro Bowl honors in 1972. His older sister is the radical political activist Angela Davis.

12. Jim Shofner (1958-63) — The Browns' first-round pick in 1958, this tall Texan, a college quarterback, had 20 interceptions, including eight in 1960, and six fumble recoveries in his six-year career. He was Brian Sipe's QB coach during his MVP year and the interim Browns coach for the end of the lamentable 1990 season.

13. Ron Bolton (1976-82) — He amassed 17 interceptions in Cleveland after some good years in New England. A wiry type, at 6'2" and 180 pounds, Bolton was a feisty competitor on the field. He led the 1980 Kardiac Kids team with six picks, then jumped a route against former teammate Jim Plunkett in the playoffs to score the Browns' only touchdown in the epic "Red Right 88" game.

14. Tom Colella (1946-48) — A member of the Cleveland Rams' 1945 NFL champions, Colella stayed in town when the Rams moved west. A versatile veteran who could also run, pass and punt, he intercepted ten passes in 1946 and six more the following year, both league highs.

Honorable mention:

- Walter Beach (1963-66)
- Leigh Bodden (2003-07)
- Sheldon Brown (2010-12)
- Clinton Burrell (1979-84)
- Oliver Davis (1977-80)
- Corey Fuller (1999-2002)
- Anthony Henry (2001-04)
- Mike Howell (1965-72), listed with safeties
- Lawrence Johnson (1979-84)
- Buster Skrine (2011-14)
- Walt Sumner (1969-74)
- Eric Wright (2007-10)

14 Best Safeties in Browns History

1. **Thom Darden** (1972-74, 1976-81) — The fifth defensive back taken in the first round of the 1972 draft, this All-American at Michigan made an immediate statement, sacking the quarterback three times in his first game. The Browns' pass defense was ranked among the league's top ten each of his first three years, but when he missed 1975 due to injury, it fell to 23rd. Darden led the NFL with ten picks in his Pro Bowl year of 1978, though his 1974 season may have been even better. In 1979, he broke Roger Staubach's streak of 150 passes without an interception by returning one for a touchdown on Monday Night Football. A lifelong Brown, the Sandusky native holds franchise career records for interceptions (45), interception return yardage (820) and seasons leading the team in interceptions (six).

2. **Ken Konz** (1953-59) — The speedy former LSU star had 30 career interceptions, hitting paydirt with four, most of any Browns safety. A first-round pick who joined the club after two years in the Air Force, the scrappy 184-pounder soon learned the importance of tackling low after meeting Marion Motley in practice. Secondary to his secondary work, Konz was one of the few players to both punt and return punts. He intercepted two passes in each of two title game triumphs.

3. **Cliff Lewis** (1946-51) — The Browns' first quarterback, the Lakewood native soon gave way to Otto Graham and served as his backup while amassing 30 interceptions at safety, including nine in the undefeated season of 1948. "He was a team man all the way," Graham said upon Lewis' death in 2002. And those teams went all the way too, winning championships every year until the 1951 title game they lost despite his last career interception.

4. **Eric Turner** (1991-95) — The first pick of the Bill Belichick era, this first-team All-American from UCLA was drafted second overall, highest ever for a defensive back. "E-Rock" became a starter during his rookie year, establishing himself as a strong tackler with good ball skills as well. He was in on 8.6 tackles per game over his Browns career. He tied for the NFL lead with nine interceptions (half of the Browns' total) — including a 93-yard touchdown return — in his All-Pro 1994 season, when the Browns' stingy defense led them to the playoffs.

5. **Ross Fichtner** (1960-67) — One of five former Purdue quarterbacks to have played for Cleveland, he had the best Browns career among them. Part of the defense that blanked the heavily-favored Colts for the 1964 NFL title, he held Hall of Fame tight end John Mackey to two yards. His impressive 21.5 yards per return of his 27 career interceptions is the highest average of any Browns safety. On Oct. 23, 1966, before a then-

record Stadium crowd of 84,721, Fichtner picked off three passes in a 30-21 win over the undefeated Dallas Cowboys.

6. **Felix Wright (1985-90)** — Undrafted out of Drake, the rangy ball hawk played three years in Canada, catching the Browns' eye by picking off four passes in a playoff win. He became part of a strong Browns secondary that included two Pro Bowl cornerbacks and ranked among the NFL's top ten pass and total defenses in the playoff years of 1987-89. Wright led the team in interceptions four times, including a league-high nine in 1989. He returned two picks for 108 yards and a touchdown in a Monday night win over the Rams in 1987. His four career playoff interceptions tie him with Konz and Ken Gorgal for second in team history behind Warren Lahr.

7. **Mike Howell (1965-72)** — This Grambling quarterback was a value find in the eighth round, racking up 27 picks, tied for sixth in team history. He played all 14 games for seven straight seasons, beginning as a cornerback and moving to safety, where he started for the playoff teams of the late 1960s.

8. **Ernie Kellermann (1966-71)** — Also a college quarterback, at Miami of Ohio he beat Purdue with an 88-yard touchdown pass as a freshman. The Cowboys drafted him and first-rounder Craig Morton in the same year. Upon his release, the hometown Browns picked up the lefty and converted him to safety, where he became a starter after a year on the taxi squad. Of his 17 interceptions as a Brown, six came in his Pro Bowl season of 1968.

9. **Don Fleming (1960-62)** — This Shadyside, Ohio, native stepped right into the Browns' lineup as a rookie and tallied ten interceptions in three seasons. The Browns retired his jersey 46 following his fatal accident on an off-season construction job.

10. **T.J. Ward (2010-13)** — Strong in run support, the second-rounder from Oregon started 16 games as a rookie and then earned Pro Bowl honors in 2013 after scoring two defensive touchdowns, including a game-sealing pick-six against Buffalo.

11. **Larry Benz (1963-65)** — The Cleveland Heights High School star led or tied for the team lead in interceptions each of his three seasons. He picked off two Eddie LeBaron passes in his second pro game, a 41-24 win at Dallas. He won the starting job after a rookie tryout, recommended by his Northwestern coach and former Brown Ara Parseghian. A member of the 1964 championship team, Benz was later left exposed to the Atlanta Falcons' expansion draft, but he left their camp after one day and never played again.

12. **Bobby Franklin (1960-66)** — The Mississippian picked off a career-high eight passes as a rookie. Three of those came in a December 1960

shutout of Chicago in which he became the first of only two Browns to return two picks for scores in the same game (along with David Bowens in 2010). The converted college quarterback was also the holder for placekicks and the emergency punter.

13. Stevon Moore (1992-95) — A solid hitter who averaged 6.3 tackles per game, he had a three-interception game in 1995 and the team's second-longest fumble return, a 73-yard score in 1992. He started all 16 games three straight years and recovered nine fumbles as a Brown.

14. Ken Gorgal (1950, 1953-54) — Though his Browns career was interrupted by Army service and shortened by an injury and subsequent trade, he was a very solid player on a dynasty's defense. Confident and collegial, he registered 11 interceptions and four more in the post-season. The former Purdue quarterback made first team All-NFL in 1953, according to UPI and the *New York Daily News*.

Honorable mention:

- Mike Adams (2007-11)
- Tashaun Gipson (2012-14*)
- Thane Gash (1988-90)
- Al Gross (1983-87)
- Sean Jones (2005-08)
- Warren Lahr (1948-59), listed with cornerbacks
- Earl Little (1999-2004)
- Brodney Pool (2005-09)
- Don Rogers (1984-85)
- Clarence Scott (1971-83), listed with cornerbacks
- Walt Sumner (1969-74)
- Donte Whitner (2014*)
- Junior Wren (1956-59)

9 Best Kickers and Punters in Browns History

Some think they're not "real" football players, but what they do is intrinsic to the game. Kicking and punting have developed into distinct specialties over the years, coinciding with expanded rosters and the emergence of soccer-style place-kicking. Though low on the salary and respect scale, punters and kickers confront enormous pressure. Whether handling a high snap on a wet day in their own end zone or trotting out for a crucial field goal with a game, season or career on the line, the men who put the foot into the football are more than window dressing: they affect outcomes, while adding to the variety of skills on display for fans of the sport. Over the years, the Browns have been blessed with some very special special-teamers.

1. Lou Groza (1946-59, 1961-67) — The exploits of this Hall of Fame placekicker and left tackle are legion in the memories of Browns fans and the team's record book: most points, most seasons played, 13 championship games (including the game-winning field goal to cap the Browns' first NFL season), scored in 107 straight contests, and converted 138 straight extra points. This nine-time Pro Bowler ranks in the very top tier of legendary Browns. Field goals were not nearly as common in Groza's day, but the strong straight-on aim of "The Toe" put the Browns in scoring position whenever they crossed midfield. He had four 50-plus-yard field goals in his first four years, when the NFL lacked a single successful kick of such distance. Though different rules and conditions affected his accuracy compared to modern kickers, his 88% FG success rate in 1953 was a team record for 41 years. Groza remained a popular and personable figure until his death in 2000 at age 76, which matches his retired jersey number. The annual award for the best college kicker is named in his honor, as is the street in front of the Browns' training facility in Berea.

2. Horace Gillom (1947-56) — Paul Brown called him the best athlete he coached at Massillon. The great Gillom, who also played end on offense and defense, was the third African American to join the Browns. His big leg helped transform the punting game. For one thing, he was the first to drop back 15 rather than 12 yards to take the snap. And though his gross average of 43.8 topped the Browns' record book until Dave Zastudil came along over 50 years later, Gillom's game was about more than distance. Long before Ray Guy, he turned the focus to what we now call "hang time," allowing the coverage to get downfield to minimize returns. One of only two Browns to lead the league in yards per punt, he did it three times. He also has the two longest punts in team history: 80 and 75 yards. (It's been over 1,300 attempts since a Brown last punted the ball even 70 yards.) The World War II Army veteran and Browns Legend has been deceased for 30 years, but his impact on the sport endures.

3. Phil Dawson (1999-2012) — He started to win over Browns fans by beating Pittsburgh in 1999 on a last-ditch field goal as the clock ran out. One of the few constants in the turbulent expansion era, this Texan found a home in Cleveland for 14 years before moving on in free agency. A pro's pro, he wasn't just some soft kicker: he recovered his own onside kick, ran for a touchdown, converted first downs passing and rushing, pooch punted to good effect, and made ten solo tackles. His most famous kick caromed off both the upright and the goal post support bar for a confusing but clutch 51-yard three-pointer to extend a crucial 2007 game

into overtime in Baltimore. Dawson only got better with age, going 14-for-15 from 50 yards or longer during his last two seasons here. Among his all-time Browns records are most field goals in a game, season and career; most consecutive FGs; and highest FG percentage for a season and career. He also ranks second in career points (1,271) and third in games played (216).

4. **Don Cockroft** (1968-80) — For most of a decade, he *was* the Browns' kicking game. One of the very last combination punter/place-kickers, he was also one of the last straight-on kickers. His 57-yard field goal in 1972 broke a 20-year-old team record by a full five yards. He still leads the franchise in career punts and yardage, though he gave up those duties in 1977. He was a steady, reliable player and person who somehow never made it to a Pro Bowl or Super Bowl. Among the most accurate kickers the NFL had seen to that point, he led the league in FG percentage three times, including his first year taking over for Groza. Many Browns fans wonder how life would've been different had he made the kick that Sam Rutigliano didn't let him try late in the last game of his career. Of course, missing it might have been even worse than what happened with Red Right 88. In 2011 Cockroft completed a 672-page coffee table book about that memorable season: *The 1980 Kardiac Kids — Our Untold Stories.*

5. **Matt Bahr** (1981-89) — To succeed Cockroft, the Browns went with rookie Dave Jacobs, who promptly missed eight of his first 12 field goal tries. In came the diminutive Bahr, who had failed to stick with two other teams, and thus Cleveland again had a long-lasting and reliable leg. Bahr, whose older brother Chris also enjoyed a lengthy kicking career, was released after the 1989 season, when he missed two field goals in overtime games the Browns lost. His playoff statistics — 46 points and 80% FG accuracy — rank second in Browns history. Of course, he's probably prouder of the Super Bowl rings he won immediately before and after his time in Cleveland.

6. **Chris Gardocki** (1999-2003) — If you had to pick an overall MVP from the reborn Browns' first five seasons, sad to say that you could make a decent case for Gardocki, the only man to play all 81 games for Cleveland during that time. A very solid punter and holder, he averaged 43.4 yards per punt. Originally a third-round pick of the Bears, Gardocki's an efficient approach kept opponents from ever blocking a punt during his 16-year career.

7. **Matt Stover** (1991-95) — Until fellow Dallas Lake Highlands High School alumnus Phil Dawson came along, Stover held team records for most field goals in a season, most consecutive FGs, and FG accuracy.

8. **Dave Zastudil** (2006-09) — The left-footed Bay Village native has the highest career average of any regular Browns punter: 44.12 yards. That's especially impressive considering that 35% of his punts pinned

opponents inside their 20-yard line. His Browns career was shortened by a knee injury, which was also the case for two other area natives signed as unrestricted free agents in 2006. But unlike LeCharles Bentley and Joe Jurevicius, Zastudil recovered to play again elsewhere.

9. Gary Collins (1962-71) — He ranks even higher as a wide receiver, but Collins was no slouch as the Browns' regular punter for his first six seasons. He led the league with a 46.69 average in 1965, still a franchise single-season record. In a 1966 game against the Eagles, he twice ran for first downs from punt formation, the second from his own 11-yard line.

Honorable mention:

- Sam Baker (1960-61)
- Steve Cox (1981-84) — His only two field goals as a Brown are — at 60 and 58 yards — the team's longest.
- Jeff Gossett (1983, 1985-87)
- Brian Hansen (1991-93)
- Reggie Hodges (2009-10, 2012)
- Tom Tupa (1994-95)

10 Best Kick and Punt Returners in Browns History

1. Joshua Cribbs (2005-12) — 10,015 kickoff return yards, 25.9 yard average, 8 TDs; 2,154 punt return yards, 11.0 ave., 3 TDs

The converted Kent State quarterback made a mighty impact with his hard-charging, relentless style as a returner, kick cover man extraordinaire, and occasional receiver and wildcat option on offense. Popular and genial, the dreadlocked Cribbs gave fans a reason to pay attention no matter how bad Browns football had become. His phenomenal 2007 season ranks among the very best years for any returner. Two years later he scored touchdowns and had plays gaining at least 35 yards four different ways. A member of the Hall of Fame's All-2000s team, he gained more yards in a Browns uniform than anyone except Jim Brown.

2. Eric Metcalf (1989-94) — 2,806 KRY, 20.2 ave., 2 TDs; 1,341 PRY, 10.6 ave., 5 TDs

The shifty speedster will forever be remembered for taking two punts to the house, including the winning score in fourth quarter, against the Steelers in 1993. He also owns the only kick return touchdown in

Browns playoff history, a 90-yarder in the third quarter of their 34-30 win over Buffalo on January 6, 1990. Opponents soon learned they needed to account for the threat Metcalf posed to score on any given play. Despite not being used as a punt returner until his third season, he ranks behind only Cribbs in total return yardage as a Brown.

3. Bobby Mitchell (1958-61) — 1,550 KRY, 25.0 ave., 3 TDs; 607 PRY, 11.2 ave., 3 TDs

Better known in Cleveland as the backfield lightning to Jim Brown's thunder, Mitchell was incredibly dangerous on special teams too, breaking over five percent of his returns for touchdowns, the highest ratio in Browns history (except for Mark Carrier's single score in 15 attempts). As a rookie, he returned both the opening kickoff and a first quarter punt for touchdowns in a 28-14 win over the Eagles.

4. Greg Pruitt (1973-81) — 1,523 KRY, 26.3 ave., 1 TD; 659 PRY, 11.8 ave.

The multi-dimensional little back out of Oklahoma made the Pro Bowl his first two seasons largely on the strength of his return game. As his role in the Browns' offense increased, his return duties were phased out, though those skills helped extend his career well into his 30s, when he earned a Super Bowl ring after being traded to the Raiders.

5. Leroy Kelly (1964-73) — 1,784 KRY, 23.5 ave.; 990 PRY, 10.5 ave., 3 TDs

The Hall of Fame running back contributed mostly as a returner until Jim Brown retired, taking punts back all the way in consecutive road wins in 1965. Though he became Cleveland's workhorse back, he still had at least one return in each of his ten seasons.

6. Dennis Northcutt (2000-06) — 26 KRY, 26.0 ave.; 2,149 PRY, 10.6 ave., 3 TDs

It's a shame that the play he's most associated with was a dropped pass in the playoffs, because Northcutt was an exciting punt returner and fairly productive receiver for several years. Without his spectacular all-around efforts in 2002, the Browns wouldn't have made the playoffs at all, nor been in a position to win that wild game in Pittsburgh. No Brown has returned more punts than Northcutt.

7. Gerald "Ice Cube" McNeil (1986-89) — 1,301 KRY, 20.3 ave., 1 TD; 1,545 PRY, 9.6, 1 TD

His memorable nickname based on both his slippery elusiveness and small stature (a clever counterpoint to "The Fridge"), McNeil is the lightest player in Browns history, listed at 143 pounds. His two return touchdowns came in back-to-back weeks in 1986 against Detroit and Pittsburgh. Each gave the Browns a lead in games they would win by three points. The Cube made the Pro Bowl for his 1987 season, which included his only two receiving touchdowns. The USFL refugee survived in the NFL long enough to rank fourth in Browns career return yards, as he rarely took a direct hit and instead tended to ricochet off tacklers.

8. Dino Hall (1979-83) — 3,185 KRY, 21.1 ave.; 901 PRY, 8.1 ave.

Another fondly-remembered bantam Brown, this speedy and courageous competitor fended off challenges for his roster spot year after year, setting team records in multiple career return categories. He also contributed in kick coverage, most notably by recovering two Bengal muffs in the division-clinching 1980 season finale for the Kardiac Kids. Though he seldom saw snaps at running back, it wasn't until 1984 that Sam Rutigliano found a worthy roster replacement for the 5'6" Hall in Earnest Byner.

9. Walter "The Flea" Roberts (1964-66) — 1,608 KRY, 25.9 ave.; 336 PRY, 8.6 ave.

Paired with Kelly as the punt and kickoff return duo for the outstanding teams of the mid-1960s, the fleet but undersized Roberts had impressed the Browns' West Coast scout, Sarge McKenzie, with his toughness by starting on all three units at San Jose State. Taken by the Saints in their expansion draft, he scored three touchdowns in that franchise's first regular-season win.

10. Keith Wright (1978-80) — 1,767 KRY, 25.2 ave.; 467 PRY, 6.0 ave.

During a brief but memorable era, this fifth-round pick out of Memphis was one of the game's best return men. As a rookie, he led the AFC in kick return average. The next year started out promising as well with four straight wins until a knee injury in the Astrodome ended his season, opening the door to Hall. The two split return duties in 1980, when Wright scored on all three of his receptions, including one against Kansas City that helped the Browns avoid an 0-3 start. He left the playoff game that year with a concussion from his head hitting the frozen field following a 20-yard punt return. More knee problems made that the last play of his NFL career.

Honorable mention:

- Randy Baldwin (1992-94)
- Travis Benjamin (2012-14*)
- Ken Carpenter (1950-53)
- Ben Davis (1967-73)
- Edgar "Special Delivery" Jones (1946-49)
- Ken Konz (1953-59)
- Billy Reynolds (1953-54, 1957)
- Glen Young (1984-88)

CHAPTER 6
FANDOM AND FRIVOLITY

10 Somewhat Apt Anagrams

In no particular order, here are ten Browns personalities whose names, when their letters are rearranged, yield some recognizable resonance.

1. Brainy Hero = Brian Hoyer
2. Cleats Concert = Clarence Scott
3. Scoring Ally = Gary Collins
4. Noise Barker = Bernie Kosar
5. Theatrics Then Memory = Marty Schottenheimer
6. Airmail On Guts = Sam Rutigliano
7. Superhero Yo = Orpheus Roye
8. A Prim Cyclone = Carmen Policy
9. Menacing Rover = Cameron Erving
10. Nothing Wasted = Ted Washington

19 Browns Players with Interesting Names

1. Cleveland Pittsburgh Crosby (1980) — This disappointing second-round defensive end was released two weeks into his rookie year and never saw regular season action as a Brown. Until turning pro he had no ties to either of the Rust Belt cities in his name, though he did show up to a Browns team meeting in a Steelers T-shirt. Cleveland was his given name at birth; Pittsburgh was later added by a stepfather.

2. Jubilee Dunbar (1974) — More productive in college and drafted higher than Southern University teammate Harold Carmichael, the receiver played just two years in the NFL, including five games with the

Browns. He arrived from New Orleans in exchange for Fair Hooker. His actual given name is Allen.

3. **Henry Ford (1955)** — This ninth-round pick was not from Detroit, but rather Pittsburgh, where he finished his playing career after appearing in just two games for the Browns.

4. **Thane Gash (1988-90)** — It's a succinct and strong moniker for a hard-hitting safety. The two-year starter opposite Felix Wright is the only Thane in NFL history.

5. **Ben Gay (2001)** — This fleeting phenom was named for his father, not the analgesic heat rub developed by French doctor Jules Bengué in the 19th century.

6. **Chip Glass (1969-73)** — With longtime DE Bill Glass at the end of his career, it was clear that the Browns ought to draft a replacement Glass. Charles Ferdinand Glass became Milt Morin's backup at tight end, averaging 20 yards per catch with five touchdowns. Not earth-shattering, but — like his name — it indicates a bit of an impact.

7. **Fair Hooker (1969-74)** — In the Monday Night Football debut broadcast, color commentator Don Meredith famously quipped, "Fair Hooker — I haven't met one yet."

8. **Barkevious Mingo (2013-14*)** — His two older brothers were named Hugh III and Hughtavious after their father, so it was his mother's turn. She added "kevious" to the first part of her name, Barbara. The premier pick of the brief Banner/Lombardi era answers to "KeKe."

9. **Earthwind Moreland (2001)** — The defensive back appeared in two games with the Browns. Reportedly, his mother's favorite band was Earth, Wind & Fire.

10. **Babatunde Oluwasegun Temitope Oluwakorede Adisa "Baba" Oshinowo, Jr. (2006)** — This Stanford defensive lineman was the sixth-round pick netted in the trade down that gave Haloti Ngata to the Ravens. His Nigerian name proved longer than his NFL career, in which he saw action in just two games.

11. **Sabby Piscitelli (2010)** — As with Hooker and Gay, this safety was named after his father. A disappointment for Tampa Bay as a second-round pick, he played five games as a Brown and later pursued a career in pro wrestling.

12. **Orpheus Roye (2000-07)** — Though he shares a name with the legendary Greek demigod best known for his music, Roye (besides being an outstanding defensive lineman) was more talented at drawing.

13. Frostee Rucker (2012) — His father, a disc jockey in the military, was known as "DJ Frost," because he was reportedly "cold on the spins." He named his son Frostee and later legally took on that name as well.

14. Pio Sagapolutele (1991-95) — The defensive tackle was born in American Samoa and raised in Hawaii.

15. Dick Shiner (1967) — The Browns sent this journeyman quarterback to Pittsburgh in the Bill Nelsen deal. There he won just three of 20 starts, setting up their selection of Terry Bradshaw.

16. Chansi Stuckey (2009-10) — This speedy little slot receiver was part of the trade that sent Braylon Edwards to the Jets.

17. Webster Slaughter (1986-91) — Over a dozen Websters have played pro football, but only for this game-breaking wideout was it a first rather than last name.

18. Spergon Wynn (2000) — This big-armed QB sported an unusual first name followed by a homophone of what he never did as a Brown.

19. Fozzy Whittaker (2013) — His official name of Foswhitt Whittaker certainly qualifies as unique and helps explain why he goes by a name most associated with a heavy metal band and a comic Muppet bear.

8 Name-Related Browns Coincidences

1. The first two men named Pruitt to play in the NFL both happened to excel as Browns running backs during overlapping tenures in the '70s and early '80s. To this day, the unrelated Mike, who wore 43, and Greg, who wore 34, rank number three and four, respectively, on the Browns' all-time rushing list.

2. Going back to 1977, only two Browns draftees have been named Joe. Thomas and Haden have proven to be no average Joes. The former top ten picks are considered the team's best offensive and defensive players of the current millennium.

3. Of the very few people to ever claim ownership of the Cleveland Browns, two of them shared a first name and middle initial. The franchise's founding owner, Arthur B. McBride, was known as Mickey, but he passed his given name down to one of his sons, who also owned shares of the Browns for a time. In 1961, a syndicate controlled by Arthur Bertram Modell purchased the team, which he uprooted after the 1995 season. Arthur was among the 20 most popular names for boys when

these ex-owners were born, but its rank has gradually slipped over the years. It dropped 22 slots to 276 between 1995 and 1996, its steepest one-year fall to that point. Modell died in 2012, and Arthur rose 32 slots to 323 the next year.

4. Only two players in Browns history were named Ross. Both of them — Fichtner and Verba — were born in October, attended Big Ten universities, won one NFL championship, and were party to (very different) off-field controversies during their time as Browns.

5. Only two players in Browns history were named Bernie. Both of them — Parrish and Kosar — played college football in Florida, started as rookies, became Pro Bowlers, were known to take initiative in calling plays, and joined Texas teams after the Browns released them.

6. Six offensive linemen in Browns history have had Anglicized nobiliary particles — that is, surnames beginning with "De." Three of them were teammates in 1974 (along with two other offensive linemen with "D" surnames, Barry Darrow and Doug Dieken).

- John Demarie (1967-75)
- Bob DeMarco (1972-74)
- Tom DeLeone (1974-84)
- Joe DeLamielleure (1980-84)
- Jed DeVries (1995)
- Enoch DeMar (2003-04)

7. In all of NFL history, only 15 players have had the first name of Preston. Three of them wore the jersey number 40 for the Browns: Carpenter (1956-59), Powell (1961) and Anderson (1974).

8. Two running backs in Browns history had the surname Hill: Calvin (1978-81) and Madre (1999). Though their careers were otherwise as different as could be, they have one other thing in common: their January 2 birthday.

23 *Sports Illustrated* Covers Depicting Browns

October 8, 1956: "Coach Brown and Quarterback Ratterman: Can they keep the Cleveland Browns on top?" — This illustration of Brown and Ratterman crouched on the sideline was an early example of the *SI* jinx. Thirteen days later, Ratterman suffered a career-ending knee injury, and the Browns had their only losing record in their first 28 seasons.

September 26, 1960: "Secrets of a Fullback, by Jim Brown" — A drawn portrait of the great runner leads in to his explanation of how he lowers his forearm, when he dives, and other technical aspects of his game.

December 14, 1964: "The Cards Fight Back" — Quarterback Charley Johnson sneaks across the goal line, stopped only by the goalpost and a rear-facing Browns player, with defender Paul Wiggin in pursuit. The Browns' loss in St. Louis tightened the Eastern Conference standings, but the Cardinals finished a half-game back.

January 4, 1965: "The Browns Are Champs! Cleveland Quarterback Frank Ryan calmly dominated the Baltimore defense" — A black-and-white photo of Ryan passing in the face of a rush by Gino Marchetti was a late editorial substitution. *SI* figured the favored Colts to win but had to pull its Shula/Unitas cover at deadline when the Browns shut them out in the NFL title game.

September 27, 1965: "Doctor Ryan of the Browns" — Cleveland's Ph.D. quarterback barks out the signals from behind his single-bar facemask. Inside is a long and interesting profile of the last man to lead the Browns to a championship.

January 10, 1966: "The Packers Are the Champs: In the mud of Green Bay, Jim Taylor barges through the Browns" — With dirt-soaked uniforms rarely seen these days, Browns MLB Vince Costello eyes the Packer fullback while being blocked.

November 21, 1966: "Pro Football's Best Deep Defenders" — Veteran safety Ross Fichtner is pictured alone and heavily featured in the cover story about the importance of his position in modern football.

November 21, 1977: "AFC vs NFC: The Rivalry Has Become a Rout" — An illustration includes the Browns' star runner Greg Pruitt among the AFC stars steamrolling the flat NFC.

October 2, 1978: "Rolling Back the Tide: USC's Charles White Runs Wild" — The future first-round pick of the Browns enjoyed his real heyday in college. The 1979 Heisman Trophy winner gained twice as many rushing yards for the Trojans as he did in eight pro seasons.

September 8, 1980: "Pro Football Issue" — The cover photo shows lanky WR Dave Logan reaching out for a one-handed catch past the Steelers' Mel Blount. Inside, Paul Zimmerman predicted the Browns to finish 8-8, behind the Steelers and Oilers, in what became the magical 11-5 Kardiac Kids season.

August 30, 1982: "Rough and Ready: Linebacker Tom Cousineau, Cleveland's $3.5 Million Man" — Shown leaping over Lions by legendary Cleveland photographer Tony Tomsic, Cousineau never quite achieved the pro potential suggested by his initial draft position, trade cost, and hype, of which this piece is a prime specimen.

December 12, 1983: "Jim Brown: You Serious? A Comeback at 47? Hey! You're just what the borrr-ing NFL needs" — He retired at the top of his game, but more than 17 years later, JB sounded off about Pittsburgh's Franco Harris possibly breaking the career rushing mark: "If Franco hangs around long enough and keeps running out of bounds, he'll get my record." He didn't.

August 26, 1985: "Banking on Bernie: Cleveland Pins its Hopes on Bernie Kosar's Million-Dollar Arm" — The 21-year-old franchise savior-in-training smiles for the camera in his clean Browns whites.

January 12, 1987: "Never Say Die: Ozzie Newsome and the Browns Rally to Beat the Jets in OT" — In the classic 77-plus-minute comeback win, Newsome caught six passes for 114 yards, the last 100-yard game of his career.

January 19, 1987: "Victory! Rich Karlis' Kick Wins in OT" — The next week's heartbreak is encapsulated by the barefoot kicker Karlis and holder Gary Kubiak jumping for joy, while the Browns' Chris Rockins signals that the field goal was wide left.

August 29, 1988: "NFL Preview" — Number 19 starts his delivery as the text asks whether Kosar is the "last of the great quarterbacks." Inside is an extensive profile piece and Paul "Dr. Z" Zimmerman's prediction that Cleveland would make the Super Bowl. Six days later, Kosar would be knocked out of the Browns' opener with an elbow injury and miss the next six games.

December 4, 1995: "Battle for the Browns: Art Modell sucker-punched Cleveland, but the city is fighting back" — Published a few weeks after the owner announced the franchise's move to Baltimore, this cartoon-style cover shows Modell landing a blow to the gut of a dawg-masked fan. The article portrays Cleveland's range of emotions to the loss of the team, including Dante Lavelli's outrage and Lou Groza's sadness.

April 19, 1999: "Pick of the Litter: The reborn Browns have the No. 1 choice. Do they take Kentucky's Tim Couch, Oregon's Akili Smith or ...?" — The photo shows Couch and Smith wearing Browns #99 jerseys, backed by masked superfan John "Big Dawg" Thompson, who (prophetically?) is turned in Couch's direction.

September 1, 1999: "Return of the Browns: A Celebration of 50 Years in Cleveland" — In this commemorative issue, a vintage close-up of Jim Brown fills the frame, while Tim Couch is inset in a passing stance.

August 6, 2007: "NFL Camps Open: Secrets and Surprises" — New Browns running back Jamal Lewis is seen charging ahead at training camp. No jinx this time, as the Browns produced their best record of the decade, with a resurgent Lewis gaining 1,552 yards in all.

September 21, 2009: "Dominator" — The Vikings' Adrian Peterson runs loose against the Browns, as D'Qwell Jackson looks up from the ground. Cleveland lost their 2009 debut to Minnesota, 34-20, as Peterson ran for a season-high 180 yards and three scores.

November 1, 2010: "Concussions" — Pittsburgh's James Harrison's illegal hit on Browns WR Mohamed Massaquoi is depicted vividly, with the background blurred for effect.

May 19, 2014: "Johnny Better Be Good: Because How Much More Suffering Can a City Take?" — The familiar draft day money-fingers shot of Johnny Manziel appears on this regional cover. Two weeks earlier, Johnny Football was the focus of the draft preview issue cover.

The 10 Best Cleveland Browns Books

Some 80 books have been published that deal substantially with the Browns — biography, memoir, history, photography, reference, fiction and more. (And that's not including children's books, media guides, or numerous recent ebooks.) Here are the best of the bunch, the essential canon for the Cleveland football fan's bookshelf and coffee table.

1. *Brown's Town: 20 Famous Browns Talk Amongst Themselves* by Alan Natali, 2001.

The most absorbing book featuring the words of ex-Browns, this 572-page chronicle serves as a biography of sorts of the legendary coach, but it far transcends that. Easily the best prose stylist among all Browns book authors, Natali lets the players speak for themselves naturally through smooth editing, set up with excellent biographical essays.

2. *The Best Show in Football: The 1946-1955 Cleveland Browns — Pro Football's Greatest Dynasty* by Andy Piascik, 2006.

This well-written work is an astute analysis of a revolutionary time in Cleveland sports, pro football and American society. Clearly, colorfully and comprehensively, Piascik makes a compelling case that the ten-year powerhouse Paul Brown built in Cleveland was superior to any other, earlier or since.

3. *The 1980 Kardiac Kids — Our Untold Stories* by Don Cockroft with Bob Moon, 2011.

The longtime Browns kicker spent years on this deep dive into the personalities, games and fan impact from a most exciting time in Cleveland sports history. The 672-page hardcover features over 650 photos, including the work of Browns great Jerry Sherk.

4. *Sundays in the Pound: The Heroics and Heartbreak of the 1985-89 Cleveland Browns* by Jonathan Knight, 2006.

Knight is among the more prolific Cleveland sports authors, and this detailed retelling of a fondly-remembered era is an interesting narrative through which to revisit names and games that may have blurred with time. Knight's books invariably reflect quality research and rely on primary sources.

5. *When All the World Was Browns Town* by Terry Pluto, 1997.

This story of the 1964 team and its championship season hit the market when Cleveland most needed to be reminded of its football glory. The veteran columnist and author, now with the *Plain Dealer*, is at his casual but authoritative best.

6. *On Being Brown: What It Means to Be a Cleveland Browns Fan* by Scott Huler, 1999.

A charming collection of short essays and interviews with fans and former players (Sipe, Graham, Warfield, Sherk, Kosar, even Mike Phipps among them), this pocket paperback connects one with the other, and reader and author, by dipping into pooled emotional essence.

7. *The Cleveland Browns: The Great Tradition* by Bob Moon, 1999.

An excellent overall combination of text and images, this handsome and highly readable history qualifies as an heirloom book.

8. *Cleveland's Browns (Photo Highlights of the First Fifty Years of the Cleveland Browns)* by Paul Tepley, 1999.

This fine coffee table book measures 26 inches across when open. The longtime *Cleveland Press* photographer's collection of his and others' work is vivid and nicely arranged. If not for Ernie Green's outstretched hands at the page's edge, the reader could half expect to catch Frank Ryan's toss and head up the dirt field himself.

9. *Legends by the Lake: The Cleveland Browns at Municipal Stadium* by John Keim, 1999.

This Lakewood native's sizable history is well worth the space it takes up. Its greatest strength lies in the frequent quotations generated from several dozen interviews.

10. *Cleveland Browns History* by Frank M. Henkel, 2005.

Though less than one-half inch thick, it excels via numerous rare black-and-white photos with descriptive captions. There's Marion Motley in a Steelers uniform helping tackle Browns QB George Ratterman, "Turkey" Joe Jones going airborne to intercept Kenny Anderson, Bernie Kosar flicking a pass under Miami's Brian Cox for a touchdown to Mark Bavaro, and Tim Couch's college notebook page in which he weighs the pros and cons of turning pro early.

Also recommended (in chronological order):

- *Classic Browns: The 50 Greatest Games in Cleveland Browns History* by Jonathan Knight, 2015 (new edition of 2008 title)
- *Tales From the Browns Sideline* by Tony Grossi, 2012 (new edition of 2004 title)
- *Things I've Learned from Watching the Browns* by Terry Pluto, 2010
- *Paul Brown: The Rise and Fall and Rise Again of Football's Most Innovative Coach* by Andrew O'Toole, 2008
- *One Moment Changes Everything: The All-America Tragedy of Don Rogers* by Sean D. Harvey, 2007
- *False Start: How The New Browns Were Set Up To Fail* by Terry Pluto, 2004
- *OttoMatic* by Duey Graham, 2004
- *Kardiac Kids: The Story of the 1980 Cleveland Browns* by Jonathan Knight, 2003
- *First and Last Seasons: A Father, A Son, and Sunday Afternoon Football* by Dan McGraw, 2000
- *The Best of the Cleveland Browns Memories* by Russell Schneider, 1999
- *Glory for Sale: Inside the Browns' Move to Baltimore & the New NFL* by Jon Morgan, 1997
- *Fumble: The Browns, Modell & the Move* by Michael G. Poplar with James A. Toman, 1997
- *Sam, Sipe, & Company: The Story of the Cleveland Browns* by Bill Levy, 1981
- *PB: The Paul Brown Story* by Paul Brown and Jack Clary, 1979
- *They Call It a Game: Shoulders the NFL Stands On* by Bernie Parrish, 1971 (reissued in 2000)
- *Off My Chest* by Jimmy Brown with Myron Cope, 1964

11 Other Brown and Orange Teams

If you see someone rocking brown and orange apparel, the odds are good that you've found a Browns fan. Though it might be someone's school colors, considering the brevity of this list, that's fairly unlikely.

1. Bowling Green State University — This northwest Ohio school was the site of the Browns' first training camp in 1946. The team continued to train there until moving to Hiram College in 1952. BGSU credits the burnt orange and seal brown color scheme to a woman's feathered hat that caught the eye of a faculty member during a trolley ride to Toledo back in 1914.

2. Heath High School — The Newark, Ohio, school's football team sports helmets remarkably similar to those of the Browns. Their suitably appropriate nickname, the Bulldogs, is not depicted on them. Hanford Dixon would approve.

3. St. Louis Browns — The American League baseball team (1902-53) is now the Baltimore Orioles. The nickname, shortened from Brown Stockings, was first used in the 19th century by the American Association and National League franchise that became known as the St. Louis Cardinals.

4. Sylvania Southview High School — The Toledo-area school calls its brown-and-orange teams the Cougars to differentiate them from the crosstown rival Sylvania Northview Wildcats, who wear black and gold.

5. Midpark High School — The Middleburg Heights, Ohio, school had brown-and-orange teams known as the Meteors. Their football helmets also closely resembled the Browns'. In 2013 its building became a junior high, with the secondary students moving to nearby Berea High School, which was renamed Berea-Midpark.

6. Weequahic High School — The Newark, N.J., school's Indians are the alma mater of the extraordinary pass rusher-turned-barbecuer Al "Bubba" Baker.

7. Trevor G. Browne High School — Named for a doctor who donated land in Phoenix for its campus, it made the obvious and right choice of school colors. It added alliteration with its nickname, the Bruins.

8. Dumont (NJ) High School — It dons brown and orange and makes frequent use of the Old English "D," ala the Detroit Tigers, on the uniforms of its sports teams, known as the Huskies.

9. Rocky River High School — The Charlotte, N.C. school opened in 2010 with the unfortunate nickname "Ravens."

10. Rochester Institute of Technology — The private university in upstate New York provides on its website the exact specifications for its official shades of brown and orange, while allowing that black, white and gray are acceptable accent colors. The student body is two-thirds male, but its sports teams, known as the Tigers, don't include football.

11. Eastfield College — This community college in Mesquite, Texas, adopted brown and golden-orange to represent the earth and the eastern horizon upon its founding in 1970. But those hues fell out of favor, and the Harvesters buried brown in favor of blue in 2012.

SEMBB's Top 10 Reasons I'm a Browns Fan

In 2012, members of the Southeast Michigan Browns Backers — website: MaybeThisYear.com — collaborated to create this list (reprinted with permission), which was featured on the club's T-shirts that year.

10. Cleveland Rocks!

9. No matter where I'm at, Cleveland's still home.

8. The suffering builds my character.

7. Barking is good stress relief.

6. Dawgs are loyal.

5. I was born and raised on the Browns!

4. We don't need no stinkin' helmet logo!

3. Real fans stick with their team!

2. Our stadium's not named after a condiment.

1. If you have to ask, you'll never understand.

19 Freaky Browns Coincidences

1. Exactly twice have the Browns drafted safeties from UCLA in the first round: Don Rogers in 1984 and Eric Turner in 1991. Sadly, they both passed away in California while still active NFL players. *(See page 30: "30 Browns Who Died Young.")*

2. Only 13 professional football games have ever ended with the score of 41-20. Two of them each were Cleveland's sixth loss of the season, were immediately followed a bye week, and came on the road against an eventual division champion: Cincinnati in 2013 and Kansas City in 2003.

3. At 1:00 p.m. on October 9, 2005, the Browns kicked off to the Chicago Bears in a game they'd win 20-10. It was the 100th regular season contest since the Browns returned to the league. Browns RT Ryan Tucker and P Kyle Richardson each played in their 100th NFL game that day. It was also the 100th career start for OLB Kenard Lang and for QB Trent Dilfer, who threw his 100th career touchdown pass that day.

4. An unwritten tradition accompanied the Browns' return to action in 1999. The first 11 season openers were all home games. The odds of that happening by chance: 0.049%, or less than five in 10,000.

5. Jerome Harrison, a 5'9" running back drafted in 2006, was dubbed with the nickname "The Ghost" by the secondary coach at Washington State, presumably because he was hard for defenders to see. Within 13 months of his donning the Browns' jersey number 35, two of its previous wearers, Galen Fiss and Alex Agase, passed away.

6. Two days after JFK's assassination in Dallas, the Browns hosted the Dallas Cowboys and beat them 27-17, a combined point total of 44. On the same weekend 44 years later, Cleveland hosted another Lone Star State team, the Houston Texans, and beat them by the identical score.

7. In both 1985 and 2005, the Browns overhauled their quarterback situation, trading for a veteran starter. In each case, the back of that veteran's jersey started with D and contained an 8 (Gary Danielson and Trent Dilfer). In both years, Cleveland drafted QBs with local ties who had grown up as Browns fans (Bernie Kosar and Charlie Frye). Their jerseys each sported a 9. In both seasons, the veteran was hurt and the rookie finished as the starter. The veteran would go into broadcasting after retirement. Each offense was very conservative and featured a running back new to the team wearing 34 (Kevin Mack and Reuben Droughns). They each topped 1,000 yards, which no other Brown accomplished in all the years in between.

FANDOM AND FRIVOLITY 157

8. Two undersized rookie linebackers competed for a roster spot on the 1981 Browns. Both Eddie Johnson, a seventh-round pick who won the job, and undrafted Sam Mills, who got cut, would became inspirational leaders for their teams. Each wore number 51, an age neither would live to see. *(See page 30: "30 Browns Who Died Young" and page 37: "12 Great Browns Who Played Only For Other Teams.")*

9. Both Kellen Winslows, father and son, inspired teams to trade up to draft them. In each case, the talented tight ends were taken with first-round picks acquired for lower first-rounders plus a second-rounder. The lower first-rounders were both used on wide receivers (the Browns' Willis Adams in 1979 and the Lions' Roy Williams in 2004). Adams and the elder Winslow both wore number 80. Williams and the younger Winslow both wore 11, until KWII switched to his father's old number.

10. It's well-known that Cleveland lost three AFC Championship games to Denver in the late 1980s. Oddly enough, though, is that on three separate occasions, the Broncos have beaten the Browns by the score of 23-20 in overtime. That includes the playoff game of January 11, 1987, a week after the Browns shot down the Jets by the exact same score. In all three OT losses (the others being in 1981 and 2003), the Browns were on their second placekicker of the season. The 2003 game was the 23rd meeting (20th in the regular season) between the two clubs.

11. The three NFL quarterbacks most recently drafted with the 22nd overall pick were all selections of the Browns: Brady Quinn (2007), Brandon Weeden (2012) and Johnny Manziel (2014). Cleveland acquired each of those picks by trade and drafted other players in the top ten.

12. In 2003, the Browns broke a lengthy losing streak by winning their season finale on the road, 22-14, as Lee Suggs rushed for over 100 yards on 26 carries. Every element of that sentence held true in 2004 as well. Those two wins, over the Bengals and Texans, respectively, were the first and last 100-yard performances of Suggs' career. And they're the only Browns games ever to end with that particular score.

13. On a snowy green and white Lambeau Field, December 23, 2001, with the temperature a crisp 30 degrees, the Green Bay Packers, in green jerseys, featured a runner named Ahmad Green, wearing number 30. Cleveland, wearing white, featured Jamel White, also wearing 30. Each back carried 21 times and gained well over 100 yards. The home team won with 30 points.

14. The straight-on placekick has long been superseded by the soccer-style technique. Three of the last four straight-on kickers happened to be Browns: Don Cockroft, Steve Cox and Mark Moseley. This seems a fitting following in the footsteps of Lou "The Toe" Groza, who was legendary for launching the field goal as a bona fide offensive weapon.

15. He's one of just four Hall of Famers whose first name starts with O. He played his whole career with the Browns. Prior to that, his coaches included Paul "Bear" Bryant. Upon turning pro, he converted to a new position, which he played no small part in revolutionizing. His name is Ozzie Newsome. And Otto Graham.

16. In 1970, Miami's director of player personnel, Joe Thomas, struck a deal with the Browns to acquire a former Ohio State wide receiver (Paul Warfield), while Cleveland drafted a quarterback from a major school in Indiana (Purdue's Mike Phipps) with the third overall pick. In 2007, the Browns used the third overall pick on another Joe Thomas. Later in that round, the Dolphins drafted an Ohio State wide receiver (Ted Ginn, Jr.), and Cleveland took a quarterback from a major school in Indiana (Brady Quinn of Notre Dame).

17. Entering the 2005 season, 49 different Browns had caught passes since the team's 1999 reincarnation. Four new skill players, including Braylon Edwards and Joshua Cribbs, were on the roster and primed to become the 50th on the list. So who was it? An ineligible receiver, but since the penalty was declined, the catch counted. Loss of a yard, but it gained an ironic stat line for number 50 himself, center Jeff Faine.

18. Of the three interim head coaches in Browns history, two — Dick Modzelewski and Jim Shofner — were the only Browns head coaches to have played for the team. The third — Terry Robiskie — was the only one whose son would.

19. Two different pro sports franchises, after five decades, abandoned their Midwestern cities, their Browns nicknames and comparable color schemes to move to Baltimore and adopt bird names. Of course, while the former St. Louis American League baseball team remains but a defunct artifact of fading memory, Cleveland's Browns are back alive, heritage and all.